6·15·72

Plant Engineering Management

Plant Engineering Management

James A. Murphy, Editor

Authors

In organizing, developing, and writing this book, the co-authors listed below
have generously donated their time, effort, and professional skills in order to
contribute to the advancement of manufacturing management.

Donald A. Bartlett, Principal
A. T. Kearney & Company, Inc.
Chicago, Illinois

George D. Botting, Plant Engineer
Detroit Steel Corporation
Portsmouth, Ohio

Harris E. Dicker, Manager
Aquatechnics
Westinghouse Electric Corporation
Hinsdale, Illinois

Donald G. Johnson, Manager
Manufacturing & Plant Engineering
John Deere Works
Ottumwa, Iowa

Mark C. Mathis, Manager
Facilities & Maintenance
Collins Radio Company
Cedar Rapids, Iowa

Florian M. Waligorski, Plant Engineer
The Heil Company
Milwaukee, Wisconsin

Published by
Society of Manufacturing Engineers
Dearborn, Michigan
1971

Manufacturing Management Series

Plant Engineering Management

Library of Congress Catalog Card Number: 74-144106
International Standard Book Number: 0-87263-027-7

MANUFACTURED IN THE UNITED STATES
OF AMERICA

Acknowledgments

Besides the co-authors listed on the title page, the following men have been instrumental in the writing and preparation of the manuscript of this book: Edward L. Barnett and Charles C. Ceedar, Associates, A. T. Kearney & Company, Inc.; Leon W. Durivage, Plant Engineer, Collins Radio Company; Dave Entrekin, President, Entrekin Computers, Inc.; David O. Gerlat, Sales Representative, Texaco, Inc.; Bernard S. Gutow and Robert B. Hill, Associates, A. T. Kearney & Company, Inc.; Fredric J. Kessler, Fry Consultants, Inc.; Robert D. Mahon, Assistant Regional Safety Engineer, United States Post Office Department; David E. Nuttall, Manager, Industrial Controls Department, Ferranti-Packard Ltd.; and Frank R. Shibilski, Engineer, Climatic Control Company. The Society wishes to especially thank these men for their contributions of time and effort toward the completion of this work.

Special thanks also goes to the men who reviewed the manuscript and contributed to its accuracy and completeness. These are B. R. Livingston, The Maytag Company; D. J. Pearse, Principal Project Engineer, Kaiser Engineers, Henry J. Kaiser Company; and Robert C. Wacker, General Sales Manager, Sterling Tool and Manufacturing Company.

Contents

vii

Figures

Tables

Plant Engineering Management

Chapter 1

Introduction

. . . When in the nineteenth century, society began to elaborate an exclusively rational technique which acknowledged only considerations of efficiency, it was felt that not only the traditions but the deepest instincts of humankind had been violated. Men sought to reintroduce indispensable factors of aesthetics and morals. Out of this effort came the unprecedented creation of certain aspects of style in the 1880's: the tool with machine-made embellishments. Sewing machines were decorated with cast iron flowers, and the first tractors bore engraved bulls' heads. That it was wasteful to supply such embellishments soon became evident; their ugliness doubtless contributed to the realization. Moreover, these flourishes represented a wrong road, technically speaking. The machine can become precise only to the degree that its design is elaborated with mathematical rigor in accordance with use. And an embellishment could increase air resistance, throw a wheel out of balance, alter velocity or precision. There was no room in practical activity for gratuitous aesthetic preoccupations. The two had to be separated. A style then developed based on the idea that the line best adapted to use is the most beautiful.

Jacques Ellul[1]

In the above quotation Jacques Ellul has effectively described the difficulty the early technologists had in making a clean break with the past. Today, in industry, the concept that form should follow function is generally accepted. However, in some areas of industry, the force of tradition is still strong. Something of the past still clings to many of our plant engineering departments. In a large number of firms the plant engineer remains an obscure figure hidden away somewhere near the boiler room. As long as anyone can recall, the plant engineer has been responsible for a wide variety of assignments, many of a nonengineering nature. These have included such items as snow removal, plant cleaning, stores control, the repair of office furniture, scheduling of company cars, etc.

Years ago, when machines and equipment were relatively simple, there

---

[1]*The Technological Society* (New York: Alfred A. Knopf, 1965), 73.

might have been some rationale for giving these additional assignments to the plant engineer. There wasn't a great deal for him to do when all of the machines were operating properly. However, today's machines are more complex; investment in plant and equipment has greatly increased. Management has begun to realize that to dilute the efforts of the plant engineer with so many extraneous tasks is to defeat his attempts to carry out his primary responsibilities. To say what these primary responsibilities should be, we must first define plant engineering.

One broad definition of plant engineering is the following: "Although this function is found to exist with unique responsibilities in almost every industrial operation, it can generally be described as being responsible for providing engineering for facilities and plant services such as power, water, heat and lighting, and maintaining the facilities including equipment and grounds."[2] This definition describes essentially what are usually considered the primary responsibilities of the plant engineering function. A listing of primary and secondary areas of responsibility for most types of industry is as follows:

Primary	*Secondary*
Facilities and equipment engineering	Safety
	Plant protection
Maintenance and construction	Plant cleaning
Power and utilities generation and distribution	Plant-wide stores control
	Transportation services
Pollution abatement	Tooling
	Cafeteria or food services

This book concerns itself mainly with the "primary" responsibilities. This is not meant to indicate that those listed as secondary are not important, but rather that this book attempts to do justice to the management of the primary functions. In addition, many plant engineering managers can attest to the fact that in specific instances the list of secondary responsibilities is often expanded to include numerous other services not shown in the above list.

RESPONSIBILITIES BY INDUSTRY TYPE

To a significant extent, combinations of responsibilities have developed similar patterns in industries of the same type. In a broad sense, these industry types are: (1) metalworking and fabricating, (2) process industries, and (3) nonmanufacturing industries and institutional operations.

In the metalworking and fabricating plants, typically considered noncontinuous process operations, the plant engineering functions are mainly traditional in type and include all of the primary responsibilities. In addition, the plant engineering manager will frequently have responsibility for plant cleaning. In these cases in which the tooling function is simple and no complex fabrication and repair is involved, it may also be included under plant engineering. Metalworking and fabricating plants tend to emphasize the engineering aspects

---

[2] Ivan R. Vernon, ed., *Introduction to Manufacturing Management* (Dearborn, Mich.: Society of Manufacturing Engineers, 1969).

of plant engineering. These activities occupy more of the manager's time than maintenance or utilities because of the relatively small numbers of personnel assigned to these last two functions.

It should be noted that the number of employees in maintenance and utilities operations are not necessarily small in an absolute sense, but rather when compared with total plant employment. Also, where plants do have small maintenance forces, 25 to 30 employees or less, larger projects such as equipment rearrangement, facility additions, and major overhauls are frequently contracted to outside firms. When such work is contracted out, the plant engineering department still retains ultimate responsibility. Plant engineering supplies designs and specifications, negotiates the contract, and maintains liaison with the contractor.

In process industry plants the plant engineering department usually occupies a relatively important position in overall plant operation. Process plants typically own large areas of real estate and have heavy investments in facilities and equipment. Three-shift operations and large-scale processes create situations making unplanned shutdowns very expensive, and for this reason the maintenance force constitutes a major portion of total employment. The greater importance of plant engineering is indicated by the fact that it is frequently the prerogative of the plant engineer to direct the shutdown of production equipment or processes for diagnosis, repair, servicing, or overhaul.

In some process plants the plant engineering and maintenance functions may be the responsibilities of two different managers. In other cases the maintenance force is divided and under control of several production supervisors. This situation frequently exists in steel mills. Power generation and utilities distribution responsibilities do not belong to the plant engineer in a number of pulp and paper manufacturing operations. In some cases a power department may have complete control and responsibility for all electrical maintenance in the plant. The engineering aspects of plant engineering tend to be de-emphasized by the large maintenance and power operations and also by the assignment of process engineering responsibilities to production departments.

The assignment of plant engineering responsibilities varies in nonmanufacturing organizations, which include service industries such as transportation and hotels as well as educational institutions, hospitals, and governmental functions. The operating objectives, types of production equipment, and other factors vary widely in these kinds of firms, and the responsibilities of the plant engineering group reflect this diversity. It is worth noting, however, that plant or facilities engineering tends to be more service oriented than in metalworking or process manufacturing. Also, in the nonmanufacturing organization there is a general lack of understanding between plant engineering personnel and operating managers. Businesses involving extensive building complexes such as hospitals and educational institutions often place the responsibility for architectural services under plant engineering.

The high degree of service orientation of plant engineering in nonmanufacturing businesses causes the function to be something of a "catch-all" for nonoperating duties; therefore, many of the primary and secondary responsibilities fall to plant engineering. In general, this tends to de-emphasize the technical aspects of engineering.

RELATIONSHIPS TO OVERALL INDUSTRY MANAGEMENT

The day-to-day relationships between plant engineering and other areas of management, particularly manufacturing management, centers around the matter of production continuity. The product must be made, the quality must be acceptable, and the rate of production must be maintained at a high level. The pressure on plant engineering is ever present to provide utilities, equipment and process operability, and process reliability on a continuous basis. This requirement can become a daily battle for the plant engineer, making it impossible for him to get ahead without placing undue restrictions on his expenditures.

In a well-run operation, daily cost reports are an ever-present incentive for maintaining production continuity. In many plants, however, the cost problem is faced only on a periodic basis, perhaps quarterly or annually. In these instances the fact that plant engineering services are inadequate for production needs, or that plant engineering costs are excessive, tends to be realized very slowly by management.

ECONOMICS—LONG- AND SHORT-TERM

The question of how much to spend for the plant engineering function involves consideration of return on investment as well as decisions relating to interruptions of production. Should servicing, repair, overhaul, or replacement become necessary, it may be feasible to defer these services until a later date, or possibly until the line must shut down due to component failure. Reliability and maintainability of new or replacement equipment must be considered when making equipment selections.

At this time, no accepted formulas exist to show how much should be spent on maintenance and repair of facilities and equipment, although some companies have developed overall targets or guidelines for use by plant engineering and maintenance management. Variations of these guidelines are used to gage the effectiveness of plant engineering management. These guidelines are established through the use of judgment and analysis of costs over the previous years.

With adequate equipment history information, the appropriate degree of preventive maintenance can be calculated against probable failure incidences for individual pieces of equipment. The optimum combination of planned maintenance and tolerated downtime costs can be determined in this manner. However, there are still repairs, failures, adjustments, and other servicing which cannot be eliminated by preventive maintenance. The maintenance or plant engineering manager is still faced with the question of, "How much maintenance is enough?" After the plant engineer has arrived at the appropriate figure, plant and production managers have to be convinced.

A great deal of management effort has gone into cost reduction in the plant engineering functions, particularly with respect to the maintenance and plant cleaning activities. While these efforts are important, they need to be balanced by consideration of other contributions of plant engineering to overall profitability. In other words, in what areas will additional dollars spent in the plant engineering function generate the most in additional return on investment?

CHANGING ROLE OF THE PLANT ENGINEER

Plant engineering has a major role to play in manufacturing management and plant operation. The computer-operated, fully automated plant is not entirely a thing of the future. In some cases it is already here; in the highly automated establishment, plant operation and plant engineering merge into a single function. In such a case, after the plant is designed and constructed and production has started, maintenance becomes a major factor.

Before all of our plants become fully automated, a semiautomatic phase will exist. This phase will require moderate numbers of operating personnel, will involve more complex equipment, and will necessitate continuous plant operation to increase utilization of the greater investment. As a result, the cost of downtime, as well as process reliability and production continuity, will assume even greater importance.

Planning of production and equipment servicing must be thoroughly coordinated and scheduled in this semiautomatic processing operation. Quality control becomes more complex as product changeovers become more costly. In-use maintainability of equipment becomes very desirable and the requirement for predictability of failure rates takes on a new dimension. The plant engineer will have to improve information resources, perform better analyses, and plan and manage in a more effective manner.

Staffing of the several plant engineering areas of responsibility is currently a problem. Trained technicians and craftsmen, as well as applicants for these jobs, are in short supply. In the past, other functions have been more attractive to engineers than plant engineering. The increased demands to be made on plant engineering as a result of increased automation and continuous process operations will make the staffing problem even more difficult. Training can be part of the solution, and finding ways to attract trainees and graduate engineers might be another solution.

In the past, the plant engineer has merely had some bothersome "water-treatment" rules with which to contend, and he or the plant manager may occasionally have sloughed off groups of irate citizens complaining about fumes or stack emissions. Of necessity this has changed. Industry is going to have to divert a significant amount of its money, talent, and effort to pollution abatement. At the plant level it is natural that plant engineering falls heir to the responsibility for pollution abatement or control. Pollutants are currently being generated for which no proven technologies exist in terms of effective control or abatement. In addition, new manufacturing processes can be expected to create additional and different pollution problems in the future.

Chapter 2

Organization

Organizations tend to evolve as an operation grows and as the changing of managers brings different emphasis to various areas of responsibility. Such evolution is not necessarily bad, but it is no substitute for the establishment of the basic organizational structure by a calculated analysis of what the function is to do and how it can best accomplish these responsibilities. After the basic structure is established, it may then have to be adjusted for some consideration of personalities or other special circumstances.

This chapter analyzes organizational structure and planning, and reviews the managerial role in integrating physical and human resources to accomplish the objectives of the plant engineering organization. The analysis deals almost exclusively with the primary responsibilities outlined in Chapter 1. Provisions for dealing with some of the secondary responsibilities are also included. A typical plant engineering organization is described, and principles are set forth to serve as guidelines to structuring the department.

ORGANIZATIONAL PURPOSES

While the design of a plant engineering organization must be tailor-made for each company, the purpose is always the same—the establishment of support-type engineering services. These services include provision of power, water, heat, and lighting and maintenance of the facilities, including equipment and grounds. Thus, while the organizational structure will be different, similarities are to be found among all such departments. The responsibility of the manager is always the same; he must see that a plan is designed and put into effect. To quote from an earlier book in this series:

Most successful managers in business, government, and education agree that there is a direct relationship between organizational arrangements and the success of an enterprise. When a functional group fails to organize properly, it is usually unable to meet the challenges that confront it. Inadequate arrangements can handicap it in making correct decisions, or in taking effective action to implement the decisions that are made.[1]

---

[1] Vernon, ed., *op. cit.*, 7.

There is some disposition on the part of lower-level managers to regard the organizational structure of their groups as fixed by upper management. Nothing could be further from the truth. Any organization, particularly a plant engineering group, must be constantly aware of the need to change in order to adapt itself to new circumstances.

The increasing rate of change—technological, economic, and social—makes it advisable to consider organizational planning as a continuous activity and to be sure the current plan is always ready to cope with new conditions. Not surprisingly, however, successful plant engineering managers give a great deal of time and attention to organizing their resources, thus providing the necessary relationship of proper organization to sound operations.

There has been a general tendency to regard the purpose for which the plant engineering group exists as that of "fire fighting." Thus, when some unforeseen incident occurs, as when a processing line breaks down, a power supply fails, or an air conditioning system malfunctions, the plant engineers are expected to come up with a quick remedy. While this is certainly part of the reason for their existence, another and more basic purpose is to prevent these mishaps from occurring. The department must be so organized that each engineer has long-term objectives as well as short-term tasks. Individuals should be able to exercise their creativity in developing needed improvements in processes and equipment.

EVOLUTION OF PLANT ENGINEERING STRUCTURE

Organizational structure is one of the means by which company objectives are achieved. Since these objectives keep changing, organizational forms must also keep changing. Such has been the pattern of growth in all areas of manufacturing, and plant engineering is not an exception. Over the 200 years that manufacturing plants have been developing, plant engineering has changed in concept from a "jack-of-all-trades" repairman to a group possessing all the skills needed to cope with a wide variety of industrial problems.

The early manufacturing enterprises were little more than shops where a small number of people worked under the direct supervision of the owner. The products they made were usually sold on the premises. The first such enterprises rarely numbered more than ten people. The owner presided over all operations, repaired equipment, and at the same time carried out all buying and selling activities. Only simple hand tools were used; one workman would make a unit from start to finish.

The industrial revolution, coming to the United States in about 1840, introduced machinery to the scene. Workers were now responsible for only one part or only one operation on a part. The production supervisor replaced the owner as overseer. A particularly handy operator became responsible for keeping the machinery in working order. In time, the amount of repair work exceeded the available time of this one operator, and a group of repairmen developed. Initially, these men reported to the production supervisor, who regarded them merely as high-grade workers.

The events which caused repairmen to become more numerous also brought other changes:

1) Machine repair became an increasingly complex problem requiring special technical skills.

2) The force supervised by the production supervisor became larger, perhaps 20 to 30 people, and the supervisor had little time to become involved in the repair or replacement of equipment.

3) The personnel required to repair and maintain the machines were more highly skilled than the production workers, and they resented taking direction from the production supervisor.

4) There was always the temptation for the production supervisor to order a new item of equipment rather than attempt to determine why existing equipment was unsatisfactory.

5) The repair and maintenance activities not directly involved in production became much greater; that is, steam, electric power, water supply, etc., all became important.

These and related conditions, plus repeated instances of production break-downs, led to the movement in the early twentieth century to create a centralized plant engineering department. This movement was sharply accelerated by the production experiences of the World War II period. Replacement machines were virtually unobtainable, spare parts were difficult to procure, and the poor results obtained from a piecemeal approach to maintenance were painfully evident. Today, plant engineering typically has sole responsibility for engineering involving plant buildings and site and usually shares responsibility for process and manufacturing equipment.

POSITION IN THE PLANT ORGANIZATION

As stated earlier, plant engineering exists primarily to provide support to the other functions of the plant organization. By definition, the function requiring most of the support services is production. In addition to production, administrative and staff groups and other production support functions such as material handling and warehousing are served by plant engineering.

In most cases the plant engineering manager reports to the plant manager or to an equivalent position with a different title. Typically, the materials manager, the quality control manager, the manufacturing manager, the manufacturing engineering manager, and the plant engineering manager all report at the same level, as indicated in Fig. 2-1. This type of arrangement seems to be best for most plants since it provides for balance and arbitration for the day-to-day differences between production and engineering. One frequent difference of opinion involves the question of whether to continue to operate equipment which is suspected of needing service or to take it out of service immediately to minimize the repairs required. In some organizations, plant engineering or maintenance reports directly to a production manager or is otherwise subservient to production. This is undesirable because as a result the immediate demands of production do not permit the arguments for shut-down to be heard.

Obviously this situation of imbalance can also exist if the maintenance function is not a part of plant engineering and does not have a direct line to the plant manager. This is even further aggravated if the maintenance function

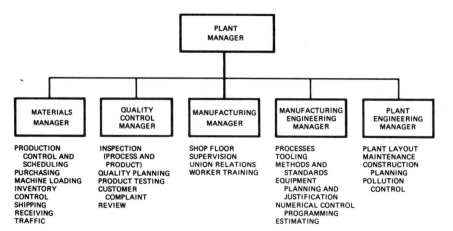

Figure 2-1. Typical manufacturing organization and functions performed at a small or medium-sized plant.

is fragmented and is responsible to various production supervisors. In this last case, maintenance service cannot readily be focused on the area of greatest need in the plant, since this determination of greatest need is viewed by a separate decentralized plant engineering function.

Owing to the size of some plants, it becomes impractical for the plant manager to have all of the major line and staff functions reporting directly to that position. In cases of this nature it may be appropriate for nonmanufacturing functions, including plant engineering, to report to a manager of manufacturing services or equivalent position, which in turn reports to the plant manager.

There are plant engineering functions in local plants which report directly to corporate or divisional engineering positions and in theory by-pass plant management. This relationship can be justified where two or more smaller plants are clustered in a metropolitan area or near a community and plant engineering management is centralized because of economics or long-range multiplant projects involved. This arrangement can also be effective in getting the plant engineering function started in a new plant. However, eventually the plant engineering department should report to the plant manager.

ORGANIZATIONAL STRUCTURE

The plant engineer managing a department providing services in the primary responsibility areas of engineering, maintenance, power and utilities, and pollution abatement should expect to organize so as to have three or more positions reporting to him. The three referred to are the superintendents of engineering, maintenance, and power and utilities. The actual position titles used should conform to titles with similar responsibility in the remainder of the plant organization. The responsibility for pollution control, contractor liaison, and similar functions that are frequently nonline or nonsupervisory may report directly to the plant engineer or to one of the primary superintendents. The question of whether such functions report directly to the plant engineer or not depends upon the size of the organization, the industry type, and the extent of ongoing programs in these staff areas. For example, if the plant is a heavy polluter and is undertaking an extensive abatement program through a plant committee, the plant engineer would want a pollution control engineer reporting directly to him either as a representative from his department or as a monitor of the projects and planning of the program. Where pollution, by nature of the process, is much less of a problem, an individual reporting to the superintendent of power and utilities or the superintendent of engineering may be sufficient.

A typical structure for functions reporting to plant engineering in a medium- to large-sized plant undertaking an active pollution abatement program is indicated in Fig. 2–2. The size of the organization obviously dictates the number

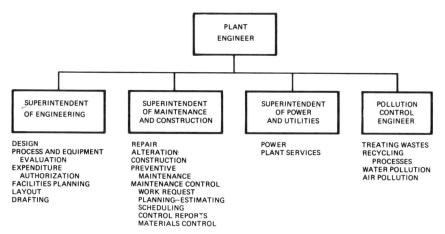

Figure 2–2. Typical line relationship of primary functions in the plant engineering department of a medium or large plant.

and relationship of the primary responsibility functions. The plant engineer may serve as supervisor of a small engineering staff as well as director of the superintendents of maintenance and power and utilities. The danger here is that the maintenance or other functions will not receive proper guidance from the plant engineer and will suffer a lack of communication at the proper level in the production organization. In plants where the engineering staff is relatively small and power is purchased, the engineering and power and utilities functions may be combined under one superintendent.

While the generation of power and the provision of utilities for the plant is stressed here as being a responsibility of plant engineering, some large plant organizations operate a separate power and utilities department. This type of structure exists even today in some continuous process plants (paper, chemical, and refining). In these cases, the power department may report to a production manager and be treated as an operating or manufacturing department or report directly to the plant manager. This structure stemmed from an earlier practice wherein plants actually sold power as a product in the local area. In this same way, the electrical source was often assigned to the power department and, in some cases, remains there today. This arrangement is not considered practical for today's operation since it splits the responsibilities for facility engineering, utilities provision, and maintenance. Also, gaps or overlaps in responsibilities are created, additional staff and supervisory positions are required, and coordination of effort is complicated.

ENGINEERING ACTIVITIES

The scope of the engineering portion of the plant engineering function is a subject of a great deal of debate and controversy, as evidenced by the many different ways in which plants establish and administer this effort. To some extent the work of the engineering section is determined by a number of nonplant engineering factors in addition to the obvious factors such as size of plant and type of process. These less obvious factors include:

1) The extent to which corporate or divisional engineering participates in engineering at the plant level
2) The scope of industrial engineering responsibility in areas such as layout, expenditure justification, and facilities planning
3) The role of production or process engineering in design, equipment, evaluation, and layout.

Obviously, it makes no sense to duplicate or unnecessarily overlap these responsibilities between various engineering sections in the plant. On the other hand, it would be unwise to segment basic facilities and equipment engineering tasks into too many different groups within the plant organization. The exact division of responsibilities must be determined in each plant; however, it is typically appropriate that the engineering section of plant engineering have significant responsibilities in the following areas:

1) Facility and process design
2) Equipment selection and evaluation
3) Facility and equipment expenditure authorization
4) Facility and equipment layout and arrangement.

Facility and Process Design

Plant engineering may get involved in facilities planning and design in several ways, which can include (1) total or partial responsibility for a new facility to be built, (2) prime responsibility for alterations or "add-ons" to present facilities, (3) participation as an advisory group to a special facilities planning task force, or (4) responsibility for the nonprocess aspects of the new facilities. In any of these cases, responsibility must be clearly defined or significant oversights can be experienced.

In established plants, operating alterations to processes are often initiated by production engineering or industrial engineering. In these cases, plant engineering often becomes the administrator or executor of the resulting project requests and later of the approved projects.

Equipment Selection and Evaluation

Since the provision of utilities, services, and maintenance of new equipment is a major function of plant engineering, it is logical that its engineering group be involved in the evaluation of prospective equipment and eventual equipment selection. What may appear as an economically justifiable new equipment purchase may change rapidly in the face of floor-load limitations and available utilities capacities. Equipment has been purchased and even installed in plants without adequate consideration of these factors.

Expenditure Authorization

In most cases the plant engineer is responsible for administering requests for expenditures in connection with additions, alterations, or major repairs to buildings and equipment. This administration may include the accomplishment of in-depth engineering investigations, completion of design and layouts, final analysis of estimated costs versus return on investment, decision as to whether in-plant forces or outside contractors are to be used, notification of and negotiation with bidders, and project control during work execution. This procedure of project authorization and control is frequently the major, continuing work load of the plant engineering group.

Facility Layout

This is one of the more variable and controversial areas of engineering responsibilities within plants. Without going into detail relative to the various arguments concerning which engineering group should have prime responsibility for facility layout and equipment arrangement, it can usually be agreed that plant engineering, process or production engineering, and industrial engineering all have important, related responsibilities. Specifically, plant engineering must deal with utilities layout and building configuration. In addition, plant engineering should be concerned with how a layout affects equipment servicing and overhaul.

Since plant engineering usually oversees the actual accomplishment of the work involved in facility or equipment additions, alterations, and rearrangement, regardless of the early design inputs from process engineering or industrial engineering, it is normally proper to involve plant engineering with specific responsibilities at the early stages of project planning and design.

Engineering Organization

Once the scope of plant engineering's typical responsibilities has been defined in the types of projects discussed (facility and process design, equipment selection, expenditure authorization, layout and process arrangement), the matter of properly organizing the personnel to accomplish those responsibilities is partly settled. Before a structure can be drawn up and staffed, other major questions should be asked. These questions include the following:

1) Should the organization be arranged on the basis of distinct engineering disciplines (mechanical, civil, electrical, structural, etc.)?
2) Should engineers be assigned to areas of the plant by process or along product lines?

3) Should engineering assignments primarily be on a project basis?

Obviously, the answers to the above questions will depend on the number of engineers in a given group; however, when there are three or more engineers involved, these considerations are meaningful.

The assignment of engineers to work by engineering disciplines can be justified for consideration by the increasing complexity of equipment and processes. Rapid technological advances within an already complex set of engineering alternatives makes it virtually impossible for the engineer to stay abreast of these disciplines. On the other hand, organization by the discipline concept requires efficient coordination of the various engineering efforts, can diffuse project responsibilities, and can cause engineers to jump from job to job. A large project can consume the entire engineering group to the disadvantage of other needed projects.

The organization of the engineering section in order to assign engineers to specific manufacturing areas of the plant involves the advantages of having the assigned engineer live with the day-to-day problems of production and maintenance personnel. This provides benefits in terms of coordination and cooperation between engineering, maintenance, and production; fixes plant engineering responsibility for the area; and assures that all major processes of the plant are brought to the attention of plant engineering. In order to utilize engineering talents to their fullest, all assignments should be flexible. Also, if individual assignments are fixed over too long a period this can tend to specialize the engineer. The organization structure designed to employ engineers strictly on a project basis has its advantages and disadvantages. In concept it gives the engineering superintendent the greatest flexibility.

MAINTENANCE AND CONSTRUCTION

In the typical industrial plant the maintenance and construction activities, particularly maintenance, make the greatest demands upon the time of the plant engineering manager. Usually, the greatest number of his personnel are in the maintenance section, which is directly tied in with manufacturing and profits and is ever-changing and demanding on a day-to-day basis. If the construction projects utilize in-plant personnel, as they usually do for all but the largest projects, the amount of attention the manager must give to this phase of his responsibilities is increased.

Reporting Level

The reporting level of the maintenance organization is a function of the type, size, and complexity of the facility to be maintained. The most noticeable difference between reporting levels for the maintenance activity occurs between process and nonprocess industries. Process-type industries include such operations as oil refining, petrochemical production, papermaking, steelmaking, and foundry. Nonprocess-type industries include such operations as electronic component or equipment production, metal fabrication, appliance manufacturing, and almost any other industry that does not have a continuous operation. The reasons for the differences in reporting levels between process and nonprocess industries are given below.

Process Industries. The maintenance activity in process industries generally reports to the plant manager through the plant engineer or, in some cases, an operations manager who may have both production and maintenance reporting to him. The reasons for this high level of reporting are:

1) The maintenance activity in process industries very often can account for between 15 and 30 percent of the total plant population.
2) Very often an emergency can shut down the entire process and, in some cases, the entire plant.
3) Maintenance, labor, and material costs are second to operating costs in most process industries.

Nonprocess Industries. By contrast, in most nonprocess industries the maintenance operation very often reports several levels down from the plant manager. One possible arrangement is to have maintenance report to the manufacturing engineering organization as part of a plant engineering or plant layout function. Another possibility is to have maintenance under a foreman who reports directly to a production supervisor. The reasons for this difference in reporting level are shown below.

1) The maintenance function in nonprocess industries generally accounts for 5 percent or less of the total plant population.
2) There are very few maintenance problems aside from electrical, gas, and air supply breakdowns that can shut down a nonprocess plant. Even then, when an emergency such as power failure does occur, the plant maintenance department will not be able to cope with the situation and will have to call for outside assistance. In this case the local power company would probably have to correct the situation.
3) Maintenance costs are generally a small part of the total plant operating costs. Very often other indirect labor functions such as shipping, receiving, or material handling have greater annual operating costs than the maintenance function.

Span of Control

A reasonable span of control for the maintenance organization is no different than it is for any other function of the manufacturing operation. A manager should be able to direct four to six supervisors. However, many "one-over-one" organizational structures are in existence as well as many so-called exalted positions. The one-over-one organizational structures are often the result of craft-oriented organizations. The exalted positions are usually the result of area maintenance wherein (and this is particularly true of the instrumentation and electrical areas) most of the craftsmen are supervised by the area multi-craft supervisor. However, it is believed by management that an additional degree of expertise is required. Therefore, often there are superintendents or supervisors of instrumentation or the electrical department who are not effectively supervising anyone since their men are all assigned to areas where they are used as technical consultants.

The same principles that apply to a production department will also apply to a maintenance department. The technical expertise for maintenance should reside within the engineering department and not within the maintenance department. An example of an organization with one-over-one positions as well as exalted positions is shown in Fig. 2–3. A preferred organization for the same department is shown in Fig. 2–4.

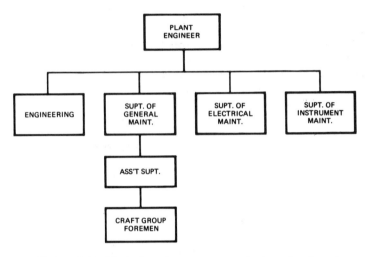

Figure 2–3. Typical maintenance organization showing the "one-over-one" and exalted position arrangements.

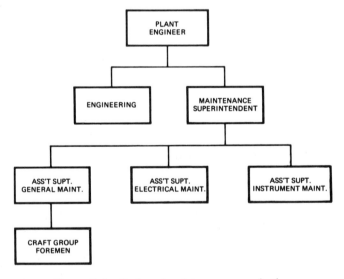

Figure 2–4. Preferred maintenance organization.

Types of Maintenance Organizations

There are four basic types of maintenance organizations: (1) area, (2) central, (3) production-assigned, and (4) a combination of these. The maintenance organization seldom consists entirely of an area, central, or production-assigned type. More often it is a combination of the three basic types. However, the extent to which a department is oriented toward the area, central, or production-assigned concept usually determines how it is organized. The following paragraphs describe briefly each type of organization and lists some of the advantages and disadvantages of each.

Area Maintenance. With this type of organization, the plant or operation has been divided into various areas of responsibility, and generally a maintenance foreman is assigned to a specific area. Employees may be assigned to the foreman on a permanent basis, or, in some cases, the best employees are assigned to an area maintenance foreman on the basis of need or daily or weekly work load. Many times, the area of assignment for an area maintenance foreman corresponds to the area of responsibility of a production supervisor. Thus, the area foreman must necessarily act as multicraft supervisor. However, this is usually limited strictly to mechanical workers such as welders, pipefitters, machinists, and millwrights. Very often the electrical and instrument crafts are organized on a plant-wide basis. Fig. 2–5 shows a typical area maintenance organization.

The advantages of area maintenance are as follows:

1) There is development of a working relationship between an area maintenance foreman and the responsible production supervisor.
2) An area maintenance foreman is intimately familiar with all equipment in a given area and accepts the responsibility for the level of maintenance of the equipment.
3) Immediate response to emergencies reduces equipment or process downtime.
4) Improved efficiency of craftsmen is due to reduced travel time.

However, the area type of maintenance organization also has certain disadvantages:

1) It is difficult to maintain central control over the entire organization and assign manpower on an as-needed basis.

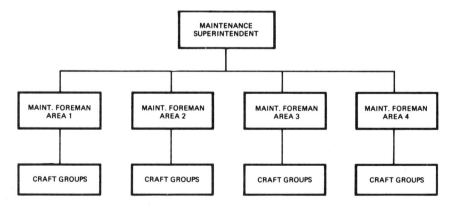

Figure 2–5. Typical area maintenance organization.

2) There is a tendency for the number of men assigned to a given area to become an established precedent regardless of the work load.

3) Production departments tend to consider the men assigned to their area as their private maintenance department.

4) Very often there is an inability to establish priorities in scheduling maintenance jobs over the entire plant.

In summary, the best area maintenance organization seems to be one in which only the area foremen are permanently assigned and the men are assigned on a daily or weekly basis as the work loads in various areas fluctuate.

Central Maintenance. This type of organization is designed to serve an entire plant on a centralized basis. Supervision and the staff supporting groups as well as the craft shops are generally located in one central area. As a rule, these organizations are craft oriented. Fig. 2–6 shows a typical central maintenance organization.

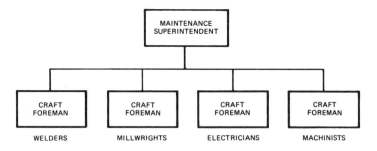

Figure 2–6. Typical central maintenance organization.

Some of the advantages of a central maintenance organization are:

1) Supervisors and workers tend to be specialists and, therefore, tend to be more highly skilled in a given craft.

2) Potentially, workers are utilized better since they are assigned on the basis of jobs which are performed in the immediate future.

3) Technical information and expertise is retained in a central location.

4) The existence of the maintenance organization tends to be ensured as a separate entity within the plant.

Some of the disadvantages of a central maintenance operation are:

1) It cannot respond as fast in the case of emergencies as an area organization.

2) It tends to create layered supervision; the one-over-one organizational structure.

3) It does not promote multicraft supervision.

4) Coordination of various crafts on a given job is more difficult since several foremen are involved in supervising their various crafts rather than having one multicraft area supervisor who is responsible for the entire job.

In summary, it can be said that the prime consideration in the selection of a central maintenance type of organization is the amount of physical area covered by the plant. In order for a central maintenance organization to work effectively, this physical area must be small enough to permit reasonable response to emergency situations.

Production-Assigned Maintenance. This type of organization is specialized and extremely inflexible. In many instances it is a result of a process having chronic maintenance problems which can become a great nuisance for the normal maintenance force. Certain men are assigned full time to the maintenance of a given piece of equipment. Very often these types of assignments result in the maintenance men simply waiting for breakdowns. According to some work sampling studies, this means the maintenance men are idle up to 90 percent of the time. The only justification for this type of maintenance organization would be in certain isolated instances in which the operation is highly critical and the production downtime is more costly than the idle time of the maintenance men.

Combination-Type Maintenance. This type of organization will be a mixture of area and central maintenance with possibly some assigned personnel. Normally the majority of personnel are assigned to various areas on an asneeded basis. Also, the workers assigned to these areas would be the major craftsmen such as welders, millwrights, machinists, instrument mechanics, and electricians. The remaining workers would be assigned to the shops or central maintenance and would be composed of such craftsmen as tinsmiths, brickmasons, carpenters, painters, and machine-tool operators. These assignments could be better handled on the plant-wide basis owing to the small number of craftsmen involved. Also, this type of organization, if properly administered, can have many of the advantages of area and central organizations with few of the disadvantages. Fig. 2–7 gives an example of a typical combination organization.

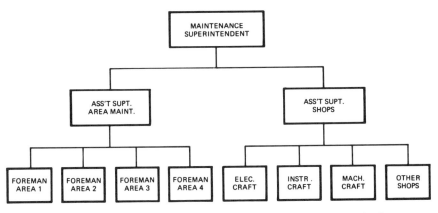

Figure 2–7. Typical combined area and central maintenance organization.

Construction Work

The organization required for the performance of construction work depends upon many factors, with company policy being the most important.

Certain industries and plants which are in a state of having programs of capital improvements or modernization very often have a separate construction force whose sole function is to work on projects of this nature.

The most common approach to manning construction and major projects is to use the regular maintenance force. All projects of this nature are manned and scheduled in the same manner as routine maintenance work. When the needs for major projects exceed the manpower availability, then the project work is contracted outside the plant as required to meet a given deadline.

Another approach would be to separate the in-plant maintenance force from all construction or major work and to contract all this type of work. The coordination of the project in these cases is generally the responsibility of the plant engineering or the industrial engineering department.

The most effective way to handle construction and project-type work is to employ what is commonly called the *leveling factor*. The leveling factor can be compared to a sine curve with a horizontal base line drawn through the center of the curve as shown in Fig. 2–8. The straight horizontal base line represents the actual maintenance force manning, and the curve with its peaks and valleys represents the fluctuating needs of the project and regular work load for that particular plant. The staffing of the maintenance department is sufficient to handle certain major projects during the valleys of the normal maintenance work load. However, when the normal maintenance work load is at a peak, construction work should be contracted out.

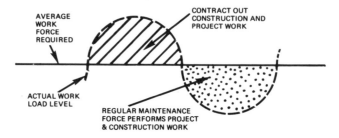

Figure 2–8. Construction and project work leveling factor.

Maintenance Staff Services

More and more plants are instituting a type of maintenance organization which involves the creation of a specialized group of individuals under the heading of maintenance staff services. The size of this group is a function of the size of the maintenance department. For example, a department of at least 20 to 25 craftsmen is necessary to justify a one-man staff services group. On the other hand, a maintenance department of 800 craftsmen could very easily have as many as 30 to 40 people engaged in staff services. The staff services organization concept is to free the first line supervisors from administrative details. This enables each supervisor to concentrate on his main task, that of supervising his people. In addition, the people in staff services become specialists and are generally better qualified for the basic functions of staff services. These functions are:

1) Scheduling of maintenance work
2) Stores administration and coordination
3) Administration of maintenance systems and procedures
4) Maintenance clerical operations
5) Preventive maintenance program development and administration

An examination of these functions and the type of personnel who would perform them are as follows:

Planning and Scheduling. Personnel with a strong craft background, and in many cases formal training in the planning of maintenance work, would be responsible for the planning and scheduling of all but emergency maintenance work. This staff can be organized and used as a central staff, or, if the organization is a large plant facility, the planners could be assigned to a given area or zone and could specialize in planning for that particular operation. In many cases the scheduling of maintenance work is performed by a specialist whose responsibility is to develop the daily or weekly schedule based upon priorities and production needs. However, the functions of planning and scheduling can be combined and performed by the planning staff. Generally, the size of the maintenance department will determine if specialization is necessary.

Maintenance Stores. In most process industries, 90 percent of the stores are maintenance items. Therefore, it is logical that the stores inventory and organization be controlled by the maintenance department. Furthermore, where a staff services group exists, it is logical that the stores organization report to the staff services manager, since a very important part of planning maintenance work is the preplanning of material needs. It is important to assure that the material is available at the time the job starts. However, in nonprocess industries, maintenance items are only a small part of stores; production supplies are the bulk of the inventory. The inventory procedures in these industries are usually quite sophisticated. Since the maintenance stores are only a small part of the overall stores activity, there is no advantage in having the stores function report to maintenance.

Preventive Maintenance Administration. For a preventive maintenance (PM) program to be effective, central control and adequate documentation is necessary. The program will include scheduling of preventive maintenance, keeping of equipment history, and reviewing and analysis of frequencies. Since staff services are located at the central control point, it is logical that preventive maintenance, which requires central control and administration, will be part of the staff services group. However, it is important to remember that the PM activity to which we are referring is only the development and administration of the program and not the execution of the program. The responsibility for insuring that PM tasks are performed is still that of first-line maintenance supervision.

POWER AND UTILITIES

The production and distribution of utilities must be continuous and uninterrupted. Thus, it is necessary to include in the plant engineering organization a supervisor for power and utilities. In a large company, a superintendent for this section may be found with lower-level supervisors. In a small company, a single foreman reporting to the plant engineer may be sufficient. Frequently, the power and utilities foreman reports to the maintenance manager.

Responsibilities for maintenance of powerhouse equipment are generally assigned to powerhouse operating personnel. This work is performed by powerhouse maintenance men in higher labor grades than the operating personnel, and some companies do employ the services of the general maintenance department. If the maintenance function is organized on an area basis, then the power plant and major utility equipment stations should receive maintenance service from the area groups in which the equipment is located.

In some process plants, the power and utility function is classified as an operating department with its own superintendent and is, therefore, out of the jurisdiction of the plant engineer. Frequently, a process industry will have a highly complex transmission and distribution network. Primary and secondary power distribution requires substantial equipment such as feeders, transformers, switch plates, and protective equipment. The proper selection of this equipment is a function of the plant's requirements and needs. Losses associated with power interruption are more serious in some process industries than others. Therefore, the type of protective equipment used is most important.

One of the major responsibilities of the power and utilities section should be provision for standby power. Because of the increased frequency with which power blackouts are encountered in the public power companies, consideration must be given to emergency procedures. Where standby power is available, as from a gas turbine generator set, each member of the section should know the procedure for cutting out of the power system and switching to the auxiliary power source. At a minimum, battery-operated lights that switch on automatically when the power fails should be available, thus eliminating the problem of workers trying to leave a darkened building. Many states require such emergency lights, and even if they are not required they are an obvious and necessary precaution. The power charge held by these battery systems should be checked routinely. A signed checklist should be filed for each inspection.

Emergency procedures should also be established for other powerhouse and utility functions. Steam-producing equipment can fail, water mains can fracture and interrupt fire fighting capabilities, and external damage can knock out electrical gear. A well-organized emergency procedure will keep production time losses to a minimum.

It is important to keep communication lines open with production supervision so that the objectives of the utility divisions are consistent with company goals and needs. Maintenance of the utility distribution system may not involve many employees, but additions and substantial changes will. The utility division must lean heavily on the plant engineering staff for design and installation, planning, and scheduling. The procurement of the material and the scheduling function should be handled by staff engineers or by an established group in the maintenance department. Most new or revised utility installations will be for machinery and equipment to be installed by maintenance division employees. The plant engineer should establish reasonable preventive maintenance schedules for powerhouse equipment and electrical substations.

Utility records should indicate the ratio between the power used to the actual available capacity. This should include particular details on specific areas of the plant in order to prevent facilities from being overloaded. This information is also useful for planning future utility additions.

In planning for new utilities, consideration should be given to the provision of fail-safe features. Any time power fails to a machine tool, even a grinding wheel, it should be necessary to actuate a reset button. If the tool simply starts up again when power is restored there is a strong possibility of damage to it or injury to the operator.

POLLUTION ABATEMENT

While the chart for Fig. 2-2 shows the responsibility for pollution abatement as a separate section within the plant engineering department, this is not always the case. Frequently, pollution abatement is associated with the power and utilities division. One of the reasons for this association is that very often pollutants are by-products of power generation, such as fly ash from power-house chimneys or cooling water for steam turbines. In steel plants the major problem is likely to be the pollution of streams by waste pickle liquor. To combat this type of problem a chemical engineer would be the best candidate. While there are aspects of pollution involving electrical, mechanical, and civil engineering, there are usually sources the chemical engineer can turn to when problems develop in these areas.

A good deal of the pollution control engineer's time will be spent in tracing local, state, and federal regulations in this area. One of the characteristics of pollution control is that it is a great deal more costly to impose upon an existing plant or process than to build into a new plant or process. If the pollution control engineer builds up a reference library of rules and regulations, books and periodicals, and manufacturers' catalogs, he will be in a good position to provide advice when problems arise. There are many consulting firms in the area of pollution control, and considerable free advice is available from the manufacturers of equipment for monitoring, treating, and recycling industrial wastes. The pollution control engineer should make it a practice to speak to local groups and to explain what the firm is doing in this area.

FUTURE ORGANIZATIONAL PRACTICE

In the future, the plant engineering department will undoubtedly be a larger group than it is today. The department will tend to report at a higher level than is common at present, and the plant engineer will be consulted more often with respect to major decisions. As equipment and processes become more complex, newer skills will be required and additional divisions will have to be formed. The plant engineering department will more than likely be headed by a manager, with several supervisors reporting to him.

In manufacturing, the project management type of organization will become increasingly important, and more personnel from plant engineering will be assigned to such groups. Fig. 2-9 shows how the plant engineering personnel will fit into a project organization, and how the project group operates almost

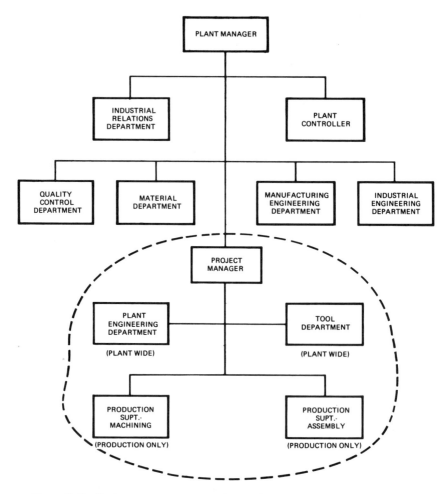

Figure 2–9. Project management superimposed upon a functional organization.

independently of the rest of the plant. The great advantage of the project organization is that it will focus responsibility upon one individual, the project manager, who knows that he is being evaluated continuously on the success or failure of his project. The greatest disadvantage of the project group is that each member of the group, except for the manager, reports to two su-periors — the functional head of his department and the project head. Authority and responsibility are not so well defined, nor is there a clear-cut hierarchical relationship between the project manager and the department heads.

Such an arrangement is generally desirable from the standpoint of the plant engineering group, in that it keeps their contribution in the mainstream of activity and makes their relationship to the success of the effort more apparent. By the nature of the project type of activity, the plant engineers have ready access to the latest and best in equipment, and they can see their ideas quickly transformed into reality.

As mentioned earlier, there is the disadvantage in detached assignment that the particular engineer will become specialized in a narrow field. There is the additional problem that the project-assigned engineer will be out of direct observation by his department head and perhaps forgotten when candidates are being considered for promotion. To guard against this, departmental meetings should be held, to which all engineers are invited and in which they would be encouraged to air their problems. Also, the manager should make project assignments on a rotating basis, not more than a year or two in duration. Unless the individual strongly desires to stay with a particular project, he should be given a variety of assignments.

Chapter 3

Engineering Management

The importance of the plant engineering department depends upon the company product line and the relative significance attached to the department by the company. Its role changes from *total*, in companies whose business is selling plant engineering services, through *partial*, in which the engineering groups are service organizations for a manufacturing facility, to *limited*, in which the firm goes outside for most of its engineering requirements.

In the case of the total concept, the company has often been founded by a group of engineers as a vehicle for marketing their services. Thus, fundamentally, the company is an engineering enterprise with all other functions, such as accounting, shipping, receiving, advertising, personnel, etc., considered as auxiliary operations.

In the case of the limited concept, the engineering department is often a repository for new and old drawings, foundation plans of the building left over from the original construction, lighting and wiring plans, and possibly some equipment overhaul manuals. Often this will be a "one-man show," with the occupant ignored except during equipment breakdowns. Occasionally, the plant engineer is consulted by a department manager or the purchasing agent on the soliciting of bids for new equipment, and he will be expected to take the state inspector on his rounds.

The contents of this chapter will be devoted to the in-between or partial role for the plant engineering department. In all probability, this represents the great majority of applications. In order to discuss plant engineering management in the 1970s in a few words, with due consideration for the wide range of businesses, the multiplicity of facilities, and the variety of products, the emphasis is on the medium-sized plant, with exceptions as noted.

If a company is medium sized, it is probably manned by skilled and semi-skilled employees who are members of a union having a contractual agreement with the company. Its products will be sold in competition with others and are therefore subject to outside influences on raw materials, wage levels, and

27

competitive selling prices. It can readily be seen that the areas where control can be exercised and changes can be made are limited and are usually restricted to the manufacturing of products and processing functions. It is in these areas that the plant engineering department can provide assistance. The department manager decides which requests deserve the highest priority and allocates his resources accordingly.

There are several areas of activity in which the plant engineering department can influence the profitability of the firm. These areas of responsibility are generally recognized as consisting of plant facilities, processes and equipment, systems and control procedures, drawings and blueprint control, and staffing and personnel.[1]

PLANT FACILITIES

The plant engineering department will ideally have multiple responsibilities including (1) the cost of new facilities, (2) the continuous operation of new facilities, and (3) the development of improvements in existing facilities. In examining the cost of new facilities, plant engineering will be involved in establishing the fundamental needs of the company. Specifications will have to be drawn up and design parameters established so that competitive bidding can be undertaken. The department's responsibility is to translate the company's requirements into drawings and other working documents.

With regard to the second area of responsibility, the continuous operation of new facilities, we are usually more concerned with the operation of equipment, per se, than with the condition of facilities. However, safe, comfortable, attractive, well-lit surroundings undoubtedly enhance morale, and good morale helps to keep production at higher levels.

In the third area, the development of improvements in facilities, plant engineering will not ordinarily be as active as in the other two areas. For example, in a manufacturing facility, changes involving walls and foundations are seldom necessary. Structural features, including heating and ventilation systems, usually remain unchanged. However, modifications may be necessary when changes occur in conveyor lines, heat loads, or exhaust systems. In this area, the mechanical and electrical designer takes the lead, with the facilities being altered in accordance with their requirements.

Building Codes

Building codes must be a major consideration in planning new facilities. For the purpose of safeguarding life and property from various hazards in residential, commercial, and industrial facilities, a number of building codes have been developed. These codes were formulated by the authorities to ensure minimum standards in the design, construction, maintenance, and operation of the facilities. Compliance with these codes will result in an installation which is essentially free from hazards although it is not necessarily the best design.

The three codes with which the plant engineer should be familiar and have

---

[1]Vernon, ed., *op. cit.*, 219–25.

immediate access to in his day-to-day operations are: The National Fire Protection Association (NFPA) *National Electric Code*,[2] The American Society of Mechanical Engineers *Boiler and Pressure Vessel Code*,[3] and the local building code of the city or municipality in which the plant is located.

The *National Electric Code* contains the following basic sections which should be of specific interest to the plant engineer:

1) Wiring design and protection
2) Wiring methods and materials
3) Equipment and general use
4) Special occupancies
5) Special equipment
6) Communication systems.

It should be noted that this code is a very widely distributed document familiar to everyone involved in electrical work. While the NFPA has no power to enforce compliance, many government bodies have adopted the code almost verbatim and do provide enforcement provisions. In addition, insurance inspectors use the code to determine the adequacy of the design and construction of electrical installations. These two considerations, in addition to the basic premise that following the code is good practice, makes familiarity with it mandatory for the plant engineer.

In addition to the *National Electric Code*, the NFPA publishes other standards under the *National Fire Code*. Though these other standards are considerably more specialized than the electrical code, the plant engineer should be aware of them and be able to refer to them when necessary.

ASME's *Boiler and Pressure Vessel Code* covers steam boilers and other pressure vessels. The code contains rules relating to safety in the design, fabrication, and inspection of boilers and unfired vessels during contruction, and offers suggestions based on good practice concerning the care and inspection of boilers and pressure vessels in service. The National Board of Boiler and Pressure Vessel Inspectors, composed of chief inspectors of states and municipalities in the United States and Canada who have adopted the code, has functioned since 1919 to uniformly administer and enforce the rules of the *Boiler and Pressure Vessel Code* under state and local laws and ordinances. Many city codes have adopted the ASME code in its entirety, adding only a permit, inspection, and testing procedure along with penalty provisions for failure to comply.

Though it would be impractical for the plant engineer to check every detail of construction when a new boiler or pressure vessel is purchased, he should determine that the unit is obtained from a reputable manufacturer and that it bears the ASME symbol indicating that the vessel meets the requirements of the ASME *Boiler and Pressure Vessel Code*. If a used pressure vessel is purchased, the plant engineer should make sure that the unit is thoroughly tested and inspected for the intended service according to the code and the local ordinance.

When a new vessel is manufactured or an existing unit modified at the plant site by the plant construction or maintenance crew, the plant engineer must

---

[2] *National Electric Code*, National Fire Codes, Vol. 5, No. 70 (Boston: National Fire Protection Association International, 1962).

[3] *Boiler and Pressure Vessel Code* (New York: American Society of Mechanical Engineers, June 30, 1967).

have sufficient knowledge of the code to be certain that the work is being accomplished accordingly, and in addition he must arrange to have the unit checked and the installation inspected by the local boiler inspector.

One of the more important tasks of the plant engineer concerning boilers and pressure vessels is to ensure, on a continuing basis, that the designed maximum allowable working pressures are not exceeded. In addition, other factors such as abrasion and signs of corrosion should be periodically checked. These factors, applied to both boilers and unfired pressure vessels, are set forth in the code.

Many cities and municipalities have a comprehensive building code incorporated into the local ordinance structure. A large portion of these local codes are composed of the major codes explained above. Additionally, a number of other items are covered, many of which are concerned with public buildings, amusement parks, apartment buildings, and so on. The fact that much of the code is not applicable does not mean that it can be disregarded.

In addition, many of these local codes also provide for the certification of individuals involved in certain types of work. Only those individuals so certified can perform this work legally under the provisions of the code. This certification is most commonly applied to electrical and plumbing construction and rearrangement workers and to the operators of boilers at pressures above 15 psi (gage).

The technical regulations mentioned earlier are taken from the national codes. The local codes explain the procedures for obtaining various permits for inspections, tests, and submission of plans. Applicable fees are listed along with penalties for noncompliance. The plant engineer needs to be particularly familiar with the procedural aspects of the local codes because complying with these procedures will be his responsibility.

If a municipal or city code does not exist in his locale, it is a good idea for the plant engineer to obtain a code from a major city to use as a guide. By following its basic provisions, he can assure himself of an accepted method of design and work performance. As one example of this, some plants outside the limits of one large midwestern city have adopted the practice of having their stationary engineers (boiler tenders) certified and licensed by the city under the provisions of its code to ensure that the engineers are qualified despite the lack of any legal regulations.

Environmental Control

One of the major responsibilities of plant engineering is the control of the physical environment within which facilities' activities occur. Controlling the physical environment requires that the plant engineer use the technologies of air conditioning, heating, ventilating, lighting, and sound and vibration control.

For example, in the manufacture of precision electronic components, such as television picture tubes, the critical considerations are air conditioning and lighting. In a maintenance machine shop, vibration control may be most critical. However, it should be remembered that obtaining the best environment in any given situation requires proper utilization and balance of all environmental control factors. The following discussion will define each control factor and outline the basic points for the plant engineer to consider in their utilization.

Air conditioning can be defined as the complete conditioning of air, including temperature and humidity control, ventilation, and air distribution. Over the years, air conditioning has taken on increased importance both in industry or in process applications such as offices and institutions. Since air conditioning is normally more complicated than the other environmental control factors, it is important that the plant engineer be knowledgeable in the design, operation, and maintenance of these systems.

Heating can be defined simply as the process of raising the temperature of air to the desired level. There are several major heating systems in general use today. These are (1) gas-, coal-, or oil-fired central hot-air systems; (2) electric baseboard systems, (3) steam or hot-water radiator systems, and (4) electric, gas, or steam suspended unit heaters.

Each of these systems has its advantages and disadvantages, and a complete analysis must be made before a selection is made. Such factors as power cost, flexibility, control, cleanliness, equipment complexity, and maintenance must be considered in detail. For example, in many areas gas is cheaper than oil, and electric power is the most expensive. However, since electric heating offers better control, this factor may outweigh the fuel cost consideration. Though hot-water heat is usually "cleaner" than hot-air heat, the cost of installing the piping system and radiators for the hot-water system might be greater than the cost of the ductwork needed for the hot-air system.

Because of the number of variables involved in determining the proper heating plant and system, the best approach is to make a detailed analysis answering the following questions:

1) What are the heating requirements?
2) What is the fuel cost comparison?
3) What is the equipment and installation cost?
4) What are the maintenance requirements?
5) How clean must the heated areas be?
6) How quiet must the heated areas be?

Ventilation refers to the process of circulating air, exhausting stale air, and introducing fresh air to remove bulk heat from the area being ventilated. Ventilation also involves the removal of dust, fumes, and odors from the air.

In selecting a ventilating system, three equipment components must be considered: (1) the fans or driving force, (2) the ductwork or distribution system, and (3) the air filtration system. Normally, in a ventilating system, the filtration is kept uncomplicated by the use of cartridge or bay filters only. The more sophisticated electrostatic and oil-film filtration devices are usually used only with air conditioning and specialized systems.

In addition to component selection, the following considerations must be analyzed:

1) Corrosive and/or abrasive atmospheric components
2) Space limitations
3) Cost of equipment
4) Temperature gradients
5) Quantity of air to be handled and the fan static pressure required
6) Noise and vibration limitations.

Proper illumination in work areas is a necessary condition for good productivity from a work force. Proper lighting involves more than simple light intensity. Factors such as cost, glare, heat generation, distribution, and ease of maintenance must also be considered. Once the lighting system has been installed, it must be properly maintained. Many well-designed systems do not furnish the intended amount of illumination because of a lack of continuing maintenance. Proper maintenance includes (1) painting of walls and ceilings in light colors, (2) washing and cleaning of ceilings and walls, (3) fixture washing and cleaning, (4) maintenance of proper supply voltage, and (5) lamp replacement schedules.

Noise and vibration control has been given increasing attention in recent years. However, the field is still in a state of flux, partially because sound and vibration have such variable effects. Whereas most individuals are uncomfortable at a temperature of 90° F and a relative humidity over 80 percent, the effect of sound and vibration is considerably less predictable.

In some cases vibration control becomes the critical consideration, as in a research laboratory where excessive vibration can destroy the calibration of delicate instruments. Vibration control has become a highly specialized technology. At the present time there are several companies engaged solely in the design and manufacture of vibration control devices which increase the life, reliability, and accuracy of the equipment on which they are installed.

Experiments in sound control have shown that reduction of noise levels causes workers to expend less energy while at the same time increasing their output. It is known too that exposure to excessive sound can cause hearing losses and other harmful effects.[4]

PROCESSES AND EQUIPMENT

The plant engineer's role in the specification and selection of processes and equipment can vary from virtual nonparticipation to full responsibility. In addition, this same statement can apply to the areas of plant layout, equipment modification, and equipment replacement. Ultimately, however, it is the responsibility of the plant engineer to provide all of the facilities required to support new processes and equipment; therefore, it is generally in the best interest of efficiency and economy that he be consulted whenever these items are being considered. The following paragraphs outline some of the ways in which he will be able to make significant contributions.

Equipment Specification and Selection

The plant engineer's knowledge of available facilities, or of the ways existing facilities can be modified to accommodate a new process or equipment, can mean the difference between an economical, fast installation or an installation which will never perform the desired function. If new facilities must be provided, he should help specify the arrangement of utility services such as electricity, compressed air, water, lighting, and any of the other process or equipment requirements. In all cases, he should make himself available for consultation in the early stages of equipment specification and selection.

---

[4]"Noise Pollution: How Much Can You Afford," *Steel,* Jan. 13, 1969, 21–25.

As mentioned earlier in this chapter, the plant engineer is also expected to be familiar with the various nationally published codes. In addition to these codes, he should also be familiar with various specifications and guidelines published by the National Electrical Manufacturers Association (NEMA) so that this information can be included, where applicable, in new process or equipment specifications. This familiarity need not be as detailed or as comprehensive as would be required for the local building or plumbing codes, but a general knowledge should be sufficient in most cases.

The plant engineer can supply detailed information on such items as water flow capacity, electrical power availability, and average lighting levels. This type of information will be required in drawing up the specifications as well as in making proper equipment selection. A good example of this is the inclusion of close temperature and humidity provisions in an equipment specification. If the air-handling system in the area where this equipment is to be installed is incapable of furnishing air to these requirements, and the equipment cannot perform its desired function without them, then the cost of modifications and refinements to the air-handling system must be included in the overall cost of the project. On the other hand, if the proposed equipment could perform just as well without the strict environmental conditions, or if the equipment itself can be manufactured to withstand less stringent environmental conditions, then the strict temperature and humidity conditions can be dropped. In any case, the plant engineer's knowledge of just what can be provided in the way of utilities and environment can play a major role in determining the final form of new equipment specifications.

When the specifications for new equipment have been submitted to various vendors and their proposals have been received, the plant engineer can still perform a vital service in the selection of the equipment to be purchased. No matter how comprehensive and restricting the specifications are, there will be plant facility-related differences between proposals submitted by the vendor. This is found to be true even when equipment specifications are written around one specific brand or model. The vendors, in their competitive bidding procedures, will recognize this and offer features and refinements not available in the preselected equipment. Many times these differences will appear in the form of greater economy of operation, and equipment that will perform the same functions while consuming less water, compressed air, or electrical energy will be highlighted in the proposal. The plant engineer is responsible for evaluating these operating economies and reporting on the possible savings if one equipment is selected over another.

The plant engineer can be of considerable assistance to the groups who are writing equipment specifications and making equipment selections. One example of this type of contribution is when power factor capacitors on large motor loads are specified. A poor-quality power factor can account for a significant portion of electrical power costs. Many electric utility companies will have low power factor penalty clauses incorporated into their rate structure. Since induction motors are the largest contributors to low power factors, power factor capacitors should be specified on the larger motors. The additional cost of the power factor capacitor is quickly regained in lower energy rates and conserved electrical capacity.

Another example of how the plant engineer can help in the specification of new equipment or processes is in the area of water-cooled equipment. The use of domestic water, whether from a well or from municipal sources, is extremely wasteful solely for cooling. If chilled water is available, the specification for the process or equipment should specify that it be used. Several benefits can be accrued from the use of chilled water for cooling. Some of these are more efficient operation, smaller piping and heat exchangers for a given cooling load, and better utilization of chilling capacity. When chilled water is not available, or the chilling capacity is not sufficient to handle the additional load, every consideration should be given to the use of cooling towers or the connection of a number of heat exchangers in series. Recent emphasis on thermal pollution by governmental authorities makes it necessary to recirculate water used for cooling purposes. There is increased pressure on industry to reduce its water consumption, and the plant engineer must always be on the outlook for means of increasing the efficiency of its use.

Another cost related to plant engineering that is not always considered in equipment selection is ease and economy of installation. Should the proposed equipment require two separate voltage inputs—for example, one 480-volt input for power and one 120-volt input for control—the cost of providing both of these voltages could easily exceed the cost of a small transformer offered as part of a competitive package. The small transformer could be used to step down the 480-volt input to 120 volts, thus eliminating the need for one of the power sources.

The plant engineer must keep open the channels of communication between himself and the engineering groups who specify and select equipment. Unless good communication is maintained between plant engineering and these other groups, there is a high probability that the equipment purchased will be unsatisfactory. Additionally, the communication between plant engineering and the purchasing department must be good, particularly where the plant has a centralized purchasing department. Clear, concise specifications will enable the purchasing agent to perform his function intelligently. Such specifications will ensure that the reliability and the quality of the equipment receive as much consideration as price.

Preventive maintenance factors such as simplification of disassembly for inspection, extension of lubrication schedules through the use of larger lubricant reservoirs, standardization of components to minimize the spare parts problem, and similar items are often neglected in the specification and selection procedures. Since in many plants the plant engineering group is responsible for implementing a preventive maintenance program, it is also the responsibility of plant engineering to include preventive maintenance considerations before any equipment is purchased. If the regreasing of a bearing for a fan involves the removal of inspection plates, shrouds, braces, and other obstructions, a fan of another manufacturer should be considered. Preventive maintenance should not be a nuisance item, to be considered only after the equipment has been installed. The proper time to take it into consideration is prior to the purchase of the equipment.

Plant Layout

The most advanced and efficient manufacturing process or equipment can fail if not properly integrated into the overall plant layout. Frequently, an industrial or process engineering group will arrange a manufacturing facility for optimum production through the use of once-through flow with a minimum of back tracks and shunt paths. Only after the layout is completed is it made known to the plant engineering department, who must then plan and install the needed utilities. This practice can create serious problems. Such difficulties as limited floor loadings, inadequate power sources, and lack of exhaust facilities are then discovered. Such discoveries make it necessary to revamp the layout, and many hours of layout time have been wasted, perhaps seriously delaying the installation of a badly needed facility.

Early consultations with the plant engineer when the plant layout is in the preliminary design stages will bring the industrial or process engineering group a wealth of useful information. The plant engineer should know if the sprinkler system is adequate, if the compressed air system can supply the new area, if the electrical distribution system has sufficient reserve capacity. Some of the other factors which must be considered when designing a new plant layout are listed as follows:

1) Adequate water supply
2) Sufficient air conditioning to handle the increased heat generation
3) Adequate make-up air to balance exhaust requirements
4) Proper lighting
5) Proper access to equipment for maintenance and repair
6) Convenient drain and waste lines.

Naturally, this list is not all-inclusive, and a machine-by-machine survey should be made to determine the exact utility requirements. A simple device which can be of great help is a utility requirement summary sheet as shown in Fig. 3–1. This listing gives a summary of what type and what quantity of utility is required, on a machine-by-machine basis. It then becomes a simple matter of arithmetic to determine exactly how much of any utility is required.

After required utilities have been determined and the locations of the equipment have been established, the plant engineer must then design the utility distribution system. This may consist of a simple specification of the size and quantity of utility outlets to be branched off from an existing distribution system. However, in the case of a major rearrangement or an installation in a new facility, a new utility distribution system must be designed. The utility requirement summary sheet has already provided the plant engineer with the type of utility that may be required and the maximum quantity of any utility which must be delivered. Then the design of the utility distribution system is simply a matter of locating the utility feeder in a position to provide economical branch runs.

The actual layout of a utility distribution system is generally determined by the location of the equipment serviced; however, there are variations and modifications of this practice which deserve some attention. One of these variations is called the *modular approach* and is shown in Fig. 3–2. In this distribution

WORK STATION UTILITY & SERVICE REQUIREMENTS

QTY. OF STATIONS	STATION NO.	WORK CENTER DESCRIPTION	ELECTRICAL POWER								SIGNAL
			115 V 1∅	208 V 1∅	208 V 3∅	KVA PEAK	480 V	28 V.D.C.	400 HZ	OTHER	100 KC

SIGNAL		D. I. WATER MIN. PSI ——— GPH	COOLING H₂0 RECIRCULATED — ± —F PSI – GPH	WATER DOMESTIC COLD 50 PSI – GPH	WATER DOMESTIC HOT 50 PSI – GPH	AIR		DRAIN WASTE MATERIAL		
100 KC	1 MEG.					90 PSI	20 PSI	MATERIAL TYPE	GPH · MAX.	TYPE

FUME EXHAUST			VACUUM	GASES DISTRIBUTED					PHONES	
TYPE	DUCT	CFM		TYPE						
				C F H						

Figure 3–1. Utility requirement summary sheet.

system, the utilities are arranged in a pattern that repeats itself over and over again, as often as required to provide a given area with the required utilities. The pattern repetition distance is generally determined by some building characteristic such as column spacing. Once the pattern repetition distance is specified and the process or equipment is arranged in a modular fashion, the utility service branches are installed. Only those utilities required for each module are installed, with space being reserved for the addition of other utilities in future installations.

The chief advantage of a modular utility distribution system is the ease with which processes or equipment may be rearranged. To rearrange an area, all that must be done is to "unplug" the equipment, move it to the new location and then "plug" it into the utility branch which will be in the same relative position as it was in the old location. The chief disadvantage of the modular system is the additional cost of providing a plug-in utility branch system. This additional cost can be deferred somewhat by installing only those utility branches required at first and then, as rearrangements dictate, installing additional utility branches. For example, if on the first installation all process or equipment modules require compressed air and 120-volt, single-phase power, and one module requires 480-volt three-phase power, only those utilities are provided even though the

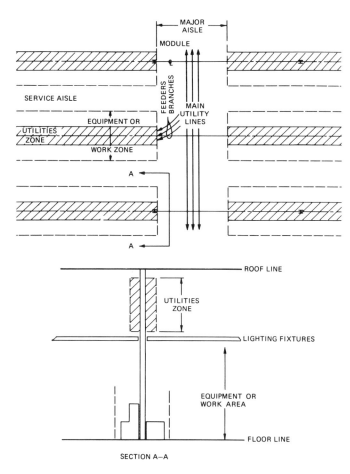

Figure 3-2. Modular utility distribution system.

main feeders are installed for all other types of utility requirements. Then for future installations requiring domestic water, an appropriately sized line branch can be installed for a specific module. Ultimately, each of the modules will be furnished with all of the utilities.

Another approach to the problem of providing utilities to an area is the *utilities floor concept* shown in Fig. 3-3. This is used in multilevel buildings where alternate levels contain only utilities that are routed up to processes or equipment through the ceiling of the utility level. The utility level is generally "thinner" than the process or equipment level, being from seven to nine feet in height. Just enough lighting is provided to enable workmen to make utility connections and provide safe movement within that level. This concept is particularly attractive where the process or equipment levels must be kept free of the clutter and confusion of an overhead utilities distribution system with its vertical utility drops to processes or equipment. A second advantage is that

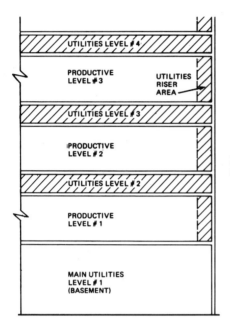

Figure 3-3. Utilities floor distribution system.

installation of new equipment or rearrangements can be carried out with a minimum of disruption to production.

The utilities floor concept of utilities distribution is suitable in installations such as hospitals, light manufacturing plants, school laboratories, office buildings, and other similar activities where a multilevel building is an economical way to house that activity. This arrangement would not be suitable for heavy industry where the process or equipment must be housed on one level or where the floor is constantly wet or flooded as in a plating facility.

Equipment Modification

After a new item of equipment has been installed and in operation, sometimes it is "not quite right." Possibly the specification was not clearly worded, so the vendor misunderstood an operating requirement. Perhaps the process requirements have changed so much that the equipment will not perform as originally intended. This is not to say that the equipment will not function at all, but rather that it will not operate as efficiently for the demands of the process standard. At any rate, it is obvious that some equipment modifications are necessary.

When the plant engineer does become involved in equipment modifications, there are certain steps he should take to ensure that the modifications will be a one-time event which will eliminate future difficulties. Obviously, the manufacturer of the equipment should be consulted when problems arise. Having designed and constructed the equipment, he is most familiar with its capabilities. Sometimes a very simple modification, such as a change in the type of time delay relay or substitution of a larger air cylinder, is all that is required. The manufacturer is in a position by his unique knowledge of the equipment to suggest better and less expensive changes in order to obtain the desired result.

If, however, the equipment is of an advanced type, it is quite possible that the manufacturer will not be able to suggest the desired changes. This is especially true when the equipment is the first of a newly introduced model line. Technology is advancing so rapidly in certain areas that the equipment is as close to the limit of the state of the art as the product or process. In cases such as these, the plant engineer must rely on the process engineering group for guidance. Since the maintenance men look to him for information and technical direction, he must be familiar with the requirements of any modifications. This, of course, means close cooperation between the plant engineer and other engineering groups. Modifications of this sort are generally of the cut-and-fit variety and will involve many blind alleys before the proper solution is found. Thus, the second step the plant engineer must take is to obtain the guidance and cooperation of other engineering groups so that he, in turn, can provide proper direction to the men.

Regardless of how simple the equipment modification is, the plant engineer must be sure that all equipment changes are properly documented. Working from marked-up drawings and diagrams is permissible while the modifications are in progress because the equipment status is fluid and may be changed from one form to another in rapid order. However, once the changes are completed, and the equipment is functioning properly, they must be incorporated in the master set of equipment drawings. Whether the drawing changes are accomplished by the equipment manufacturer and reissued as a new set or are made "in-house" on a set of reproducible drawings is immaterial. The prime concern is that the drawings are brought up to date after the modifications are completed. The reason that the plant engineer· is interested in properly revised drawings is that he is generally responsible for the maintenance and repair of the equipment. There is nothing more frustrating or time-consuming than trying to work on equipment that is not properly documented with current and legible drawings. Thus, the third step the plant engineer must take in regard to modifications is to ensure that all changes are reflected in revised drawings, diagrams, and schematics.

The preceding paragraphs were written with new equipment modifications in mind; however, the above also applies to changes made to older equipment. There are many reasons for modifying older equipment. A few of these reasons are the need for more efficient operation; the fact that the cost of making a change is less than the cost of new equipment; the possibility that the equipment, when modified, will be superior to anything available on the market; and the advantage that modified equipment will require fewer repairs and be on line a greater proportion of the time. Regardless of the reason for modification, the plant engineer should be certain that the steps outlined above are followed as completely as possible.

One reason for modifying equipment is ease of maintenance; this is a primary concern of the plant engineer. Here again, close liaison with the equipment manufacturer will provide much valuable assistance. Most reputable manufacturers want feedback from the field regarding the maintenance of their equipment. Some will go so far as to provide field-engineering help and other technical assistance free of charge. The growing trend toward automated, continuously operating equipment and processes makes maintenance and repair costly operations, and any modification which can reduce these expenses will be favorably received.

Some examples of modifications that can ease maintenance and repair are the addition of cleanout and access ports in large hydraulic cylinders, the use of vapor-proof enclosures for electrical controls instead of ordinary sheet metal enclosures, the replacement of light-duty components with heavy-duty rated components, and the extension of lubrication fittings with tubing to more accessible locations.

Many times, a modification is suggested by the maintenance mechanic or the machine operator. The plant engineer must be especially careful that he keeps an open mind in such cases. The mechanic or operator has direct experience with the equipment and can readily see where improvements can be made. Because a modification is suggested by a nonprofessional does not mean that it will be unsatisfactory. Sound, objective judgment should be made regarding all proposals for equipment or process modifications, especially where these changes will affect ease of maintenance.

To summarize, when modifications are to be performed and the plant engineer must assist in implementing these changes, he must be sure that the following steps are taken: (1) the manufacturer of the equipment should be consulted, (2) the product or process engineering group must be consulted, and (3) all equipment or process modifications must be promptly documented.

Equipment Replacement

Of the many economic decisions that a plant engineer must make, the replacement of equipment is perhaps the most troublesome. In the case of production or process equipment, this decision is already made, and all he must do is provide technical advice in the removal of the old equipment and the installation of its replacement. However, in the case of plant or facilities equipment, he is responsible for the entire process from the original decision to replace the equipment to the final check-out of the replacement.

In many cases, the decision to replace equipment is clear-cut. For example, small fractional-horsepower motors which fail should be replaced rather than rewound; however, it may be more economical to rewind a larger or more complex motor. In fact, an older motor rewound with newer, high-temperature insulated wire may run cooler than a new-model, small-frame motor. If an equipment fails or no longer meets operating requirements, the plant engineer has no difficulty in deciding that it must be replaced. Most of the time, replacement decisions will fall into this category. However, in some cases there will be no such compelling reason; the decision will have to be based on an analysis of the situation.

The first factor that the plant engineer should consider is maintenance cost. A quick review of the maintenance history may reveal that repair costs have been increasing. If the maintenance costs over a year are a substantial percentage of the replacement cost, then obviously new equipment is indicated. Plant- or facilities-related equipment will generally have an expected life of ten years or more; during this period it should be relatively maintenance free. Additionally, any maintenance performed on new equipment should be routine in nature—drive belt replacement or greasing, for example. Any out-of-the-ordinary repairs should be noted by the plant engineer. It is on the basis of such nonroutine repairs that he will make his replacement decision.

A second factor that a plant engineer should consider is the ability of a piece of equipment to perform its required function. One example of this factor would be an older air compressor which, although performing in a satisfactory manner, does deliver a small amount of oil with the compressed air. In certain operations, a small amount of oil in the air is not objectionable. However, when the compressed air is supplying a number of pneumatic control instruments, fine orifices and other delicate devices under such circumstances quickly become clogged and nonfunctional. Thus, either the older air compressor should be rebuilt with a special oil filter added, or a new oilless-type air compressor should be installed. In many cases, complete replacement may be justified because of the increased operating efficiency of a new air compressor.

Increased operating efficiency brings up the third factor that a plant engineer should consider when deciding if a machine or piece of equipment should be replaced. One of the areas where he can make significant contributions to manufacturing or operational economies is in the realm of utilities conservation. Any time an older machine or equipment can be replaced with a significantly more economical version, a very detailed cost comparison should be drawn. The cost comparison should include at least the following items:

1) Operating costs per hour
2) Operating costs per unit produced
3) Maintenance costs
4) Remaining life of the existing unit
5) Rated life of a new unit
6) Total operating cost per unit produced over the life of the unit, including maintenance costs
7) Removal and installation costs.

Comparison of the items listed above plus any other items dictated by local conditions will enable the plant engineer to make a sound economic decision.

Other, less obvious factors may be of some assistance to the plant engineer in deciding whether or not to replace equipment. A tax advantage may be obtained if an older, fully depreciated machine is replaced with a slightly different, more efficient machine requiring a capital expenditure. Installation of new, more advanced antipollution devices in place of older devices may well bring tax advantages or lower utility rates. Many corporate or company accounting and legal departments can provide the plant engineer with these and other reasons for replacement.

To summarize, a plant engineer will have to consider maintenance costs, operating effectiveness, operating efficiency, and other individually determined factors when making a decision concerning equipment replacements. If thorough study is made, the correct answer will generally be self-evident.

SYSTEMS AND PROCEDURES

The engineering group should have a procedures manual which covers the processing of all communications with which the plant engineering department deals. In addition, the department should have its corporate or plant reference manual of engineering standards containing authorized construction specifications, equipment installation methods, and company drafting techniques. This will not only eliminate overlapping and inconsistent engineering and drawings on routine items, but will also require conformity to properly established engineering practices. Fig. 3–4 is a page taken from a typical standard practices manual.

The engineering project control procedure should be detailed in the procedures manual. Most plants do a satisfactory job of processing orders via plant

Joint Design	Base Metal, Use, Etc.		Filler Metal	Weld Pos.	Inch Thk Range
Single Vee Double Welded Manual	ASME	SA 240, Type 304, 304 L	R - 389	F	3/16 - 7/8
	ASME	SA 300, Gr. D & E 3 - 1/2% Ni Steel	R - 186	F	3/16 - 3/4
	Non-Code	Cr Steel, Type 430	R - 389	All	
Single Vee Backed Manual	ASME	Cr Ni Steel Type 304, 304 L	R - 389	F	3/16 - 7/8
	ASME USCG, ABS	3-1/2% Ni Steel	R - 186	F	1/16 - 3/4
	Non-Code	Cr Steel	R - 389	All	
Single Vee Backed M. I. G.	ASME	3-1/2% Ni Steel	R - 721	F	3/16 - 1
Double Vee Manual	Non-Code	Cr Steel	R - 389	All	
Single Bevel Single Welded Manual	Non-Code	Cr Steel	R - 389	All	
Single Bevel Double Welded Manual	ASME	3-1/2% Ni Steel	R - 186	F	3/16 - 1-1/2
	ASME	Cr Ni Steel Type 304, 304 L	R - 389	F	3/16 - 1-1/2
	Non-Code	Cr Steel	R - 389	All	
Single Bevel Backed Manual	ASME	3 - 1/2% Ni Steel	R - 186	F	3/16 - 1-1/2
	Non-Code	Cr Steel	R - 389	All	
Fillet Weld Manual	ASME USCG, ABS	3-1/2% Ni Steel	R - 186	F	1/16 - 1-1/2
	ASME	Cr Ni Steel Type 304, 304 L	R - 386	F	3/16 - 1-1/2
	Non-Code	Cr Steel	R - 389	All	

Figure 3–4. Page from typical standard engineering practices manual.

engineering on the basis of criteria such as capital work and dollar levels. However, too many so-called minor jobs which involve significant alterations to process, equipment, or plant services systems are not routed through plant engineering. This short-circuits the systems that ensure proper specification of materials and reduces the opportunities for design improvements in repairing or replacing equipment or components. It can also create inaccuracies in drawings which may cause engineering problems at a later date.

For these reasons, the engineering project control procedure should be designed to encompass construction, alteration, or repair work which (1) requires capitalization, (2) involves an expenditure over a specified amount (this figure frequently ranges from $1,000 to $2,000), or (3) includes potential design and related drawing changes.

The typical steps involved from the conception of a project through the final engineering audit and closing report are shown in Fig. 3–5. This procedure, which may form the basis for the use of Critical Path Methods—Progress Evaluation and Review Techniques (CPM–PERT) networks when justified by the size of the project, may be logically divided into the following four phases:

    Phase I – Preplanning for Approval
    Phase II – Project Engineering
    Phase III – Design Drafting
    Phase IV – Installation

Phase I – Preplanning for Approval

As soon as a decision has been made to begin work on a project, the project engineer enters a description of the job and the date on the project control record shown in Fig. 3–6 and takes the record to the manager of the user department and the chief engineer for approval. These entries are the start of a project history which will be summarized on this form for the duration of the project. These two approvals authorize the work required in phase I, which is concluded with the presentation of the appropriation request for approval. To start these tasks, the chief engineer, or an appropriate engineering supervisor, assigns the work to a project engineer, who assumes primary responsibility until completion or termination.

It is first necessary for the project engineer to estimate the time required and the completion date for phase I in addition to assigning the job order number and priority. He then must prepare the preliminary drawings, sketches, and specifications to define and estimate the job. Estimating should be done according to the categories listed under the job summary on the project control record. As soon as the approximate cost has been determined, the project engineer should evaluate this cost figure. Does it appear reasonable? Does the magnitude of the cost indicate the need to search for another engineering approach? Do the anticipated benefits of the project justify the expenditure which is indicated?

If the project is expected to produce reductions in cost or improvements in profit, it is necessary at this point to utilize quantitative methods for justifying the project. Three common methods should be considered. These methods are (1) payoff, (2) rate of return, and (3) discounted cash flow.

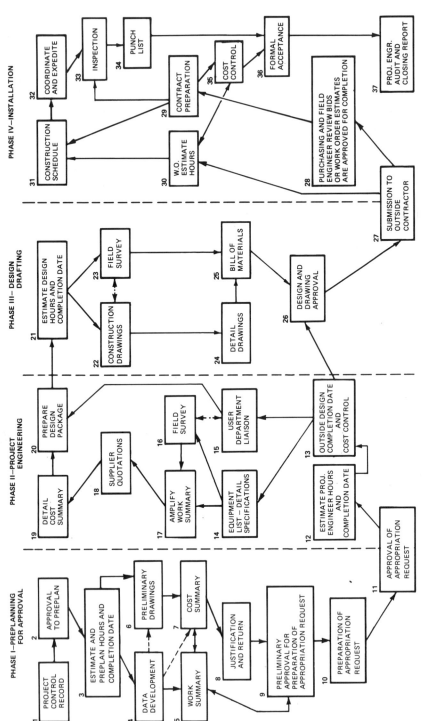

Figure 3-5. Engineering department project control procedure.

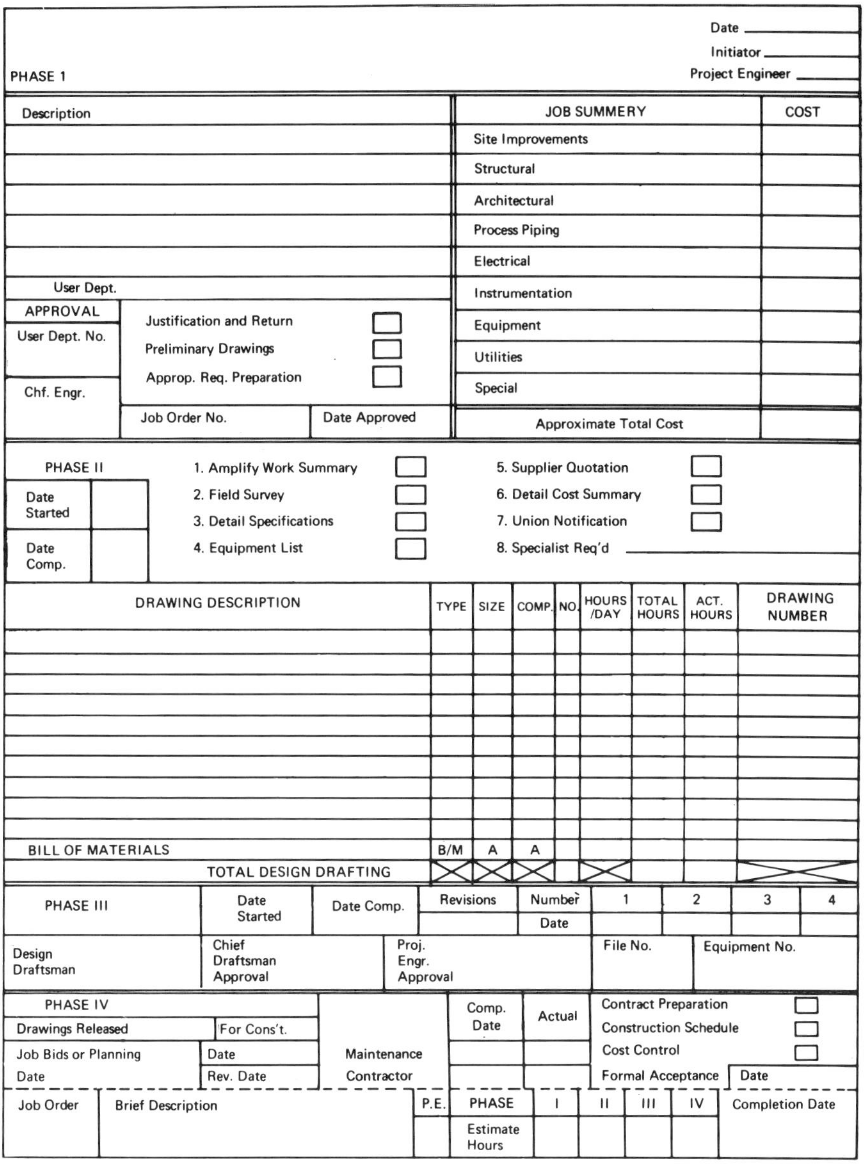

PHASE 1
Date
Initiator
Project Engineer
Description
JOB SUMMERY
COST
Site Improvements
Structural
Architectural
Process Piping
Electrical
Instrumentation
Equipment
Utilities
Special
Approximate Total Cost
User Dept.
APPROVAL
User Dept. No.
Chf. Engr.
Justification and Return
Preliminary Drawings
Approp. Req. Preparation
Job Order No.
Date Approved
PHASE II
Date Started
Date Comp.
1. Amplify Work Summary
2. Field Survey
3. Detail Specifications
4. Equipment List
5. Supplier Quotation
6. Detail Cost Summary
7. Union Notification
8. Specialist Req'd
DRAWING DESCRIPTION
TYPE
SIZE
COMP.
NO.
HOURS /DAY
TOTAL HOURS
ACT. HOURS
DRAWING NUMBER
BILL OF MATERIALS
B/M
A
A
TOTAL DESIGN DRAFTING
PHASE III
Date Started
Date Comp.
Revisions
Number
Date
1
2
3
4
Design Draftsman
Chief Draftsman Approval
Proj. Engr. Approval
File No.
Equipment No.
PHASE IV
Drawings Released
For Cons't.
Job Bids or Planning
Date
Date
Rev. Date
Maintenance
Contractor
Comp. Date
Actual
Contract Preparation
Construction Schedule
Cost Control
Formal Acceptance
Date
Job Order
Brief Description
P.E.
PHASE
I
II
III
IV
Completion Date
Estimate Hours

Figure 3–6. Project control record.

To illustrate these methods, the following situation is assumed. It is proposed that a plant install a conveyor system having an estimated cost of $85,000. An analysis of all factory labor and expense accounts shows a net estimated savings of $25,000 per year, excluding the effect of depreciation and income taxes. The equipment should have at least a ten-year life with a $5,000 salvage value at the end of this period.

Payoff Method. Primary consideration is given to the original investment and annual savings as follows:

$$Payoff\ years = \frac{Original\ net\ investment}{Initial\ annual\ earnings}$$

$$Payoff\ years = \frac{\$85,000}{\$25,000} = 3.4$$

A variation of this formula uses annual earnings after taxes as follows:

$$Payoff\ years = \frac{Original\ net\ investment}{Initial\ annual\ earnings\ after\ taxes}$$

$$Payoff\ years = \frac{\$85,000}{\$25,000\ (.50)} = 6.8$$

Note that a tax rate of 50 percent is assumed.

Still another variation deducts both taxes and depreciation from the annual earnings in calculating the years required to pay off the investment:

$$Payoff\ years = \frac{Original\ net\ investment}{Initial\ annual\ earnings\ after\ taxes\ and\ depreciation}$$

$$Payoff\ years = \frac{\$85,000}{(\$25,000 + \$8,000)(.50)} = 10$$

Regardless of which form of the payoff formula is used, the calculation gives a rapid indication of the risk involved and functions effectively as a coarse screen in the rough evaluation of various projects. Many companies rely completely on this method of evaluating cost reduction and profit improvement projects. This reliance should be avoided for the following reasons: (1) the ability of the project to liquidate the project cost becomes the prime consideration, (2) profitability of investment beyond the payoff period is ignored, and (3) the demand for short payoff periods often causes good investment opportunities to be rejected.

Rate of Return Method. Utilizing the reciprocal of the results obtained in the payoff formula, this method yields figures which are usually consistent with the company's accounting approach.

$$Rate\ of\ return = \frac{Initial\ annual\ earnings\ (100)}{Original\ net\ investment}$$

$$Rate\ of\ return = \frac{\$25,000\ (100)}{\$85,000} = 29.4\ percent$$

As with the previous method, rate of return can reflect the effect of taxes and depreciation if desired.

While this approach to cost justification is useful, it is limited in the following ways: (1) earnings resulting from the project are considered to be constant for each year, (2) no consideration is given to the time-value of money or the time-shape of earnings, and (3) projects with a faster write-off show disproportionately higher returns on investment. For example, a project costing $100,000 and estimated to have an effective life of two years with net earnings of $150,000 during that period will show a return on investment of 75 percent. On the other hand, the same investment in a project with a life of five years and net earnings of $300,000 during that period will show a return on investment of only 60 percent. Under normal circumstances, the conclusion drawn from this analysis is misleading.

Discounted Cash Flow. More and more companies are using the method of discounted cash flow to evaluate potential project investments. This method is based on the procedure by which predicted increases in profit (or decreases in cost) are discounted at a certain percentage for each future year. The theory, of course, is that tomorrow's money is worth less than today's. This is illustrated by the fact that a businessman would prefer to receive a dollar due him today rather than a year from today, but would prefer to pay a dollar of debt a year from today instead of today.

For the conveyor system in the example previously described, the financial analysis using discounted cash flow is shown in Fig. 3–7. It was necessary to know the minimum acceptable return on investment for the company, which in this example was assumed to be 13 percent. From this analysis it may be seen that an incoming cash flow of $170,000 will be generated over the ten-year period as a result of the initial investment of $85,000. On a discounted basis, the return will be greater than required for the minimum return on investment by the amount of the excess present value, or $6,000. A negative figure for excess present value indicates that the return is less than required to meet the discount rate.

Determination of the exact rate of return by the method shown in Fig. 3–7 would require trial and error using different discount rates until the rate is found that produces a value of zero for excess present value. However, a faster and easier solution to this problem can be obtained through the use of a computer. Fig. 3–8, which shows the calculation made by a time-sharing computer, indicates a return of 14 percent on investment. The advantages of discounted cash flow are the following:

1) Potential investment in plant and facilities is analyzed in a sophisticated manner.
2) Considerable flexibility is provided. Such factors as time, of investment, status of project, unlike alternatives, and addition or subtraction of facilities can all be accommodated. Furthermore, cash receipts and expenditures are accurately reflected at the time they are predicted to occur.
3) The characteristics of the project throughout its life become part of the input data.

There are certain disadvantages of the discounted cash flow method which should be recognized. These disadvantages are the following:

1) It is often difficult to forecast future income and expense accurately by year.
2) The income forecast required for this method is generally inconsistent with accounting practices.
3) Only one rate of return can be used throughout the analysis.
4) Slow-starting programs are placed at a disadvantage.

End of Year	Income Before Depreciation	Depreciation	Incoming Cash Flow After Taxes			Outgoing Cash Flow	Net Annual* Cash Flow	Present Value of $1 Discounted† at 13%	Present Value of Annual Cash Flow
			Income	Depreciation	Total				
0 Investment Return Cash Flow	$25,000	$8,000	$12,500	$4,000	$16,500	$85,000	$-85,000	1.00	$-85,000
1	25,000	8,000	12,500	4,000	16,500		16,500	.88	14,500
2	25,000	8,000	12,500	4,000	16,500		16,500	.78	12,900
3	25,000	8,000	12,500	4,000	16,500		16,500	.69	11,400
4	25,000	8,000	12,500	4,000	16,500		16,500	.61	10,100
5	25,000	8,000	12,500	4,000	16,500		16,500	.54	8,900
6	25,000	8,000	12,500	4,000	16,500		16,500	.48	7,400
7	25,000	8,000	12,500	4,000	16,500		16,500	.43	7,100
8	25,000	8,000	12,500	4,000	16,500		16,500	.38	6,300
9	25,000	8,000	12,500	4,000	16,500		16,500	.33	5,400
10 Disposal of Equipment	25,000	8,000	12,500	4,000	16,500	-5,000	21,500	.30	6,500
Total Incoming Cash Flow							$170,000		
Excess Present Value									$ 6,000

*Positive number indicates net incoming flow.
†Obtained from Present Value tables found in accounting textbooks and handbooks.

Present value of $1 at end of year $x = \dfrac{\text{Present Value at End of Year } (x-1)}{(1.00 + \text{Discount Rate})}$

Figure 3-7. Discounted cash flow financial analysis for a conveyor system—manual.

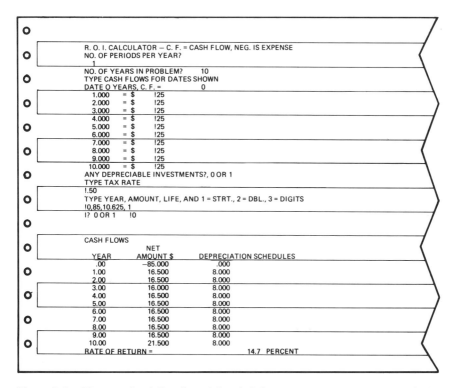

Figure 3-8. Discounted cash flow financial analysis for a conveyor system — computerized.

Summary. Comparing the results obtained from each of these methods shows a wide range of answers. It becomes obvious that care must be used in discussing these figures or in comparing them to similar figures for other projects. Obviously, the statement "We can pay for the conveyor system in 3.4 years" is misleading unless it is pointed out that cost of depreciation and federal income taxes have been ignored. Similarly the statement "The conveyor system will return 29.4 percent on the investment" must be amplified to explain the costs included and the method of calculation. Failure to exercise this kind of care will lead to incorrect conclusions. Although there are some engineering projects which can be adequately evaluated using the payoff or rate-of-return methods, the flexibility and precision of the discounted cash flow method dictates its use as a normal procedure.

The project engineer should be satisfied with all aspects of the project, especially the relationship between the cost and anticipated financial and non-financial benefits to the company, before proceeding further. If dissatisfied, he should prepare and present to his immediate supervisor a recommendation for an alternate approach or even termination of the project. Only when he is completely satisfied (or has been instructed by his superior to proceed) should he prepare the appropriation request. It is important to remember that this document is prepared specifically for the use of top management in deciding whether to approve the expenditure of capital funds for the project. Not only must the request provide a clear and concise explanation of the project and contain the answers to all relevant questions, but it must also sell the project and the capabilities of the project engineer.

Basic requirements of the appropriation request include the following: (1) concise description of the project, (2) estimate of project costs, (3) economic justification when applicable, and (4) proposed project timetable. A typical form for an appropriation request is shown in Fig. 3–9. Often supplementary printed forms are available for showing the project cost estimate and economic justification in a standard form.

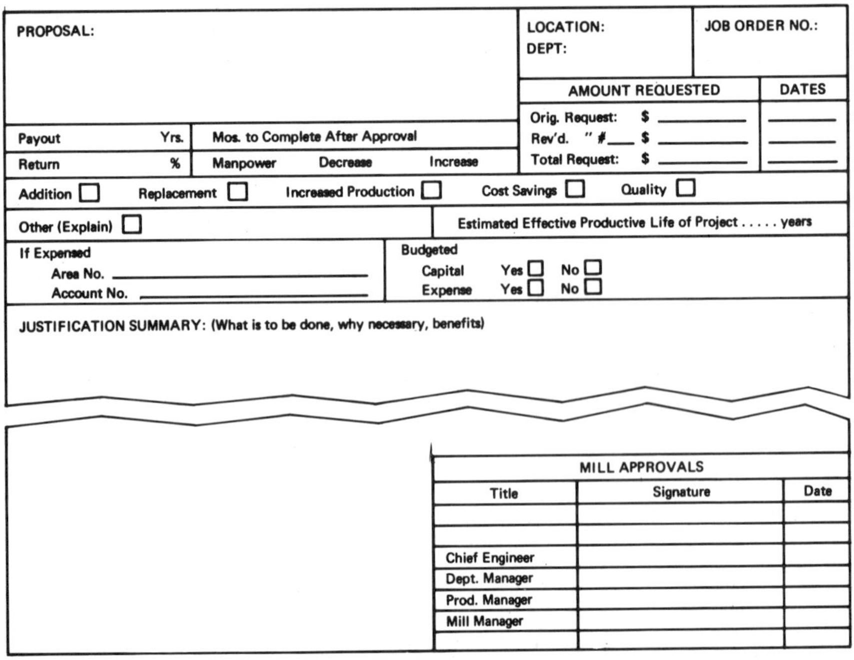

PROPOSAL: | LOCATION: DEPT: | JOB ORDER NO.:

AMOUNT REQUESTED | DATES
Orig. Request: $ ______ | ______
Rev'd. " #___ $ ______ | ______
Total Request: $ ______ | ______

Payout ___ Yrs. | Mos. to Complete After Approval
Return ___ % | Manpower Decrease Increase

Addition ☐ Replacement ☐ Increased Production ☐ Cost Savings ☐ Quality ☐

Other (Explain) ☐ | Estimated Effective Productive Life of Project . . . . . years

If Expensed
Area No. ______
Account No. ______
Budgeted
Capital Yes ☐ No ☐
Expense Yes ☐ No ☐

JUSTIFICATION SUMMARY: (What is to be done, why necessary, benefits)

MILL APPROVALS		
Title	Signature	Date
Chief Engineer		
Dept. Manager		
Prod. Manager		
Mill Manager		

Figure 3–9. Appropriation request form.

Normally, the number and level of approvals, based on the amount of money requested and the type of project, are included in company procedures. With the submission of this request, the project engineer has completed the normal work in Phase I and must wait for approval before proceeding with the project.

Phase II – Project Engineering

The notification of approval of the appropriation request triggers the start of project engineering. After posting the date of approval on the project control record, the project engineer prepares an estimate of the hours required and scheduled completion date for this phase. At this time he consults with other engineering specialists, such as electrical and instrumentation engineers, to obtain their input into the schedule. Because he is primarily responsible for preparing and administering the schedule, the project engineer should continue work on it until he is satisfied that it is reasonable and can be met.

At this point full engineering work should be started. Depending upon the size and scope of the project, the work may range from a small job for the project engineer to the use of a consulting engineering firm or a full-time team of engineers from the various departments within the company.

Most projects require considerable work with vendors during this phase, but too frequently this need is inadequately met. Certainly the idea of getting help from vendors is nothing new; in fact, many companies are making strenuous efforts to encourage vendors to develop ideas and products which they can buy. However, many engineers seem to prefer to design their own equipment and project components.

A more reasonable approach would be to inform vendors who have the proper accumulation of skills and type of equipment of the functions required together with the pertinent constraints and limitations. Based on this information, the vendor will provide suggestions and quotations, with costs often amounting to 25 to 50 percent of the cost of in-house work.

It makes sense to use and pay for the vendor's skill and knowledge to the greatest practical extent (even at the expense of the pride of a project engineer) for the following reasons:

1) Special knowledge exists in every field, and much of this knowledge is not possessed by people in other fields.

2) Only a relatively small amount of the total knowledge bearing on any technology exists in any one place at any one time.

3) Special machines, fixtures, tooling, and equipment exist in large numbers.

4) Good vendors develop new machines and techniques which might be used in the future. They can be used only if the vendors are called into the job to which they are applicable.

Locating the best-qualified vendors is a difficult task which is usually performed most effectively with the cooperation of the purchasing department. By combining the detailed knowledge of both vendor and purchasing with the project engineer's specific knowledge of the project requirements, it should be possible to pinpoint appropriate vendors.

After a vendor has been contacted and the requirements have been explained to him, it is important that he have an opportunity to ask more questions and that his technical personnel be given time to study alternative solutions. If the vendor arrives at the best answer and submits a fair quotation, he should be given the business. In such cases, it is both self-defeating as well as unethical to (1) send his ideas to other vendors for quotations, or (2) use them to build the equipment "in-house."

The roles played by the project engineer and purchasing relative to working with a vendor have a real potential for conflict. Normally, the project engineer should follow the procedure favored by purchasing, provided that he is given ample opportunity to work directly with the vendors in determining how the needs of the project can be met, and provided purchasing follows the specifications of the engineer in placing the order.

Besides working with vendors, the project engineer and his team will be detailing equipment specifications, preparing design sketches in sufficient detail for efficient drafting, and maintaining a close liaison with the management of the user department. At the conclusion of this phase, the following data should be prepared: (1) the equipment list shown in Fig. 3–10, (2) the job order cost summary shown in Fig. 3–11, and (3) the drawing list and drafting time estimate on the project control record.

Job Order No. _____

Dept. _____

Sheet _____ of _____

Date _____

Proj. Engr. _____

EQPT. ITEM	NO. QUAN.	DESCRIPTION	Weight (lbs)	Price (Inc.Frt.)	Erect'n Costs	Eqpt.Bldg Costs	Total	Promised Receipt Date
1	2	3	4	5	6	7	8	9
		TOTALS – THIS SHEET						

Note: Column # 7 includes foundations, anchor bolts, piling,
roof slabs, concrete fills, etc., for equipment.
FWE: Furnished with equipment.
D&E: Delivered and Erected.

Figure 3–10. New project equipment list.

Phase III – Design Drafting

This phase should begin with a complete review of the job by the project engineer's supervisor to ensure that the work is complete and of good quality. After the review, the project engineer meets with the chief draftsman to discuss the work and to give him all data required by the draftsmen. During the drafting period, the project engineer checks periodically with the chief draftsman to determine that the work is on schedule and to provide the additional clarification and information needed.

When the drawings are completed, they should be approved by the chief draftsman and then given to the project engineer for approval. In addition, the chief draftsman should close out phase III on the project control card and return it to the project engineer.

Job Order No. _____					Sheet _____ of ____			
Dept. _____					Date _____			
					Prep. By _____			

C — Contractor   Designate One Of Following:
M — Maintenance; O — Outside Contractor; P — Supplied by Vendor

DESCRIPTION					DESCRIPTION			
EQUIPMENT COSTS					PIPING COSTS			
Eqpmt.—All Types*					Process Piping			
Freight					Instrument Piping			
Erection					Water Sply. Piping			
Painting					Pipe Insulation			
Safety Guards					Painting			
Insulation &								
Prot. Ctg.					Subtotal			
Unlisted & Misc.								
					AREA COSTS			
EQUIP, BLDG, COSTS					Grading			
Piling					Landscaping			
Other Equip.					Sidewalks			
Bldg. Costs					Fencing & Gates			
					Railroads			
Subtotal					Underground			
					Fire Protection			
BUILDING COSTS					Process Drains			
Demolition					Storm Drains			
Piling					Sanitary Sewers			
Substructure					Foundations and			
Superstructure					Exploration			
Structure Steel					— Tests			
Painting					Cost of Land			
Other Bldg. Costs								
Sprinklers					Subtotal			
Subtotal					INSTRUMENTATION			
					Instruments			
ELECTRICAL COSTS					Installation:			
Control Eqpmt.					Mechanical			
Switchgear					Electrical			
Motors								
Motor Control					Subtotal			
Unit Substation								
Bldg. Lighting					Total Direct Cost			
Outside Lighting								
Power Wiring					Contingencies			
High Voltage Fdr.								
Telephone, Alarm					Engineering & Const.			
Clock, and					Supervision			
Call Systems								
Painting								
Subtotal					Total			

Note: *Includes Process; Mechanical; Heating & Ventilation
and Occupancy Equipment

Figure 3-11. Project job order cost summary.

Phase IV — Installation

This phase begins with a meeting between the project engineer and his superior (in addition to any other concerned executives) to establish the time that will be allowed for completion and to determine what portion of the project will be given to the maintenance department and what portion will be done by outside contractors.

It is the responsibility of the project engineer to follow through after this meeting to secure the necessary estimates from the maintenance department, and, in conjunction with purchasing, to request bids from outside contractors.

After the bids have been opened and the contract award decisions are made, purchasing prepares and executes contracts for the work. At the same time, the project engineer must see that an overall installation schedule is prepared which coordinates the activities of the various contractors and the maintenance department. All construction and installation work must be coordinated by the project engineer. Inspection reports, such as the one illustrated in Fig. 3–12, are prepared and reviewed regularly. Corrections indicated by these reports, or other revisions or changes, are passed on to the contractor.

JOB ______

PROJECT NO. ______
JOB ORDER NO. ______
PROJECT ENGINEER ______
DATE ______
SHEET ______ OF ______

Item No.	TIME		DESCRIPTION AND LOCATION OF WORK	ACTION			CPL
	AM	PM		1	2	3	

1. Work approved with exeptions as noted above.

2. Work rejected pending compliance with above requirements–
subject to reinspection

3. ______

Figure 3–12. Project inspection report.

A key element of the project engineer's responsibility during phase IV is the control of costs. A convenient form for this purpose (Fig. 3–13), may be used in a manual system or adapted to the computer. Assuming a manual system is used, a clerk would use this form as a work sheet during the month,

Approp. Number	Date Approved	Description	User Dept.	Expenditure Approved			Scope Adj.	Expenditure To-Date			Complete		Schedule Compl. Date	
				Material	Contract	Maint. Labor		Material	Contract	Maint. Labor	$ - %	Est.	Orig.	Crnt.
				$ (1)	$ (2)	$ (3)	(4)	$ (5)	$ (6)	$ (7)	(8)	(9)		

DEFINITIONS:

(1) Expenditure Material refers to the total estimated amount which must be purchased to complete the job based on quotations secured by the project engineer.

(2) Expenditure Contract refers to the total preliminary bids secured to develop the expenditure from outside contractors supplying material and labor.

(3) Expenditure Maintenance Labor refers to the dollars of plant labor estimated to complete the job and supplied by the Planning and Scheduling Division.

(4) Scope change will be checked if such occurs. The addition or deletion of approved amounts should be carried as a separate entry below the original approved expenditure.

(5) To Date Material includes all invoices which have been approved for payment.

(6) To Date Contract includes all invoices which have been approved for contractor services.

(7) To Date Maintenance Labor includes all labor charges in dollars accumulated against the appropriation number.

(8) The Dollar Percentage complete is developed by comparing the total contracts and estimated maintenance labor to be expected to that expended at the time of the report preparation.

(9) The Estimated Percentage Complete is the project engineer's opinion of the current physical status of the jobs.

Figure 3–13. Project cost control and summary status report.

posting all costs by phases as incurred. At the end of the month, totals would be determined and posted on a summary report, which could be arranged in the same format.

After completion of the work, the project engineer makes a thorough inspection and prepares a list of additional work required from the contractor or maintenance department. Upon satisfactory completion of this list, he recommends the acceptance of the work and prepares a final report.

DRAWINGS AND BLUEPRINT CONTROL

An effective plant engineering department is dependent upon a well-organized plan for identifying equipment and maintaining comprehensive files on repairs and maintenance. This necessitates a filing system that quickly and easily locates any information relative to the departmental responsibilities. For assigning general responsibilities, a filing code should be established which uses either a numerical system or an alphabetic system. The system selected should also provide for a breakdown into subheadings under the broader categories. The following is an example of a suggested plant engineering department filing code system.

Filing Code System

When the filing code (see Table III–1) has been established and the proper numbers assigned to the correct departments and equipment, the file drawers are appropriately marked. Now all drawings and documents should be coded as they originate to make it easier for a clerical worker to file them. Plant equipment may have asset numbers in addition to the file code numbers. It is advisable to use the file code number as a prefix to any other identification number to simplify access to all information pertaining to the equipment. In order for the engineering department to function effectively, it is necessary that all records be kept up to date, as there is very little opportunity to effectively plan a project without having this information readily available.

Table III–1. Filing Code System.

A. Personnel Relations
   1. Union negotiations
   2. Vacations
   3. Job classifications
   4. Job evaluation
   5. Personnel – monthly report
   6. Policy
   7. Personnel

B. Plant Safety
   1. General
   2. Plant protection
   3. First Aid
   4. Guards – machinery, etc.
   5. Safety Director
   6. Fire Protection
      6.1. Fire extinguisher locations
   7. Insurance (see also G2)
   8. Accidents
   9. Civil Defense
   10. Key system
   11. Flammable liquids, vault, solvents, etc.
   12. Noise control
   13. Technical data
   14. Housekeeping
   15. Dusts, fumes, vapors

C. Main Plant General
   1. General correspondence
   2. Machinery and building maintenance
   3. Machinery and equipment
   4. New construction/old construction
   5. Building codes
   6. Boiler and associated apparatus
   7. Plant layout
   8. Utilities
      8.1. Boiler (see also F9)
      8.2. Electric
   9. Insurance matters

D. Material Cleaning and Protection
   1. Steel storage and protection
   2. Government service parts
   3. Rust prevention
   4. Metal cleaning (see also H3, H4)

Table III–1. Filing Code System *(Continued).*

E. Plant Engineering
    1. General
    2. Plant layout (see M)
    3. Preventive maintenance
    4. Design, etc.
    5. Oxygen and acetylene reports
    6. Engineering literature, symbols, etc.
    7. Cost standards and std. installation costs
    8. Chemicals
    9. Air handling and air conditioning
    10. Painting, processes, etc.
    11. Hydraulic mechanisms
    12. Dust, fumes, vapors (see also B15, E9, H7)
    13. Production test material
    14. Contractors. Index of large concerns – technical (engr. and constr.)

F. Heating and Ventilating
    1. Unit heaters
    2. Air conditioners (see also E9)
    3. Fans
    4. Monthly fuel reports
        4.1. Weather reports
        4.2. Fuel specifications and contracts
    5. Boilers and associated apparatus, water treatments, etc.
    6. Steam lines
    7. Piping
    8. Compressors
    9. Boiler insurance
    10. Codes
    11. Toxic gases (see B11 for solvents and E12 for vapors)
    12. Heating – plant
    13. Heating – office

G. Building and Properties
    1. New construction and engineering
        1.1. Estimates
        1.2. Company contractor
        1.3. Old building construction and cost data – tax data
        1.4. Floor loads
    2. Building maintenance
        2.1. Insurance coverage, certificates, waivers, etc.
        2.2. Insurance maps
        2.3. Guarantees (other than machinery)
    3. Sewers
    4. Parking lots
    5. Snow removal
    6. Chimneys
    7. Photographs
    8. Surveying notes – land, etc.
    9. Permits
    10. Insurance – claims
    11. Testing farm
    12. City, state, county
    13. Roads, streets, driveways, parking privileges
    14. Storage tanks and pressure tanks
    15. Signs

Table III–1. Filing Code System *(Continued)*.

16. Washrooms
17. Roofs and skylights
18. Warehouses and storage
19. Elevators
20. Dumping grounds
21. Building codes
22. Septic tanks
23. Manufacturing dept. maps, also sq ft and acreage
24. Footings and borings
25. Railroads
26. Lockers
27. Office partitions
28. Landscaping
29. Furniture
30. Painting – buildings, etc.
31. Scales

H. Facilities
   1. Paint booths, drying and baking ovens
   2. Sand blasting booths, associated apparatus and material
   3. Phosphatizers
   4. Washers
   5. Incinerators
   6. Air lines (see also E9)
   7. Dust control equipment
   8. Welding equipment (see also J10)
   9. Metal spinning

I. Utilities
   1. Gas
   2. Electricity
      2.1. Substations
      2.2. Bus duct layouts
      2.3. Codes
      2.4. Literature
      2.5. Power distribution
      2.6. Lighting
   3. Water
      3.1. Water conditioning service reports
      3.2. Hot water heater piping
      3.3. City and fire line mains
   4. Monthly reports
   5. Telephones
   6. Oxygen lines and cascades
   7. Paging system

J. Machinery
   1. New machinery
   2. Used machinery
   3. Repairs and overhauls
   4. Preventive maintenance
      4.1. Lubrication
   5. Cranes and monorail cranes
   6. Air compressors and allied apparatus
   7. Estimates and quotes
   8. Filters and separators
   9. Shear maintenance
10. Welders

Table III–1. Filing Code System *(Continued).*

K. Housekeeping
   1. Window washing
   2. Pest control
   3. Sanitary services
   4. Sweepers
   5. Floor surfacing
   6. Monthly reports

L. Fleet
   1. Repairs and overhauls
   2. Preventive maintenance
     2.1. Lubrication
   3. Fleet rentals
   4. Tires
   5. Gas and oil
   6. Repair parts
   7. Monthly gas reports
   8. Licenses
   9. Motor vehicle laws
  10. LP fuels, gases
  11. Radios

M. Plant layout
   1. General
   2. Departmental rearrangement
   3. Plant maps
   4. Machinery rearrangement
   5. Shop photographs

N. Material Handling
   1. Skids, pallets, tote boxes, racks, jib booms
   2. Ladders, packing boxes
   3. Chains, cables, ropes, hooks
   4. Fork and pallet trucks
   5. Conveyors
   6. Engineering (material handling)
   7. Material handling correspondence
   8. Lifting devices

Large manufacturing and processing plants are experiencing storage problems with the great amount of paper work required to control their operations. It may also be too time-consuming to locate information if the files become too large or complex. Several methods are available to overcome these problems. They should be evaluated independently relative to their time and space savings versus their costs. Economics should be the basis for the decision as to which system is best suited to the company's needs.

Microfilming can reduce mountains of paper storage to small cabinets of film magazines. This compact system permits a more convenient method of handling and transferring large volumes of information. The most recent method of organizing records is the microfiche system which can be viewed or duplicated rapidly with a code identification on the microfiche cards. Also, filing and sorting of information can be improved to a great extent by using this system. Another advantage is that information can be duplicated and transmitted to distant offices that have Teletype terminals installed.

Further reduction of paper work and timesaving advantages are realized by computer output microfilming (COM). Several auxiliary machines are required in addition to the computer that feeds information from magnetic tape through a cathode-ray tube (CRT) onto unexposed film. Film developer, film duplicator, microfilm viewer, and microfilm retrieval machine are required to complete the microfilm information system. Effective maintenance control requires an up-to-date information system to minimize delays in servicing equipment.

STAFFING AND PERSONNEL TRAINING

In order to examine the staffing needs for the engineering department, reference should be made to the description given earlier to the partial role of the plant engineer. Taking the plant engineering concept to be one of total involvement with the company's goals, it is fairly easy to establish the types of skills required. These include: (1) specification writers, estimators, and bid analysts, (2) design engineers—mechanical, electrical, civil, and electronics, (3) layout and detail draftsmen, and (4) mill or works engineers.

Upon examining the first category, we see that to be able to define and write specifications competently one must be in a position to both analyze the bids received and to prepare one's own estimates for comparison purposes. The work of an estimator is a difficult role to perform adequately, for usually the available information is in a very sketchy form. The estimator often relies upon his own personal experience stored in his own "black book" and more likely has to draw from his catalog of previous performance for similar jobs. A clearly defined specification will pay dividends when cataloging cost figures after the work is performed, and the rates, quantities, and unit prices determined can be used for future estimates.

Unit price structures can be established quite easily for such items as reinforcing bar, concrete, structural steel, etc. For example, a review of similar jobs may reveal a unit price of $120/cu yd for reinforced concrete for heavy foundations. Hydraulic piping assemblies can be measured by dollars per foot run per inch of diameter including fittings and valves.

Only years of experience will bring the skills necessary for the important tasks of specification writing, estimating, and bid analyzing, and the knowledge of one paves the way for competency in the others. An experienced estimator can readily spot an error in a contractor's bid documents upon analysis and likewise will be better equipped to establish clearly defined specifications for the next job.

Design Engineers

The staffing of this department can be done on a different basis because here a blend of young and old in terms of experience can be applied to advantage. Certainly experience comes with age, but often new ideas are held back because of previous methods and "tried and true" attitudes. The saying "If you have been doing it this way for 25 years, it is time for a change" applies to the design group. New methods, materials, and machining techniques are always appearing, and advantage should be taken of them.

The introduction of plastics in the engineering field has revolutionized many so-called tried and true techniques—the uses of gears, couplings, and bushings, to name a few. Even in the basic steel industry, which for many years has been noted for its conservative attitude, the advent of nylon, Teflon,[5] and the like has brought overnight change. For example, sparks can be minimized in an explosive atmosphere by the use of plastic gears, pins, and pump parts.

A design group will ideally comprise field-trained men brought up in the world of "hard knocks" as well as recent graduates. The ability of the staff to observe the results of the efforts in the field is in itself a great experience. Many designers began their training as detailers. Their job is to make part or detail drawings under the wing of the designer. To graduate to a designer status is a worthwhile goal, but an experienced detailer can save considerable expense in the machine shop and is himself an important asset to the design group.

Layout and Detail Draftsmen

This group is often the hard core or nucleus for the engineering department; usually the greatest number of men are employed here, and the group can be given basic training here for other roles in the future. Layout work is a most interesting job and often presents the greatest challenge when the task is to shoehorn a facility into an inadequate space. The field is open for ingenuity and skill.

A good knowledge of operation procedures is necessary when establishing layout needs; for example, a manufacturing facility will require raw material storage, the processing unit itself, inspection and packaging units, storage and shipping, as well as auxiliary needs such as maintenance shops, spare parts storage, and tooling setup areas. Materials flows have to be established and the types of handling equipment decided upon. Overhead cranes for handling materials obviously provide maximum free use of floor areas but increase the building support column costs. By the same token, payloaders, tractors, or other wheeled vehicles often are available at a reduced capital expenditure, but aisle space and clearly defined roadways have to be provided plus rebuilding and service areas.

Today's computing devices are coming into their own as aids in creating drawings for machine-shop use, and tape-controlled machine tools can have programs designed around two plane coordinates which define the shape of an object without the use of a conventional detail drawing. The employment of draftswomen in a detailing office is often beneficial; women sometimes show a special aptitude for repetitious work that is not often found in men, and they are often employed for making final drawings and record drawings from rough pencil sketches.

Mill or Works Engineers

This staff service is often employed in the heavy industries and chemical engineering field and its particular function is that of a link between the manufacturing end of the business and the engineers' office. Personnel training is an important feature which is often neglected in the face of mounting requirements

---

[5] Registered trademark, E. I. du Pont de Nemours and Company.

from the engineering department. All too often, a young man's training is merely progression through the ranks from print boy to detailer or from draftsman to designer by virtue of years of on-the-job experience. A progressive, forward-thinking office will have its own school for the instruction of its members in engineering drawing, hydraulics, stress theory, and strength of materials, together with geometry and trigonometry.

Machine-tool operation in the form of a short apprenticeship is often found to be beneficial if the company is a machine-tool builder. Foundry practice and patternmaking are essential ingredients of training in the heavy industries, and with the increasing use of fabrication techniques, welding theory and practice will pay handsome dividends in the design office.

Chapter 4

Maintenance Management

The challenge of keeping expanding industrial facilities in good repair is rapidly growing in cost, complexity, and sophistication. There has been a marked change in management's attitude toward the importance of the maintenance function. Industry has experienced a tremendous growth in mechanization. The point has been reached in some plants that maintenance man-hours now exceed production man-hours. The trend toward automation will continue at an accelerated rate, and maintenance will be a major cost factor. This intensifying importance has brought into focus the necessity for better management in order to increase the effectiveness of this expanding segment of industry.

The maintenance cost increase has not been limited to the industrial community. Hospitals, retail outlets, transportation, hotels and motels, and government — both local and federal — are all searching for means to control the upward spiral of cost involved in maintaining their facilities.

MAINTENANCE FUNCTIONS

Snapshots of several maintenance functions separated geographically would show a number of unrelated activities. While the purely maintenance-type activities may be found in all cases, the hodgepodge of activities often lumped together under maintenance tend to cloud the picture. The inconsistency of responsibility assignments to maintenance functions has made the application of universal indices impracticable. How should the wide variety of activities classified as maintenance be defined? In general, the maintenance function is responsible for the satisfactory functioning of the machines, buildings and services needed by other segments of the organization.

Responsibilities

Responsibility assignments will vary from industry to industry, from plant to plant, or even within the same plant from year to year. Also, the size of the plant would determine some types of assignments. In a small plant, activities may be grouped for economy. In a large industrial company, the activities are more apt to be separated to provide better visibility and control. But in many cases, despite the growth from a small to a large company, the hodgepodge of activities has simply remained intact because no one has examined the reasons for making the original assignments.

A review of responsibility assignments is made here to help clarify these points. The functions will be classified as *principal* or *related*. The principal functions are the ones most commonly assigned, and the related responsibilities are those which have been assigned over the years for reasons of expediency. The list is not intended to be complete but is merely indicative of the type of service rendered by some maintenance organizations.

Principal responsibilities include the following:

1) Environmental control
2) Housekeeping
3) Preservation of existing structures and grounds
4) Maintenance of existing plant equipment
5) Services generation, distribution, and conservation
6) Modification of existing structures and equipment
7) New installation of structures and equipment

Some related responsibilities may be listed as follows:

1) Plant protection
2) Waste and pollution control
3) Material and parts control
4) Salvage
5) Food service
6) Fleet service
7) Safety

Many of the above items are not really maintenance-type activities. This fact has been pointed out in preceding chapters wherein the proper assignment of these responsibilities was described. Only housekeeping, preservation of existing structures and grounds, and maintenance of existing plant equipment are purely maintenance functions.

An amplification of the various responsibilities, both principal and related, will bring out the reasons they are included.

Environmental Control. This function includes control of the temperature, humidity, odor, and cleanliness of the plant's atmosphere; the control of illumination through the use of proper relamping procedures; and noise abatement. While environmental control includes some elements which could be construed as pure maintenance, basically this activity has more of an operational or engineering overtone.

Housekeeping. This is a pure maintenance function which maintains existing facilities in good condition. The cleaning and preservation of surfaces is the main element of this category. Other elements which could be included are rodent and insect control, waste removal, bacterial control, janitorial service, and promotion of good housekeeping practices.

Preservation of Existing Structures and Grounds. Another pure maintenance function, this activity embraces the elements of repair, restoration, inspection, and care. These elements are applied to internal and external parts of structures (roofs, walls, service distributions, etc.) and to external property (roads, landscaping, rail spurs, parking lots, signs, etc.). This function would normally include snow removal.

Maintenance of Existing Plant Equipment and Machinery. The maintenance activity is, of course, the basic reason for the existence of the maintenance department. Keeping equipment in good order includes preventive, corrective, and emergency maintenance; routine inspections, checking, and adjusting and proper record keeping are all important elements of this function.

Services Generation, Distribution, and Conservation. This activity is often included in the maintenance department. The size of power requirements frequently governs the organizational position of this responsibility. While the need to care for the equipment would tend to make this a maintenance function, the engineering-operational aspects would tend to remove it from maintenance, and in larger plants it may be a separate department. Areas of responsibility include generation of normal, special, and critical or emergency power; generation of process services such as gases, deionized water, steam, etc.; operation of the thermal capabilities; distribution of the generated and purchased services, including domestic requirements; and conservation of the various services as a very significant element.

Modification of Existing Structures and Equipment. Modifications and re-arrangements of existing facilities are a responsibility which makes it difficult to determine the true cost of maintenance. This type of activity is most often associated with the maintenance function, and therefore was listed as a principal responsibility. In many plants both modifications and repair of facilities are performed by the same personnel. The elements of moving equipment, changing walls, routing services, etc., should be separated from pure maintenance for purposes of control. It may be desirable to assign this responsibility to maintenance, but it is necessary that the costs be clearly segregated so the true maintenance activity can be defined.

New Installation of Structures and Equipment. As in the previous modification category, segregation to promote visibility is most important. In many plants or institutions, the new installation is assigned to outside contractors and coordinated by maintenance. In large plants, there is frequently a separate department for new installations, and the work is performed by either company employees or outside contractors. Again, as in other categories discussed, economics plays the major role.

Plant Protection. The main areas of responsibility are security and fire protection. Because NLRB regulations require separation of a guard union from production or maintenance, security is often part of personnel or industrial relations. Fire protection requires maintenance, testing, inspection of fire protective equipment. Also, the fire brigade must be drilled and trained. Since the fire brigade is made up largely of maintenance personnel, the fire protection function is most commonly assigned to maintenance.

Waste and Pollution Control. The waste pickup in the buildings is a function of housekeeping, but the disposal responsibility is normally assigned to the grounds maintenance group. The category is a broad one, and assignments of responsibilities vary widely. Elements in this category are waste disposal, waste treatment—both chemical and industrial—and air pollution control. Government interest in pollution will require that more emphasis be given to this area.

Material and Parts Control. The support of a maintenance organization is desirable in the area of materials and parts. While stores is sometimes part of maintenance, more frequently it is a manufacturing material support function. The elements normally included are material and supplies control, spare parts control, and interface with purchasing for the purchases of stores. Additionally, because from a cost standpoint outside contractors are sometimes classified as materials, the administration of service agreements, such as typewriter repairs, may be included.

Salvage. The salvage of precious metal, obsolete equipment and materials, valuable waste, and scrap will, at times, fall under the control of the maintenance function. Even if the function is not assigned to the maintenance activity, the responsibility of the actual salvage operation will normally fall within its jurisdiction.

Food Service. This is a function most commonly found assigned to industrial relations, but it is also sometimes assigned to the maintenance area because of the latter's "catchall" aspect.

Transportation. The major purpose of this service is to transfer personnel from one building to another. The main reason for assigning this function to maintenance is probably because of its close association with automotive maintenance.

Safety. The relationship of safety and maintenance is one of safety practice establishment and maintenance implementation. This relationship has established safety as part of the maintenance function to accomplish the common goal of safe facilities and practices.

There are numerous other responsibilities frequently assigned to maintenance by management because of the catchall tradition attached to this function. But regardless of the number of additional responsibilities, the main task of maintenance management is to protect the investment in plant and equipment.

Organization

Good management requires a good organization structure. The subject of organization has been covered in a preceding chapter, but some of its aspects should be mentioned here because of their importance to maintenance management.

There is no single type of organization which is suitable for all maintenance departments. The diversity of responsibility described is the main reason for organizational differences. Also, the approach to work accomplishment by functional, geographical, or some combination method will have an effect on organizational structure. Any organizational attempt should work toward the following objectives:

1) Simple structure
2) Good communications
3) Clear definition of lines of authority
4) Clear relationship with other segments of the organization
5) Well-established internal responsibilities.

It is good practice to display the structure of the organization so that everyone understands his role in it.

Budgeting

Budgeting is essential to a well-managed maintenance department. A budget is a target or a cost goal which forecasts the expected cost for a particular project or organization for some future period. The process of preparing budgets implies that responsibilities have been defined and the maintenance activity is so organized that the budgets are meaningful. How well you budget depends on many factors, but mainly on the manager's understanding of his total responsibilities.

Budgets normally fall into three categories:
1) Capital requirements
2) Major expense requirements
3) Operating requirements.

Capital budgets are required when an investment is made in some major piece of equipment. Descriptors normally used in capital budgeting are improve, purchase, modernize, install, construct, upgrade, erect, provide, build, and fabricate. Capital budgets are normally project related and require justification as to the nature and schedule of payoff.

Major expense budgets are more frequently prepared by the maintenance manager than are capital budgets. A major expense budget is required when an expenditure exceeds some dollar amount established by management — perhaps anything over $1,000. Descriptors normally used in expense budgeting are repair, relocate, renovate, rearrange, remodel, replace, refurnish, and revise. An expense budget can be either project or operation related. Justification is also required in this category, but the payoff aspect is not as important as it is in the capital area.

The capital and major expense budgets are normally portions of larger budgets. Individual capital budgets are part of an annual total capital forecast which is approved at the corporate level when the initial capital funding availability is determined. The major expense budgets normally obtain their funds from an established operating expense budget.

The operating budget is the major indicator of a manager's position relative to the cost goal he has established. This budget contains the financial plan of the total work planned over a period of time. The basic elements of preparing an operating budget include:

1) Cost control units to accrue cost related to the responsibilities assigned to that unit. This elemental breakdown is necessary so that proper analysis can be made.

2) Supporting information such as sales forecasts, planned facilities installations and planned maintenance activities. These data must be available to form the basis for the financial plan.

3) Manning plan to accomplish the tasks to be performed over the next period. The plan should numerically define the type of manning required and the amount of overtime expected. The manning plan will be the basis upon which the requirements in terms of materials, tools, and administration are determined.

4) Review of historical information and actual cost incurred. The plant engineer should understand the basis for previous cost levels and update

this information based on knowledge of what is expected in the next period.

5) Realistic budgeting estimates. A budget with a large hedge factor may eliminate some embarrassment, but will be less useful as a guide throughout the year.

The chart of accounts shown in Table IV-1 represents only a partial listing of costs. It is important that all costs be categorized into major accounts for each cost control unit. Table IV-2 breaks down the labor cost into more descriptive elements. The account-number approach provides a means for segregating charges and facilitates the collection of costs.

Table IV-1. Major Control Accounts.

Account Number	Account Title
7000.00	Salaries
7100.00	Transfer of salaries to direct labor or to auxiliary order related to prime jobs
7200.00	Indirect labor and clerical
7300.00	Supplies
7400.00	Outside services
7500.00	Utilities
7600.00	Telephone and telegraph
7700.00	Postage
7800.00	Travel
7900.00	Transportation
8000.00	Professional services
8100.00	Retirement plan
8200.00	Advertising
8300.00	Dues and subscriptions
8400.00	Donations
8500.00	Insurance—payroll
8600.00	Insurance—other
8700.00	Taxes—payroll
8800.00	Taxes—other
8900.00	Rentals
9000.00	Amortization of emergency facilities
9100.00	Depreciation
9200.00	General expense
9300.00	Charges transferred to asset accounts
9400.00	Expense of service departments
9500.00	Services purchased from other divisions
9550.00	Services purchased from subsidiaries
9700.00	Services sold to other divisions
9750.00	Services sold to subsidiaries

Budgets are of two types—fixed and variable. The fixed budget consists of a definite amount based on a relative unchanging set of circumstances over the fiscal period. In some cases it can be adjusted if a major change occurs. A variable budget is possible when a good base has been established. The maintenance cost can increase or decrease depending upon the size of the base. Some examples of bases are number of pieces of equipment to maintain, square-foot

Table IV-2. Subsidiary Accounts.

Account Number	Account Title
7200.00	Indirect labor and clerical
7203.00	Tool expense
7205.00	Tool repair
7206.00	Furniture and fixture maintenance
7207.00	Transportation equipment maintenance
7208.00	Building maintenance
7208.13	Roof maintenance
7208.21	Glass maintenance
7209.00	Machine maintenance
7214.00	Publications
7216.00	Equipment installation
7217.00	Furniture and fixture expense
7228.00	Customer service
7235.00	Test equipment expense
7236.00	Test equipment maintenance
7238.00	Industrial engineering
7251.00	Overtime premium
7252.00	Vacation allowance
7253.00	Inspection
7254.00	Inventory work
7255.00	Idle time
7256.00	Personnel policy
7257.00	Packaging and crating
7258.00	Material handling and storeskeeping
7259.00	Sweeping and cleaning
7260.00	Watchmen and guards
7261.00	Scrap collection and salvage labor
7263.00	Night work premium and special work week bonus
7267.00	Retroactive pay adjustments
7270.00	Setup time
7272.00	First aid and matrons
7273.00	Clerical
7274.00	Drafting
7277.00	Holiday pay
7278.00	Labor adjustments
7280.00	Union business
7290.00	Engineering

area of buildings to clean, production levels, average number of beds occupied in a hospital or hotel, etc.

The period of time covered by the budget will vary. The most popular operating budget period is one year, as most fiscal periods are of 12 months' duration. The yearly budget in many plants allows periodic adjustments to occur during the year with the most common interval being semiannual.

It is important to note that the recording of variance (actual finances versus budget) is a sound approach for determining the effectiveness of a maintenance organization. Also, it is important that if the cost yardstick is used alone for measuring effectiveness, one may be trapped—other yardsticks along with cost must be used to determine the true picture. Additionally, budgetary procedures will not correct inefficient maintenance; improvements must come through better planning and scheduling, methods improvements, preventive action, work measurements, etc.

SYSTEMS AND PROCEDURES

The effectiveness of any maintenance function depends largely on the application of the proper systems and procedures. These controls are vital in obtaining full value from the maintenance dollar. An illustration can be found in the parable of kite flying. Imagine a kite speculating, "I could really fly if it were not for this ridiculous string and that fellow standing in the field holding me back." There is restraint in the string, and it does seem that if the string were cut the kite would really soar. But every boy who ever flew a kite knows what happens when the string breaks. It is the healthy relationship between kite and string which makes the flight possible. So it is with controls—many feel that systems and procedures are burdensome, useless restraints that do not contribute to the completion of the work. Actually, however, they are a necessary form of discipline. Without controls the maintenance effort would falter and decay.

Work Request/Order Control

A work request is the basic document for communication between the requester and the maintenance function. The documentation of the work requested is the first step. The work request should be so designed that the initiator can transmit all vital information for planning purposes. An example of a work request form is given in Fig. 4–1. This form is in four parts for continuity of communication. When the request is made out by the originator, he retains one copy for follow-up. The action copy will initiate planning or request accomplishment or other action. The maintenance file copy is held for control purposes. The completion notice is returned to the originator when the work has been accomplished. The maintenance number block is used to insert a maintenance control number. This number becomes the significant identifier; it is assigned when the request is submitted. All references to the request will carry this identifier even after the charge number has been established.

Internal maintenance requests, as shown in Fig. 4–2, are forms which are suitable for use with an automatic message output center. The request, usually one which requires immediate action, is converted to an authorized work document with the main emphasis on work accomplishment.

Work orders of the type illustrated in Fig. 4–3 differ from work requests in that the work has previously been authorized. The three-part form is used to ensure that the work is charged to the correct number, that the cost is accumulated to the proper department, and that visibility is given to the job. The document becomes the initiator of the control procedure and is designed to describe the pertinent information for computer insertion. In some plants, a data processing card is used in order to eliminate one data conversion step.

The authorization permitted by a work order may be limited to a certain dollar amount. The level which determines the need to account for a job varies, but it must be based on what benefits will be derived from spending money to formally control the job. The work order normally comes into existence only after planning has been carried through and a cost estimate has been prepared.

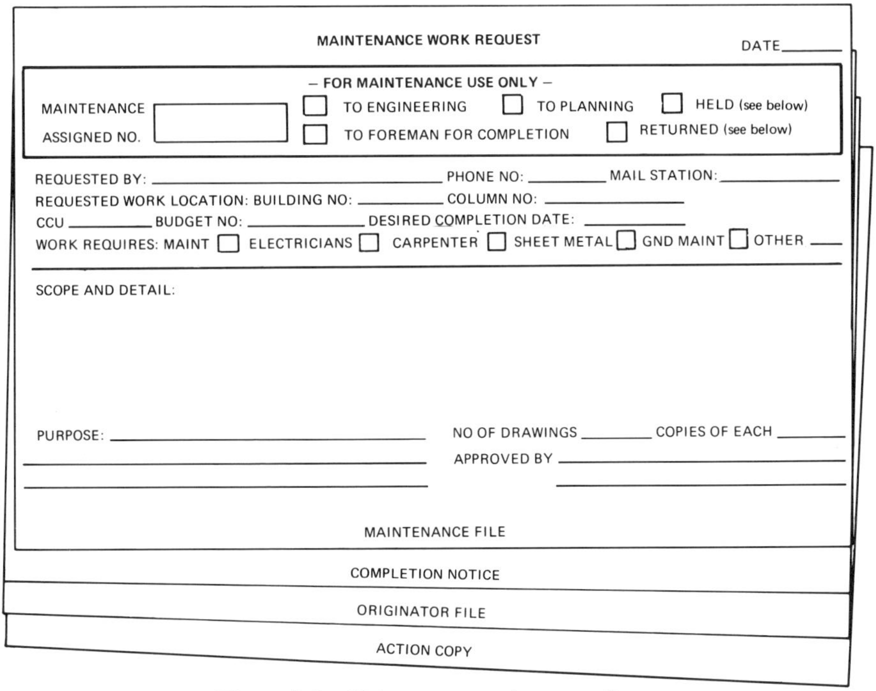

MAINTENANCE WORK REQUEST DATE____

– FOR MAINTENANCE USE ONLY –

MAINTENANCE ASSIGNED NO. ☐ TO ENGINEERING ☐ TO PLANNING ☐ HELD (see below)

☐ TO FOREMAN FOR COMPLETION ☐ RETURNED (see below)

REQUESTED BY: ____ PHONE NO: ____ MAIL STATION: ____

REQUESTED WORK LOCATION: BUILDING NO: ____ COLUMN NO: ____

CCU ____ BUDGET NO: ____ DESIRED COMPLETION DATE: ____

WORK REQUIRES: MAINT ☐ ELECTRICIANS ☐ CARPENTER ☐ SHEET METAL ☐ GND MAINT ☐ OTHER ____

SCOPE AND DETAIL:

PURPOSE: ____ NO OF DRAWINGS ____ COPIES OF EACH ____

APPROVED BY ____

MAINTENANCE FILE

COMPLETION NOTICE

ORIGINATOR FILE

ACTION COPY

Figure 4–1. Maintenance work request form.

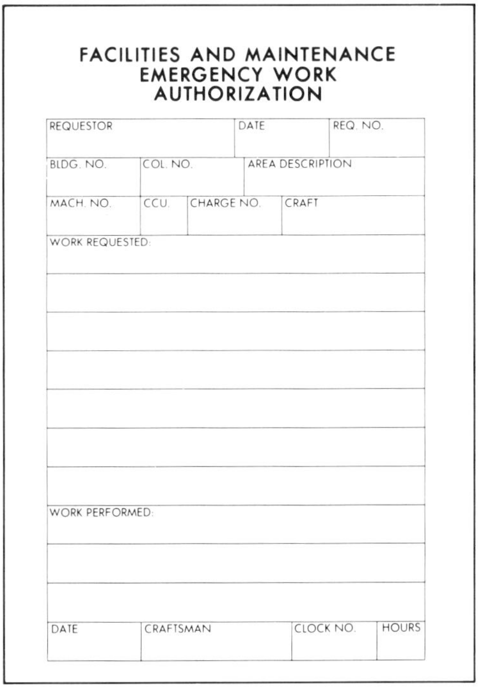

FACILITIES AND MAINTENANCE EMERGENCY WORK AUTHORIZATION

REQUESTOR		DATE	REQ. NO.
BLDG. NO.	COL. NO.	AREA DESCRIPTION	
MACH. NO.	CCU.	CHARGE NO.	CRAFT

WORK REQUESTED:

WORK PERFORMED:

DATE	CRAFTSMAN	CLOCK NO.	HOURS

Figure 4–2. Internal maintenance request form.

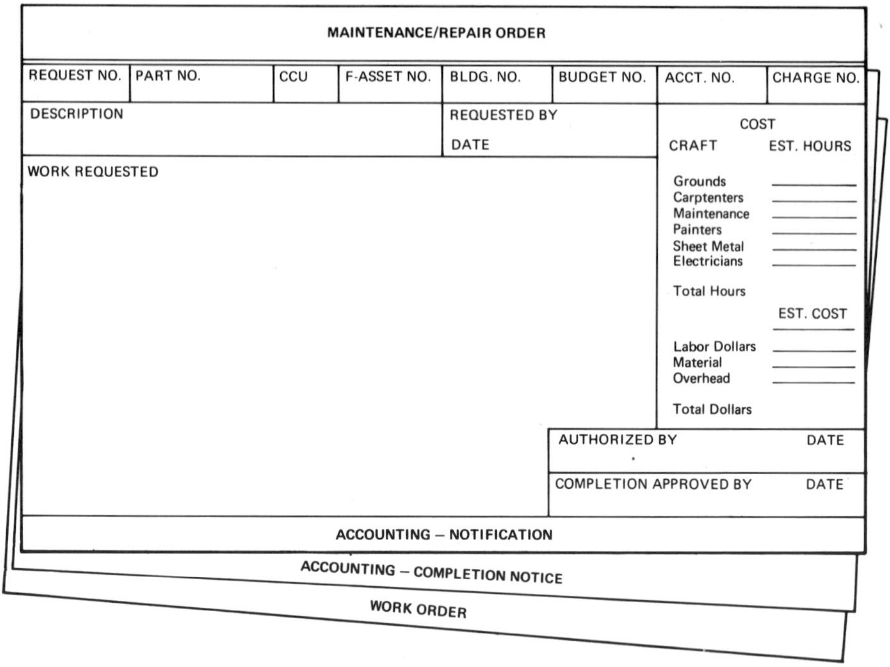

MAINTENANCE/REPAIR ORDER								
REQUEST NO.	PART NO.	CCU	F-ASSET NO.	BLDG. NO.	BUDGET NO.	ACCT. NO.		CHARGE NO.

DESCRIPTION

REQUESTED BY

DATE

COST

CRAFT   EST. HOURS

WORK REQUESTED

Grounds   _____
Carpenters   _____
Maintenance   _____
Painters   _____
Sheet Metal   _____
Electricians   _____

Total Hours

EST. COST

Labor Dollars _____
Material   _____
Overhead   _____

Total Dollars

AUTHORIZED BY   DATE

COMPLETION APPROVED BY   DATE

ACCOUNTING – NOTIFICATION

ACCOUNTING – COMPLETION NOTICE

WORK ORDER

Figure 4–3. Maintenance work order.

Therefore, a job to tighten a bolt on a machine would not require a formal work order, but the work request or some other document would initiate the action. A manager should attempt to determine what it costs to control an individual work order and then establish a benchmark which determines if a formal control procedure is necessary.

The cost of the work done without the benefit of a work order need not be lost. General work orders or standing work orders can be established at the beginning of the year to accumulate costs on all miscellaneous items, buildings, or equipment. These general work orders will provide information about how much cost has been incurred at any given time. Preventive maintenance, repetitive work such as cleaning and snow removal, and small jobs are all good candidates for this type of treatment. It is important that all standing orders be reviewed or rewritten each year. This will allow planning to review the tasks, check the methodology, and improve it where necessary.

The simplified chart of Fig. 4–4 shows the movement of the information generated by the work request/order form. The following steps are encountered when a request is processed:

    1) Request submittal
        a. Request received by central clearing agency (CCA)
        b. Preliminary review
        c. Assignment of maintenance number
    2) Review and action by CCA
        a. Review of scope of request

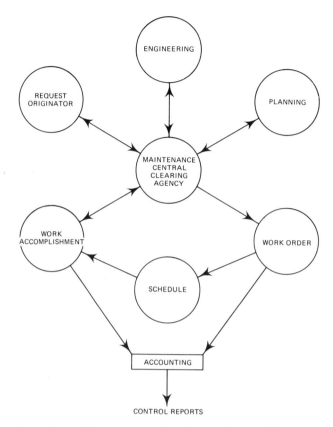

Figure 4–4. Maintenance work order – work request flow chart.

 b. Assignment to labor force. Individual work order control is not
  required, a general work order number is assigned
 c. Assignment to engineering when required
 d. Assignment to planning
 e. Log request disposition
 f. Filing of appropriate copies
3) Engineering
 a. Reception and recording
 b. Appropriate action is taken
 c. Request and engineering information is returned to CCA
4) Planning
 a. Reception and recording
 b. Investigation and review
 c. Development of plan package
 d. Request and plan package is returned to CCA
5) Preparation of work order by CCA
 a. Preliminary package review
 b. Preparation of budget if dollar amount dictates

       c. Assignment of charge number
       d. Preparation of maintenance work order
       e. Recording of pertinent information
  6) Review and approval
       a. Review of total package for completeness, quality, policy, etc.
       b. Securing of proper approval
       c. Activation of accounting control
  7) Schedule
       a. Entering work order into preliminary schedule
       b. Assignment of work order priority
       c. Elements of work order are distributed to proper functions
  8) Work accomplishment
       a. Initiated by CCA as described in step two or by the schedule
       b. Performance of work requested
       c. Completion of time and material control cards
       d. Return of request to CCA when completed
  9) Completion and close-out by CCA
       a. Recording of completion
       b. Forwarding of request completion notice to originator
       c. Forwarding of work completion notice to accounting
       d. Closing of all record files
 10) Accounting
       a. Receipt of basic information inputs
       b. Distribution of costs to proper CCA
       c. Generation of cost control reports

Job Planning

Job planning covers the what and how of job methods. This is where engineering must be applied to maintenance because the development of a job plan requires an investigation of the tools, materials, manpower, and techniques best suited to the job. This procedure will enable the maintenance function to effectively realize the potential of the skilled crafts by providing them with the support that will free their time for actually applying their skills.

It is best to have a separate planning function which is manned by specialists in the area. The planner is responsible for the preparation of the job plan which includes the following steps:

1) Investigation at the job site, looking at the job, and ascertaining what work is required.
2) Preparation of a step-by-step procedure which will accomplish the work with the most economical use of manpower and materials. Includes one-line diagrams and sketches.
3) Preparation of a list of material required
4) Estimation of the time required to accomplish the task
5) Preparation of a list of special tools required
6) Provision for necessary safety devices and safety instructions.

The type of individual selected to accomplish the planning effort depends largely on the sophistication desired. He can be selected from the craft, supervision, or engineering groups, but in all cases he must possess an analytical mind and a good understanding of the craft for which he will plan jobs. Also, training in work measurement, work simplification, safety requirements, material availability, etc., should be a prerequisite to the job assignment.

The role of the job planner has been misunderstood in many maintenance circles. It has been erroneously stated that the main job of the planner is to apply standard data so that the job can be time rated. This misconception is quickly corrected by taking a detail look at how the planner spends his time in a typical maintenance planning function. Table IV–3 shows the result of a work sampling study conducted on a maintenance planning group. The study indicates that 50 percent of a planner's time is involved in investigation and methodizing the job. The standard data application represents only 12.7 percent of his time. The work measurement aspect of planning will be discussed later in this chapter.

Table IV–3. Summary of Planner's Time.

Planning Elements	Percentage of Time
Job investigation	24.4
Plan development	25.6
Standard data application	12.7
Bill of materials preparation	18.3
Follow-up	6.5
Personal and miscellaneous	12.5

The sequence of the job is an important element of job planning. A detail summary form, as shown in Fig. 4–5, can be used to indicate the sequential steps involved in accomplishing the job. The planner uses this form to summarize his planning effort, and, along with sketches, information sheets and material list make up the complete package which will be sent to craft supervision. The summary also provides the basic information for work order generation.

The planning effort acts as the heart of the maintenance function, providing vital information to all areas of the organization. By using a complete program based on an elemental breakdown of work by standard data, the planner knows that his plan is complete, that the job has been properly time rated, that the material cost and special tool requirements are complete, and that the work will be consistent with past practice.

WORK MEASUREMENT

Work measurement is currently one of the most discussed topics in maintenance. Some of the questions raised at seminars and conferences are: How do you measure maintenance labor performance? How do you measure the effectiveness of what you are doing? How do you know if the standard data is reliable? Certainly work measurement is the foundation on which successful management is based, for as Lord Kelvin once said, "If you can measure that of which you speak and can express it by a number, you know something of

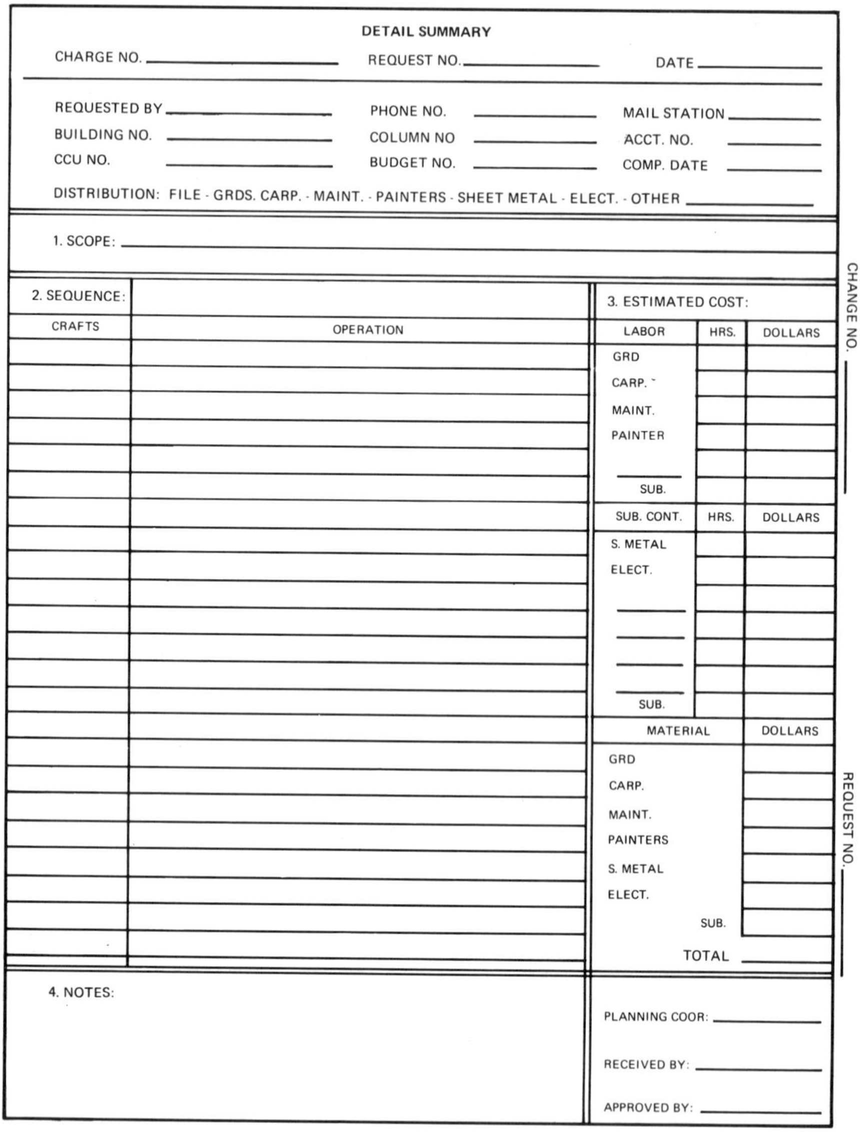

DETAIL SUMMARY

CHARGE NO. _____   REQUEST NO. _____   DATE _____

REQUESTED BY _____   PHONE NO.   _____   MAIL STATION _____

BUILDING NO.   _____   COLUMN NO   _____   ACCT. NO.   _____

CCU NO.   _____   BUDGET NO.   _____   COMP. DATE   _____

DISTRIBUTION: FILE · GRDS. CARP. · MAINT. · PAINTERS · SHEET METAL · ELECT. · OTHER _____

1. SCOPE: _____

2. SEQUENCE:		3. ESTIMATED COST:		
CRAFTS	OPERATION	LABOR	HRS.	DOLLARS
		GRD		
		CARP.		
		MAINT.		
		PAINTER		
		SUB.		
		SUB. CONT.	HRS.	DOLLARS
		S. METAL		
		ELECT.		
		SUB.		
		MATERIAL		DOLLARS
		GRD		
		CARP.		
		MAINT.		
		PAINTERS		
		S. METAL		
		ELECT.		
			SUB.	
			TOTAL	___

4. NOTES:	
	PLANNING COOR: _____
	RECEIVED BY: _____
	APPROVED BY: _____

CHANGE NO. ___

REQUEST NO. ___

Figure 4–5. Job planning detail summary form.

your subject; but if you cannot measure it, your knowledge is meager and unsatisfactory."

A manager must have a system by which he can measure his work effort. Once, work measurement was entirely concerned with production. Today, however, it is an accepted practice to use work measurement in the maintenance function as well. Standard data is available, and meaningful results are now obtainable. However, overemphasis of labor control without consideration of the other factors which influence labor can occur and would have a detrimental effect on the program. All aspects of job analysis must be included with the application of work standards. Materials, equipment, methods, etc., are all a part of a work measurement program. Establishing a time standard without consideration of other factors is inexcusable.

Methods of Work Measurement

Frank Gilbreth, the father of motion study, subdivided the time elements first developed by Frederick Taylor into basic motions which he called *therbligs*. These therbligs were used to build up an operation standard. The expansion of the Taylor and Gilbreth methods has resulted in predetermined elemental times for a great many factory operations. Methods-Time-Measurement (MTM), Work Factor (WF), Motion-Time Analysis (MTA), and Basic Motion Timestudy (BMT) are some of the best-known systems using this approach.

The use of predetermined elemental standard data in the maintenance area has grown in popularity. The approach is more costly than some other systems because of the time it takes to apply the standards and the paper work involved. However, the additional cost is small compared to the benefits obtained. A task is broken down into its parts, and a time value is applied to each element. The sum of these values, plus allowances for job conditions, travel times, fatigue allowances, etc., represents the time it should take to accomplish the work. The benefits gained in applying engineered time standards include the following:

1) The job times are consistent and accurate
2) The standards require job methodizing
3) The standards are necessary tools for reliable planning
4) They provide impartial benchmarks
5) They supply a reliable basis for evaluating methods, equipment, or contractor performance.

These elemental time values become the building blocks for the planner. The standard data base gives the planner confidence in his final product because he knows that the job was time-rated objectively.

Other systems of estimating are less costly, but all have substantial drawbacks. Subjective estimating can be done cheaply and easily, but the estimates tend to be inconsistent and inaccurate. Historical data-based estimates are somewhat better than pure estimating, but past mistakes are retained and improvement in methodology is hampered. Job slotting is another method which can be used if all that is required is a time value and the planner is not interested in job conditions. It is possible to use a combination of systems to provide an overall coverage of the operation.

The application of standard data to repetitive types of work can be very beneficial financially. The cost to establish the standard becomes insignificant because of the repetitive nature of the work. Janitorial work, certain preventive maintenance tasks, operational aspects of maintenance, etc., are all good candidates for the application of standards. The elimination of bad practices which have occurred repetitively can save a maintenance function a good deal of money. Applying this method to repetitive work will accomplish two favorable results: (1) return on investment will be realized quickly, and an (2) evaluation of the application of standard data can be accomplished in a short time, thereby developing confidence in the program. The janitorial area is an especially good starting point where the work is predominantly repetitive and labor frequently constitutes up to 90 percent of the cost.

Nonrepetitive work is, of course, a difficult and costly area for standard data application. It is essential to plan a nonrepetitive job because of the unfamiliarity of the task to the supervisors and workmen. If the job is not planned and the method is not established based on standard data, the burden of planning will fall on the supervisors or craftsmen, and the planning will normally be done in a haphazard manner. The results will be a more expensive job and less manpower to do other work.

Some maintenance functions utilize standard data to determine what the efficiency was on particular jobs. This practice is rarely helpful, however. By the time the standard is established, the job has been forgotten, and it will be hard to generate interest in why certain things went wrong. Application of standards after the fact can be beneficial as an auditing technique for a planned job. The auditing process should be conducted on a random sampling basis, with the results reviewed with the planner to help him improve his techniques.

Another widely used method of measuring labor effectiveness is work sampling. Work sampling is a technique for observing and recording what a worker is doing at a particular time. The observations are collected and are expressed in percentages such as working—55 percent, idle—20 percent, travel—15 percent, and so on. Work sampling (ratio delay) is based on the laws of probability. The key to the accuracy of the technique is in the number of observations. The greater the number of observations, the higher the degree of accuracy. However, fewer observations will be required if the activity definitions are fairly broad ones such as work, idle, travel, and the like.

In every kind of measurement work a certain tolerance or margin for error is accepted. Since random sampling is a way of measuring, a tolerance is accepted. This tolerance is called *percentage deviation*. With random sampling there is a chance that the observations will be outside the allowable percentage deviation (acceptable tolerance) even though the actual composition of the population is within the tolerance. This is called the *probability of statistical error*. Percentage deviation and statistical error are related through what is known as the *standard error of deviation*.

The number of observations required depends directly on the accuracy desired. Most authorities recommend a ±5 percent (twice the standard error as a tolerance) accuracy level as an acceptable standard. To illustrate, if the percentage occurrence of a particular element or activity is 30 percent, then the chances are 95 out of 100 that the true value will lie between 38.5 and 31.5 percent for a ±5 percent accuracy. Table IV–4 shows the required number of observations for this tolerance.

Work sampling is a good technique for helping to identify problem areas. However, this particular method will not solve any problems by itself. The most to be gained by it is an approximately 15 percent increase in productivity due to improvements made as a result of these studies. Work sampling is essentially an

Table IV-4. Observations for Work Sampling.

Percentage Occurrence	Observations for 5% Element Tolerance
1	158,000
5	30,000
10	14,400
20	6,400
30	3,680
40	2,400
50	1,600

inexpensive method for monitoring other work measurement systems to determine their effectiveness.

Another application of work sampling can be found in the use of foremen as observers. The foremen can be taught the technique of making observations as they follow up on their work assignments. While the observations will not be random, the activity will cause the foremen to be more conscious of time and productivity. Many foremen will be surprised when a goal of three observations per day per man is hard to obtain. Good sampling procedures require that observations be taken at random times. The random samples are preferably scheduled by means of a table of random numbers.

Some general comments and conclusions should be made to emphasize certain points:

1) Work measurement is a tool, an ineffective tool unless used properly.
2) Performance data application involves many factors such as method establishment, material and equipment analysis, and supervision involvement.
3) Management consultants are a good source of performance data if you are not staffed to develop your own data.
4) Ultimately, the standards developed should be accurate enough so that they may be used as a basis for incentive plans.
5) Before you can properly apply performance data you must streamline your control system.
6) Once the program is installed, follow up, document, and obtain the most benefit possible out of the system.
7) Maintain a work sampling program to monitor the effectiveness of your program.
8) As managers, you must support your program so *your* interest permeates *your* organization.
9) Students who do well in school do not cringe at test results. This application of proper performance bench marks recognizes job effort and is a reward to the ones who have earned that recognition.

Scheduling

Scheduling covers the "when" and "who" of job tasks. Effective scheduling requires realistic thinking based upon substantial data. It is generally agreed that scheduling is an inherent part of overall planning and is basic to good maintenance management. Therefore, if a manager desires to have scheduling work for him, he must not apply wishful thinking to the process of determining the likelihood of meeting completion dates.

The scheduler must have access to certain facts before he can begin to operate. The more salient facts are the following:

1) Manpower availability by craft, location, shift, and overtime authorized
2) Manhour backlog of current jobs
3) Availability of machine or area where work is to be performed
4) Availability of material
5) Availability of special equipment
6) Manhour requirement of new jobs
7) Completion date required by customer.

Manpower Availability. This information concerns how much manpower is available, normally expressed in hours, and must be known. The availability of hours must also be broken down by craft, geographical location if significant, and the shift position. The overtime authorized is also a part of the manpower availability equation.

Man-hour Backlog of Current Jobs. This backlog consists of the mathematical summation of the hours required to complete the jobs presently on the schedule.

Availability of Machine or Area. Knowledge of when a machine, system or area is available will determine when the job can be scheduled. This area of scheduling can be very difficult, and it is important to maintain close cooperation with the operating functions.

Availability of Material. Awareness of this key factor is essential. The availability of material, such as manpower, will establish whether or not the job can be scheduled. To overlook this aspect of scheduling will produce gross inefficiency and will make the scheduling effort virtually worthless. Material availability is one of the most important parts of the scheduling equation.

Availability of Special Equipment. To accomplish some of the more complex jobs, certain special equipment is often required. Lifts, compressors, concrete saws, cable-pulling equipment, high-potential devices, etc., are examples of such equipment. The availability of such equipment must be determined prior to any scheduling effort.

Man-hour Requirement of New Jobs. As in the second item, the new job man-hour input must be made. The merging of the new with the current requirements will give the complete needs for proper scheduling.

Completion Date Required by Customer. The due date, if not considered, can be detrimental to good scheduling. It must be determined if the requested completion date is realistic and necessary. Once the authenticity of the date has been established, the scheduling of the job should be motivated by that requirement.

Job scheduling is accomplished in many ways. Maintenance functions can be scheduled daily, weekly, or monthly; or they can be scheduled for different periods such as four-, five-, and seven-day weeks. The schedule can be geared to geographical location, craft relationship, shift position, or functional grouping; or it can be totally responsive to priority requirements.

Thus, scheduling must be tailor-made to fit the circumstances in your plant. There is no single scheduling scheme which can embrace all aspects and objectives desired. A maintenance function must determine the objectives desired by the organization and then establish a scheduling method which can best help to obtain those objectives.

An example of a scheduling printout sheet is shown in Fig. 4–6. The example is a page of a weekly schedule. The following elements are included:

1) FY-WK – The fiscal week of the schedule
2) Type – Title of the function which will perform the work
3) Maintenance No. – This is the number of the related work request, if applicable.
4) Charge No. – This is the work order number to collect the job charges
5) Date Scheduled – Date job put on schedule
6) Building No. – Location where the job is to be performed
7) Description – Brief description of the work
8) Priority – The priority assigned to the task. Priorities used in this scheduling application are as follows:
   A+ – Carry over a job priority of last week.
   A – Job to be accomplished this week.
   B – Job not scheduled this week; no limiting factors exist, and work can be performed on the job if manpower becomes available.
   C – Material or equipment not available.
   D – Job on a hold for some reason other than availability of maintenance related items.
   X – Denotes completed or used as an indicating mark.
9) Hours Scheduled – Hours scheduled for current week
10) Hours Planned – Estimated hours to complete job
11) Hours Worked – Accumulated hours from previous scheduled weeks
12) Hours Balance – Balance of hours between planned and worked
13) Planned – X indicates if standard hours are applied and a detailed plan was established.
14) Completed – X indicates job completion
15) Remarks – Remarks as necessary

The schedule in Fig. 4–6 is designed to allow daily flexibility by the performing department. In areas such as machine maintenance, where the date and time are essential to allow for production shutdowns, a daily shift schedule must be prepared. Because of the desirability of having the schedule sensitive to a number of elements, the scheduling function is ideal for electronic data processing. This aspect will be discussed in a later section.

There are other techniques available to assist the scheduling function. Gantt charts, milestones, and the Critical Path Method (CPM) are some of the techniques generally used by maintenance organizations. These techniques are normally found associated with job planning but in actuality are more closely related to scheduling. The usual practice is to combine the planning and scheduling into one operation. Combining these two activities will work as long as the manager can recognize them as distinct functions. Job planning produces the "what and how"; the product of scheduling is the "when" and "who." Also, the planning effort must always precede the scheduling effort.

MAINTENANCE DEPARTMENT WORK SCHEDULE
FY-WK 0-21   TYPE: MAINTENANCE & OPERATIONS   PAGE 3   DATE 12/18/69

MAINT. NO.	CHARGE NO.	DATE SCH.	BLD. NO.	DESCRIPTION	GRDS	CARP	MAINT	PAINT	S.M.	ELECT	OTHER	HOURS SCHEDULED	HOURS PLANNED	HOURS WORKED	HOURS BALANCE	PLANNED	COMPLETED	REMARKS
-- --	0956--	8/2	105	Machine Repair Fab			A			A		140.0		192.8				See Daily Schedule
-- --	087641	8/2	120 122	Building Operation FY-WK 21								88.0		85.0				
95721	069591	8/13	138	Paint Old White Room				B					135.2	0	135.2	X		
				Janitor							B		51.5	0	51.5	X		
00799	096854	9/18	106	Repr. 20 gal. Cooking Pot			D						16.0	3.0	13.0			F & M
01026	069917	10/2	111	PM Chiller Starter #2MWO 6689						B			50.0	0	50.0			F & M
01931	087859	11/12	108	Retile Floors – Jan. Closet		A+						2.8	15.8	13.0	2.8	X		F & M
02229	087879	12/3	139	Repl. Worn Treads on Stairs		C							4.5	0	4.5	X		
02231	087888	12/3	106	Repl. Absolute Filters			C						24.0	0	24.0			Req. 12/9
02266	096954	12/17	105	Repair Vapor Degreaser			A					26.0	26.0	0	26.0			12/21
02390	096940	12/10	105	Paint Booth Schedule FWO-20			A+					42.0	45.0	3.0	42.0	X		
02453	087895	12/10	105 133	PM Week #20			A+					80.0	143.0	54.5	88.5	X		
										X			119.8	0	119.8	X	X	
02501	096947	12/17	105	Paint Booth Schedule 0-21			A					35.0	35.0	0	35.0	X		
02548	060528	12/17	120	Paint Office Marketing				A				4.6	4.6	0	4.6	X		12/19
02549	087910	12/17	105 133	PM Week #21			A					97.1	97.1	0	97.1	X		
										A		153.1	153.1	0	153.1	X		
02560	060537	12/17	110	Replace Exit door—Yellow Rm.		A						7.7	7.7	0	7.7	X		
								A				2.7	2.7	0	2.7	X		

Figure 4-6. Typical maintenance department work schedule.

These additional scheduling methods provide a more descriptive (primarily a more graphic-type) technique. They are used when the manager is faced with uncertainty regarding labor availability to accomplish a time objective, when interdependency of activities exists, when visibility of a multielement task is to be gained, and when the job is mainly sequential in nature.

The Gantt chart was developed by Henry Gantt during World War I. The chart is normally a bar graph with descriptives entered vertically on the left and time increments entered at the top. The plot would normally be a bar, outlined for the scheduled time and filled in as the task progresses. The graphic presentation is an exceptionally good method for displaying progress and controlling projects. Milestones are used in conjunction with the Gantt chart to subdivide the horizontal bars into well-defined checkpoints. These checkpoints show the scheduler if the project is progressing satisfactorily in relationship to the time objective. Milestones can be used alone as subgoals, and in some cases they are expressed as calendar dates.

The critical path method is a graphic presentation of an arrow diagram representing the interrelationships between tasks of a multitask job. A simple critical path diagram is shown in Fig. 4–7. Each arrow of the diagram repre-

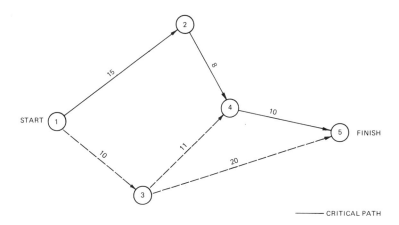

Figure 4–7. Simple critical path method diagram.

sents an activity or job, and the sequence is indicated by the manner in which they are connected. Circles or nodes (events) are used to mark a start or the completion of one phase of a task. The critical path is shown as a solid line and takes 33 units (sum of 15, 8, and 10) to complete. The other two paths take 30 and 31 units, respectively. The determination of the critical path allows the scheduler to analyze the job to see if the longest path can be shortened to improve the completion date. Analysis will also quickly show where delays may result, permitting the scheduler to watch these particular areas and take action to possibly prevent the delays. The method provides good flexibility in that it can be updated easily.

MATERIALS AND PARTS CONTROL

The area of materials and parts control must be emphasized along with the labor functions. The proper control of supplies and spare parts is essential to allow the maintenance department to realize savings on any labor control program which they may install. The use of labor standards is predicated on a material and parts control system.

The maintenance manager must insist on a system which will provide good inventory control. A system which tends to overstock will produce a number of ill effects. The requirement of higher investment at high interest rates will waste capital which could be used in other areas, more area will be required to stock the material and parts, management will be critical of high inventories, scrapping of materials and parts due to obsolescence will be higher, and an indifferent attitude may be created toward material and parts conservation because of the overabundance of supplies. If the system tends to understock, another set of ill effects will be produced. The loss of efficiency in labor utilization will increase the cost of jobs, unnecessary or excessive downtime of production equipment will be experienced, rush orders to obtain the material and parts will increase costs because of transportation and lower quantity orders, and there will be a chronic inability to meet schedule commitments. Obviously, the main objective of a supplies control system should be to maintain the inventory level at the proper maximum and minimum levels which are consistent with the operating and financial requirements of the maintenance function.

A principal component of a good control system is a well-organized stocking area. The storeroom should be centrally located to permit convenient access by maintenance personnel. Ideally, the stocking area should be one large storeroom which receives all incoming items. The stockroom then issues selected parts to various satellite areas. The flow of material and the travel of craftsmen must always be considered when determining the location of a stocking area.

The storage of the material and parts within a stocking area should be geared to the administrative system. Material should be stocked in accordance with the part numbering or identification system and the bins should be arranged so that the storeskeeper can locate and withdraw material conveniently. For example, plumbing fittings should be located in one area, with the bins of fittings grouped together by size. The storeskeeper would then fill a order requiring a number of $\frac{1}{2}$-inch fittings with a minimum of travel. The spare parts section, tool room, and related supplies such as sanitation items, etc., should all be segregated from the main material stock. This segregation is required so that the material or parts will be withdrawn for their intended use.

A stockroom should always include some open floor space. This space is required to provide a queue for incoming material or outgoing issues or job kits. This open floor space is often too small because of the pressure of space utilization. The control system should be designed to accomplish the following:

1) Establishment of what items are to be carried in inventory
2) Identification of materials and parts
3) Establishment of inventory levels and reorder points
4) Provision of information for purchasing of items
5) Receipt of stock and issue of items

6) Identification and disposal of slow-moving, obsolete, and damaged items
7) Control reporting.

The system should be computerized to receive full benefit of the program. Manual analysis is almost impossible with any medium-to-large stocking function. Computer application to material control is widely accepted and used in industry today. The first step in establishment of a control system is to determine what items should be carried in inventory. The items should be identified in major categories and subcategories. The following is an example of category codes:

Code	Category
0900	Paint and coating
1000	Fuels, lubricants, and coolants
1100	Hardware
1200	Electrical
1300	Plumbing
1400	Mechanical
1500	Equipment and machine spare parts
1600	Building materials
1700	Yards and grounds
1800	Sanitary supplies (janitorial)
1900	Health and safety

An example of subcategory codes is as follows:

Code	Category
1100	Hardware
1102	Anchors, toggle bolts
1104	Cap screws
1106	Carriage bolts
1108	Eyebolts, S-hooks, and turnbuckles
1110	Lag screws
1114	Nuts
1116	Sheet metal screws
1118	Machine screws
1120	Threaded rod
1122	Washers
1124	Wood screws

Each item should be identifiable by a single part number and further described by a component specification to aid purchasing in buying the item. Fig. 4–8 shows an example of a supplies specification form used to establish an item's existence in a control system. The 30-character narrative description and supporting data would be retained in the computer and available to all concerned as an output in catalog form.

Much data must be derived on the item to allow the system to determine usage rates, maintain proper inventory levels, and purchase replacements. As an example, the response code is a number representing a weighted rela-

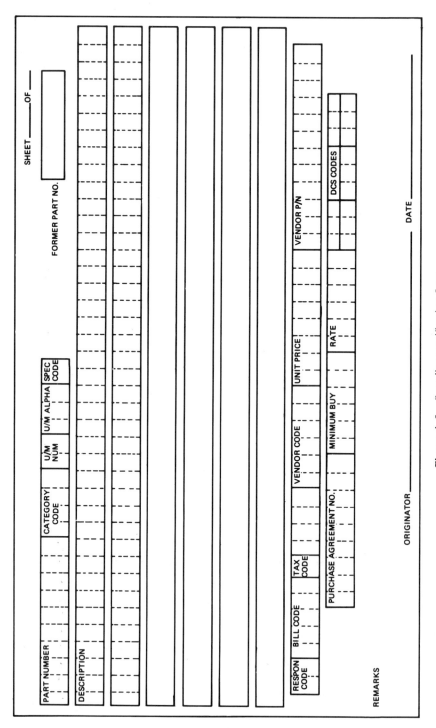

Figure 4–8. Supplies specification form.

tionship between historic usage rate and current usage rate on an item. This number is then used in a mathematical formula to determine the projected usage rate. The system would then allow a buyer to make purchases in economical lot sizes.

The material and parts consumer must be aware of the key piece of information—the part number. A supply user's catalog will provide the information required. Fig. 4–9 is a sample page of a catalog which shows the listing for

Category 1124. Flat-Head Wood Screws

Part No.	U M	U/M Abr	Unit Price	S C	Description	Wood Screws
344-0713-010	7	PCS	.43000	1	FHWS 2 × ½	PLATED BOX 100
344-0713-020	7	PCS	.44000	1	FHWS 3 × ½	PLATED BOX 100
344-0713-030	7	PCS	.47000	1	FHWS 3 × ⅝	PLATED BOX 100
344-0713-040	7	PCS	.42000	1	FHWS 4 × ¼	PLATED BOX 100
344-0713-050	7	PCS	.45000	1	FHWS 4 × ½	PLATED BOX 100
344-0713-060	7	PCS	.48000	1	FHWS 4 × ⅝	PLATED BOX 100
344-0713-070	7	PCS	.44000	1	FHWS 5 × ⅜	PLATED BOX 100
344-0713-080	7	PCS	.45000	1	FHWS 5 × ½	PLATED BOX 100
344-0713-090	7	PCS	.49000	1	FHWS 5 × ⅝	PLATED BOX 100
344-0713-100	7	PCS	.51000	1	FHWS 5 × ¾	PLATED BOX 100
344-0713-110	7	PCS	.60000	1	FHWS 5 × 1	PLATED BOX 100
344-0713-120	7	PCS	.47000	1	FHWS 6 × ½	PLATED BOX 100
344-0713-130	7	PCS	.50000	1	FHWS 6 × ⅝	PLATED BOX 100
344-0713-140	7	PCS	.52000	1	FHWS 6 × ¾	PLATED BOX 100
344-0713-150	7	PCS	.57000	1	FHWS 6 × ⅞	PLATED BOX 100
344-0713-160	7	PCS	.62000	1	FHWS 6 × 1	PLATED BOX 100
344-0713-170	7	PCS	.74000	1	FHWS 6 × 1¼	PLATED BOX 100
344-0713-180	7	PCS	.90000	1	FHWS 6 × 1½	PLATED BOX 100
344-0713-190	7	PCS	.49000	1	FHWS 7 × ½	PLATED BOX 100
344-0713-200	7	PCS	.56000	1	FHWS 7 × ¾	PLATED BOX 100
344-0713-210	7	PCS	.60000	1	FHWS 7 × ⅞	PLATED BOX 100
344-0713-220	7	PCS	.64000	1	FHWS 7 × 1	PLATED BOX 100
344-0713-230	7	PCS	.77000	1	FHWS 7 × 1¼	PLATED BOX 100
344-0713-240	7	PCS	.90000	1	FHWS 7 × 1½	PLATED BOX 100
344-0713-250	7	PCS	1.20000	1	FHWS 7 × 2	PLATED BOX 100
344-0713-260	7	PCS	.59000	1	FHWS 8 × ¾	PLATED BOX 100
344-0713-270	7	PCS	.64000	1	FHWS 8 × ⅞	PLATED BOX 100
344-0713-280	7	PCS	.68000	1	FHWS 8 × 1	PLATED BOX 100
344-0713-290	7	PCS	.81000	1	FHWS 8 × 1¼	PLATED BOX 100
344-0713-300	7	PCS	.92000	1	FHWS 8 × 1½	PLATED BOX 100
344-0713-310	7	PCS	1.09000	1	FHWS 8 × 1¾	PLATED BOX 100
344-0713-320	7	PCS	1.21000	1	FHWS 8 × 2	PLATED BOX 100
344-0713-330	7	PCS	1.48000	1	FHWS 8 × 2½	PLATED BOX 100
344-0713-340	7	PCS	.62000	1	FHWS 9 × ¾	PLATED BOX 100
344-0713-350	7	PCS	.71000	1	FHWS 9 × 1	PLATED BOX 100
344-0713-360	7	PCS	.66000	1	FHWS 10 × ¾	PLATED BOX 100

Figure 4–9. Page from supplies users' catalog.

Category 1124, flathead wood screws. The part number and other information is retrieved for supplies requisitioning.

Requisition forms come in all shapes and formats. Some examples are shown in the following figures:

Fig. 4–10 – This form is used primarily by the planner to call out material or parts for a job.

Page ____ of ____						SERIAL NO. 8673		
CHARGE NO: _____ MAINTENANCE ASSIGNED NO: _____ CURRENT DATE: _____								
MATERIAL DELIVERY DATE: _____ JOB SCHEDULE DATE: _____								
JOB LOCATION: _____ FUNCTION: _____								
PLANNER: ENGINEER _____ CCU _____ BUDGET NO: _____ ACCT. NO: _____								
JOB SCOPE: _____						SCS ISSUE BY		
P/N	MATL. SOURCE	QTY. ORDER	QTY. ISS.	DESCRIPTION		UNIT COST	TOTAL COST	STD. MIN.
JOB FOLDER								

CHARGE NUMBER

MAINT. ASSIGNED NUMBER

Figure 4–10. Material list and stock requisition form.

Fig. 4–11 – This form can be used by anyone; it is normally used in the field to secure parts and materials on small repair or emergency work.

DATE _____									**113502**	
DELIVER TO:	NAME		MAIL STATION			DCS. DOC ID CODE				
IRU/SPEC. REQ.	CCU	STORES RETURN (CHECK IF) SPECIAL REQ. ☐ ☐	APPROVED BY					DATE REQ.		
QTY. ORDERED	PART NUMBER		DESCRIPTION	LOC.	QTY. ISSUED	QTY. BACK OR'D	ACCT. NO. JOB CHARGE	UNIT COST	TOTAL COST	

ISSUED BY _____ DATE _____

Figure 4–11. Standard supply requisition form.

Fig. 4–12 – This form is used in conjunction with a telescriber system between satellite and central stocking areas.

A requisition form, regardless of the format, should provide space for the insertion of all basic information necessary for any type of control system; date, location of material, delivery, charge number, identification of items, and quantity for issue are some of the items in this category.

The planner is one of the key submitters of requisitions. The combination of his material-required list and requisition reduces paper work and labor (Fig. 4–10). The planner should be completely familiar with the material and parts in the system. This familiarity will increase his effectiveness as a planner and provide the right material for the right job.

If electronic data processing is not currently being used in your supplies system, the manual method used should be geared as closely as possible to a computerized system. This approach will make the transition into the EDP area an easy one. The use of EDP is a proven tool in reducing cost in the material control area, and a maintenance manager should consider the use of a computerized program to allow his company to stay competitive.

CONTROL REPORTS

Reporting on how well the department has performed against an established goal is a cardinal objective of a well-organized maintenance department. The

SUPPLY REQUISITION

NO. 3801

DATE	DELIVER TO: NAME AND MAIL STATION	
DCS-DOC ID CODE	IRLL/SPEC.	CCU
ACCT. NO.- JOB CHARGE	DATE REQ'D	

ORDER QTY.	PART NUMBER	PART DESCRIPTION	ISSUE QTY.

ISSUED BY:	DATE ISSUED:

Figure 4–12. Telescriber supply requisition form.

reporting must be such that a manager can quickly gain the visibility required to determine his effectiveness in the areas where control systems have been employed. The visibility will permit the manager to take action to correct out-of-control areas. The reports should be timely and easily interpreted.

Expenditures

Expenditures both of a capital and expense nature should be compared against a budget, goal, or estimate and reported on a periodic basis. The operating expense budget is a good example of such a report. The report can occur on a weekly or monthly basis showing actual expenses versus the budget with emphasis on the variance. A graphic presentation such as that shown in Fig. 4–13 depicts the accepted variance of two sigma limits of ±5 percent and shows the budget versus actual. The manager establishes the control limits (in this case ±5 percent), and when the variance falls within the limits no

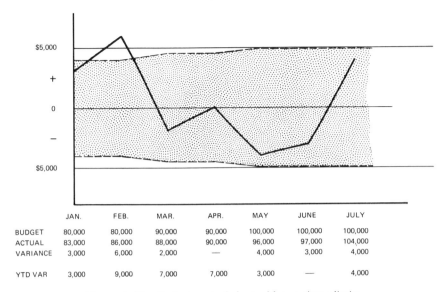

	JAN.	FEB.	MAR.	APR.	MAY	JUNE	JULY
BUDGET	80,000	80,000	90,000	90,000	100,000	100,000	100,000
ACTUAL	83,000	86,000	88,000	90,000	96,000	97,000	104,000
VARIANCE	3,000	6,000	2,000	—	4,000	3,000	4,000
YTD VAR	3,000	9,000	7,000	7,000	3,000	—	4,000

Figure 4–13. Budget control chart with two sigma limits.

variance explanation is required. Only when the variance falls outside of the control limits (for example, in February in Fig. 4–13) should a detailed explanation be required. This type of chart will eliminate unnecessary review of expenditures, but it also demands that the budget and tolerance limits be established realistically. Bar graphs (Fig. 4–14), actual versus budget plots

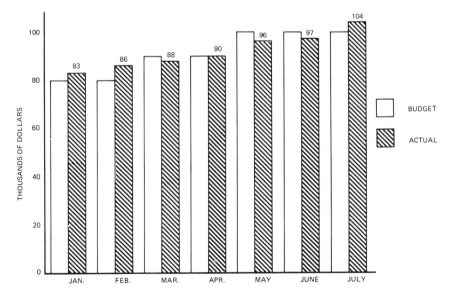

Figure 4–14. Bar chart of budgeted vs. actual expenses.

(Fig. 4–15), and pie charts are all used in reporting or analyzing expenditures. Costs are graphically depicted by year to show trends. Individual job costs should be subjected to the variance approach so that out-of-control jobs can be analyzed and improvements made. The main point to remember when devising control reports is to make them meaningful and simple enough that they can be quickly and easily interpreted.

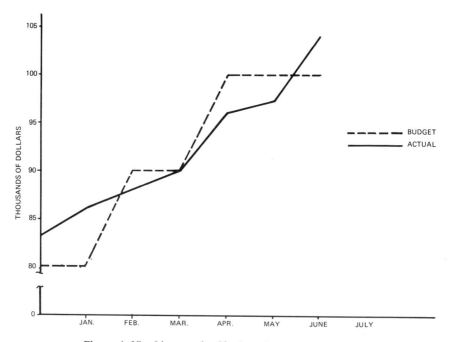

Figure 4–15. Line graph of budgeted vs. actual expenses.

Performance

The evaluation of labor performance is effective only when reports are issued and management acts upon the results. A manager must be interested in his labor performance and review reports which will enable him to take positive action to correct a deficiency or recognize an accomplishment.

Table IV–5 shows labor performance for a janitorial section. The report gives the daily and project earned minutes per area of responsibility, the total earned minutes, the minutes worked, and the performance expressed as a percentage. The report covers a period of five working days. In conjunction with the janitor labor performance report, it is advisable to issue an area quality rating report. The area quality rating could be shown on the labor performance report. Most janitor area loading programs have a direct relationship between efficiency and quality, and the integration of the two will give the overall performance of the individual.

As in expenditure reporting, graphics can effectively indicate labor per-

Table IV-5. Sanitation Performance Results.

Area or Title	Name		Earned Minutes Daily	Project	Minutes Earned, Total	Minutes Allowed	Performance (percent)
1	Lane		1532.8	159.7	1692.5	1920	88.2
2	Kircks		2029.5	805.6	2835.1	2400	118.1
3	Jones		1843.0	120.9	1963.9	2400	80.7
4	Smith		2005.0	——	2005.0	2400	83.5
5	Johnson		1092.6	107.7	1200.3	1440	83.4
6	Franks		2070.0	143.7	2213.7	2400	92.2
7	Morris		1734.5	398.6	2133.1	2400	88.8
8	Hanks		2371.0	149.5	2520.5	2400	105.0
9	Rivers		2004.0	130.6	2134.6	2400	88.9
10	Fields		1710.5	169.6	1880.1	2400	78.3
11	Links		1284.8	267.0	1551.8	1920	80.8
12	Abbot		2035.5	376.6	2412.1	2400	100.5
13	Parks		1808.5	287.3	2095.8	2400	87.3
14	Hopkins		1434.9	——	1434.9	1440	99.6
15	Lardy		2094.5	770.3	2864.8	2400	119.4
	Robinson	S.T.*		1386.0	1386.0	2400	57.8
	Dacker	S.T.		1534.7	1534.7	1920	79.9
	Cook	S.T.		1932.7	1932.7	2400	80.5
	Hardy	U.T.†			2400.0	non-standard	
Total Nonstandard Hours:				40.0			
Total (Hours):					596.5	664.0	89.8

*S.T.—scrub team
†U.T.—utility man

formance. Various charts and graphs can be employed to show accomplishment against a standard or performance based on a standard. Fig. 4–16 shows an example of a performance graph with a coverage plot also shown. The graph is a four-week running average plot to smooth out the peaks and valleys. The coverage plot is important when standard data application does not include all manpower. The relationship between performance and coverage is important to the manager so that he will be able to determine the effectiveness of his work measurement system. Coverage is a percentage; it consists of the manhours covered by standard data divided by the total manhours available. If the coverage percent is low, there could be a tendency by the workers to manipulate the hours in order to load the nonstandard jobs.

Control reports can also be used to determine labor backlog information, planning accomplishment, work request status, etc. The application of graphic presentation in all areas where control reports are necessary will aid the reviewer in interpreting the results.

TIMEKEEPING PROCEDURES

It is imperative that a maintenance organization be geared administratively to handle a work measurement or control system. The proper allocation of labor charges is a most important aspect of a control program. Timekeeping

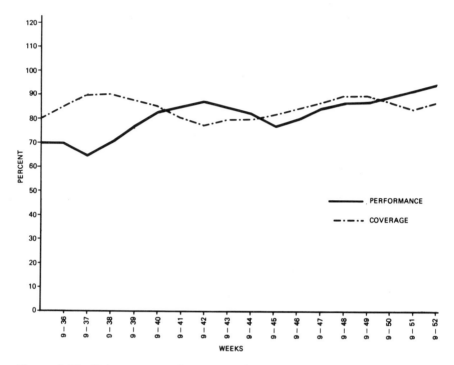

Figure 4-16. Maintenance performance and coverage graph—four-week running average.

can be handled in various ways, but the end result should be to properly account for all the man-hours worked and have them recorded against the actual job for which they were spent.

In most maintenance areas timekeeping is handled through the use of a time card which is filled out by the worker and is checked by the supervisor. The timekeeping system should include a time clock or timekeeper. Some plants use a dispatcher system in which the employee receives assignments and reports complaints. Hours worked should be reported to the nearest tenth of an hour. Thus, the time reporting will be consistent with most standard data practices of rounding off to the nearest tenth.

PERFORMANCE APPRAISAL

The determination of a maintenance department's overall effectiveness is most difficult. The comparison of the maintenance effort with some base is the usual procedure. But deciding what figures to use in the numerator and denominator in order to provide a meaningful indication is where the problem lies. Most managers would like to have one significant indicator which would give a true measurement of their organization's performance. In some industries this may be possible, but in most cases a number of indices are required. Managers would also like to match their results with similar plants for comparison, but usually this is not possible because of the differences in practice from one plant to another. The type of industry, the location of the plant, the organization of the function, the method of operation, the philosophy of management, and differences in terminology are all factors which make comparisons difficult. The variance between industries when maintenance and repair costs are expressed as a percentage of sales is shown in Table IV–6. The variance between industries when maintenance and repair costs are expressed as a percentage of plant and equipment value is shown in Table IV–7. In both cases wide variations can be seen. It is also interesting to note the variance in ranking of a particular industry such as petroleum in the two charts.

Table IV–6. Maintenance and Repair Costs as a Percentage of Sales.*

Industry	No. of Firms Represented	Five-Year Average, Percent	Range by Plant Per Year, Percent	
			High	Low
Radio-television	4	0.9	1.2	0.2
Shoe	3	1.3	2.9	0.6
Meat packing	4	1.3	1.6	0.6
Aircraft	5	1.5	2.6	0.4
Foods	5	1.8	2.9	0.8
Pharmaceutical	6	1.9	3.4	0.6
Electrical mfg.	5	2.2	3.0	1.5
Rubber	5	3.2	4.1	2.6
Petroleum	7	3.3	5.8	2.5
Automotive	4	6.3	9.3	2.0
Chemical	6	6.8	10.5	2.4
Glass	5	7.3	10.6	4.5
Steel	5	12.8	16.8	8.8

*Reprinted from *Effective Maintenance Management*, McGraw-Hill Book Company.

Table IV–7. Maintenance and Repair Costs as a Percentage of Plant and Equipment Value.*

Industry	No. of Firms Represented	Five-Year Average, Percent	Range by Plants Per Year, Percent	
			High	Low
Petroleum	7	2.6	3.9	1.5
Radio-television	4	3.2	3.9	1.3
Chemical	6	3.8	7.9	3.1
Pharmaceutical	6	3.9	4.9	2.1
Foods	5	5.3	10.0	4.7
Electrical mfg.	5	5.8	7.0	3.7
Shoe	3	6.1	9.1	4.8
Rubber	5	6.2	13.4	4.2
Meat packing	4	7.5	10.9	5.8
Aircraft	5	7.6	13.3	2.0
Glass	5	7.9	20.0	4.5
Steel	5	8.6	15.1	6.3
Automotive	4	12.8	20.0	5.3

*Reprinted from *Effective Maintenance Management*, McGraw-Hill Book Company.

The indices of maintenance cost to sales and capital investment are widely used. But it is difficult to justify an increase in percentage when the sales volume goes down. Maintenance cost is not normally a function of sales. Sales may go down without any decrease in facilities, equipment, or demand for service. Again, this is an instance where several indices should be used for proper appraisal.

There are many indices used in appraising elements of a maintenance function; some of those most frequently used are the following:

$$\frac{Maintenance\ material\ dollars}{Maintenance\ labor\ dollars} = Percent$$

$$\frac{Housekeeping\ dollars}{Facility\ square\ footage} = Dollars/sq\ ft\ or\ floor\ space$$

$$\frac{Standard\ labor\ hours}{Actual\ labor\ hours} = Percent\ performance$$

$$\frac{Total\ maintenance\ dollars}{Company\ employees} = Dollars\ per\ employee$$

$$\frac{Machine\ failures}{Machines\ available} = Percent\ failures\ for\ a\ given\ period$$

$$\frac{Spare\ parts-Dollar\ inventory}{Investment\ in\ equipment} = Percent$$

$$\frac{Preventive\ maintenance\ hours\ expended}{Total\ maintenance\ hours\ expended} = Percent$$

$$\frac{Utilities\ cost\ in\ dollars}{Sq\ ft\ of\ building\ space} = Dollars/sq\ ft$$

$$\frac{Breakdown\ hours\ (emergency)}{Preventive\ maintenance\ hours\ expended} = Percent$$

$$\frac{Grounds\ maintenance\ dollars\ expended}{Unit\ of\ land} = Dollars/unit$$

$$\frac{Overtime\ hours}{Straight\ time\ hours} = Percent$$

$$\frac{Backlog\ of\ labor\ hours}{Total\ hours\ available\ per\ period} = Number\ of\ periods\ of\ backlog$$

$$\frac{\text{Craft hours planned by planner}}{\text{Hours worked by planner}} = \text{Ratio of planner effectiveness}$$

$$\frac{\text{Maintenance cost in dollars}}{\text{Unit of production}} = \text{Dollars/unit}$$

$$\frac{\text{Maintenance people}}{\text{Plant direct people}} \text{ or } \frac{\text{Maintenance payroll}}{\text{Plant payroll}} = \text{Percent}$$

$$\frac{\text{Outside contract labor}}{\text{Internal maintenance labor}} = \text{Percent}$$

The most important aspect of using indices is to have good definition of the numerator/denominator. Any elements within the definition which could be manipulated must be eliminated or segregated. For example, maintenance material is compared to labor and expressed as a percentage. The material definition includes outside contractors and therefore is not pure material. The use of the outside contractors in manipulating the expression could occur with respect to any of the goals established. Definition of the numerator/denominator is essential when comparing plant with plant or industry with industry.

The use of graphics in presenting the output of industries can depict the trends. Analysis of the plots over a period of time will quickly show the manager if established goals are being accomplished or if an out-of-control condition is imminent.

PREVENTIVE MAINTENANCE

Preventive maintenance carries the connotation that some action must be taken now to prevent a more severe problem at a later date. The acronym PM means about the same thing to the maintenance field as it does in the medical field, where it stands, of course, for preventive medicine. If the records of a physician were to be reviewed, their similarity to those of industrial maintenance would be surprising. In both cases the purpose is to eliminate the need for radical treatment sometime in the future.

The practice of preventive maintenance in industry means different things to different people. Preventive maintenance means inspections, adjustments, lubrications, and major overhauls to most of us. But others may think of painting, waxing, replacements, chemical solution monitoring, and water treatment. The term is broadly used, but it essentially represents a philosophy of providing care which will protect and maintain the essential quality of the equipment.

Some of the benefits to be gained from a preventive maintenance program are the following:

1) *Equipment, machinery,* and *buildings* will be kept functioning properly.
2) *Higher production* will be achieved due to the continuous availability of operating equipment.

3) *Higher-quality end products* will be realized as a result of properly adjusted equipment which maintains tolerances.

4) *Waste material and rejects* due to malfunctioning equipment will be reduced.

5) *A better-controlled environment* will permit maximum efficiency to be reached both by personnel and equipment.

6) *Capital investment* will be protected by the increased productive life of equipment.

7) *Quicker reaction time* will be developed for emergencies due to the familiarity gained by the maintenance men in performing routine tasks.

8) *Overall maintenance costs* will be reduced because preventive maintenance is performed by in-house personnel, whereas breakdowns will often require specialists.

9) *Conditions* that could lead to a major breakdown will be discovered and corrected before damage occurs.

10) *Equipment information* will be collected to enable decisions such as purchase of new equipment to be made more accurately.

11) *Proper scheduling* will be provided so maintenance can be conveniently performed with available personnel and materials.

12) *Safety conditions* will be improved.

The scope of the items mentioned must meet some economic criteria. Some items do not warrant preventive maintenance because the expense would exceed the replacement cost. Noncritical fractional-horsepower motors are an example of equipment for which preventive maintenance would not be warranted because of the economics of the situation. Additionally, progress and technological advancement has focused attention on the need to carefully weigh the possibility that a particular process or piece of equipment may become obsolete prior to the end of its normal life span. Obviously it will not be necessary to spare or PM a process or piece of equipment after it has been withdrawn from service.

Engineering Inputs

The most valuable engineering input is the original design of the equipment and buildings. Preventive maintenance will be facilitated if provisions for performing it are incorporated during the design phase. Designers often overlook the need for maintenance or sacrifice the maintenance aspect to emphasize aesthetics or reduce initial cost. Later, maintenance must modify the design to provide a workable system which can be maintained at a reasonable cost. Obviously, such modifications will be much more costly at this time.

Some of the blame for the frequency with which design and construction shortcomings are encountered must lie with maintenance itself. The maintenance segment of industry has not promoted the need for a better review of the initial phases of a new project as strongly as it should. This lack of interest has cost industry millions of dollars in unnecessary PM cost. The educational process must be more vigorously promoted by maintenance management. Presenting the proper historical facts can do much to improve the situation.

Designers with a good understanding of maintenance have contributed greatly to reduction of maintenance time. Sealed motors, modular components, and built-in diagnostic test units are just a few of the innovations which have made maintenance an easier task. As the cost for maintenance becomes increasingly significant, more such innovations will be forthcoming.

Good engineering judgment must be utilized in a preventive maintenance program. Techniques such as Mean Time Between Failures (MTBF), Technical Data Accumulation and Analysis, Work Methods, and Time Evaluation are necessary parts of such a program.

A facilities maintenance manual is an engineering input and serves as the basic preventive maintenance document. Documentation of pertinent information and procedures is essential to a good program. The great advantage of a maintenance manual is that all essential information is included under one cover. Additionally, related information such as vendor booklets, prints, or schematics is referenced. The related information would also be identified as to its file location. The format of the document is not important, but collecting together the pertinent data is most significant. Computerization of the data would be still more beneficial in that the data would be rapidly available and would facilitate the use of electronic data processing for the total PM program.

Equipment History

A PM program attaches new significance to individual pieces of equipment. Each item of equipment takes on an identity which enables maintenance to be scheduled, costs to be accumulated, information to be referenced, and so forth. For example, one piece of equipment might be assigned a ten-digit PM number, such as 064 1805 005. Note that one must be careful not to limit the digit number; always have a block of numbers large enough to absorb any future requirements. The number identification system is really the first step in moving towards a PM system. Application of the numbers to individual items of equipment is accomplished during the initial survey of the plant to obtain equipment data and location. An example of a survey is shown in Fig. 4–17, but the format is not important as long as the required information is included. The particular form used here is a master/work copy that is used for survey and other information that will be transferred to a similar master record.

An example of an equipment record used in maintaining historical information on an individual piece of equipment is shown in Fig. 4–18. This record provides general information data, associated accessories information, frequencies of inspections, crafts involved, time elements, appropriate spare parts information, and a history of repairs to the equipment. The historical information provides the basic data required to make the proper evaluations of the equipment or system. The information shown can be part of a computerized program. The information would be the basic data set for such a program. At all times, a maintenance organization considering or involved in a manual program should be recording the data and establishing the procedures with the possibility in mind of ultimately converting to a computerized system.

Another history-type record is the PM "part-used-on-record." Fig. 4–19 shows the record for the temperature control associated with a chiller; it quickly indicates the activity of the particular spare part. This history enables the material control personnel to better establish inventory levels.

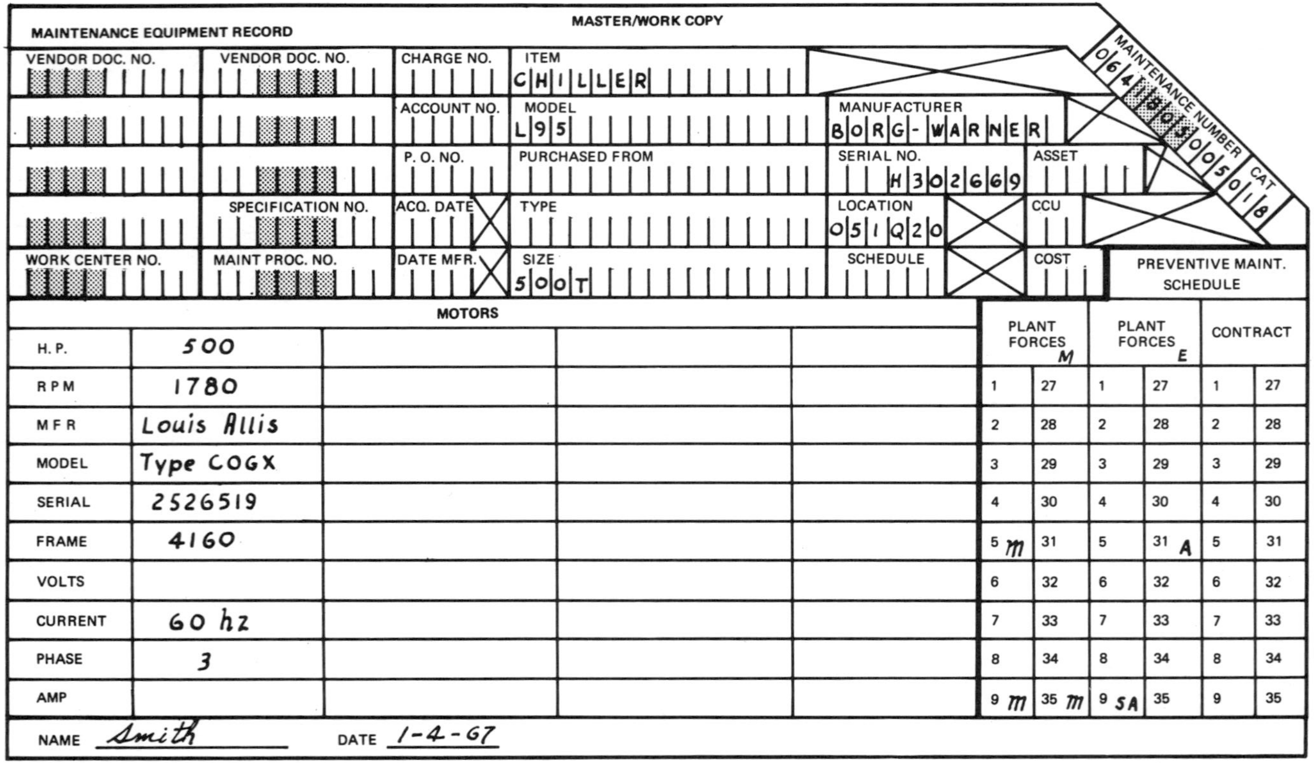

Figure 4–17. Plant equipment survey form for equipment data and location.

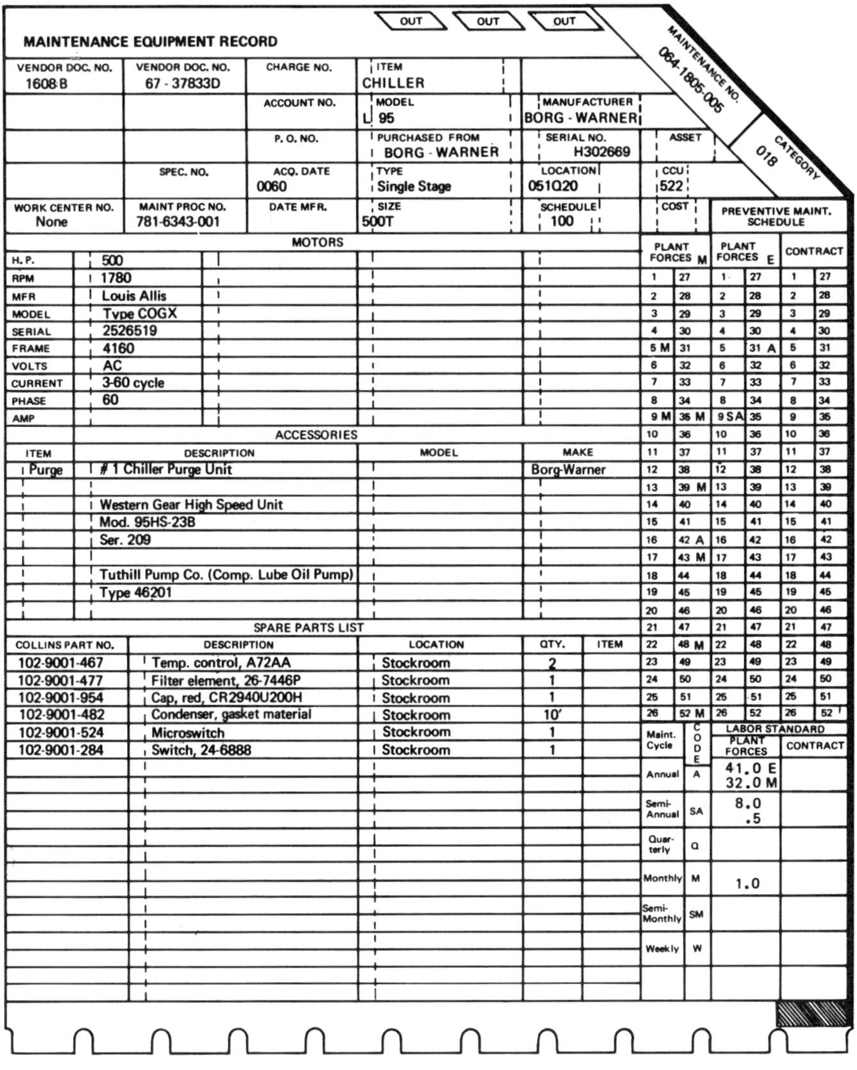

MAINTENANCE EQUIPMENT RECORD

OUT OUT OUT

MAINTENANCE NO. 064-1805-005

CATEGORY 018

VENDOR DOC. NO.	VENDOR DOC. NO.	CHARGE NO.	ITEM	
1608 B	67 - 37833D		CHILLER	
		ACCOUNT NO.	MODEL L 95	MANUFACTURER BORG - WARNER
		P. O. NO.	PURCHASED FROM BORG - WARNER	SERIAL NO. H302669
	SPEC. NO.	ACQ. DATE 0060	TYPE Single Stage	LOCATION 051Q20
WORK CENTER NO. None	MAINT PROC NO. 781-6343-001	DATE MFR.	SIZE 500T	SCHEDULE 100

ASSET | CCU 522 | COST

MOTORS

H. P.	500
RPM	1780
MFR	Louis Allis
MODEL	Type COGX
SERIAL	2526519
FRAME	4160
VOLTS	AC
CURRENT	3-60 cycle
PHASE	60
AMP	

ACCESSORIES

ITEM	DESCRIPTION	MODEL	MAKE
Purge	# 1 Chiller Purge Unit		Borg-Warner
	Western Gear High Speed Unit		
	Mod. 95HS-23B		
	Ser. 209		
	Tuthill Pump Co. (Comp. Lube Oil Pump)		
	Type 46201		

SPARE PARTS LIST

COLLINS PART NO.	DESCRIPTION	LOCATION	QTY.	ITEM
102-9001-467	Temp. control, A72AA	Stockroom	2	
102-9001-477	Filter element, 26-7446P	Stockroom	1	
102-9001-954	Cap, red, CR2940U200H	Stockroom	1	
102-9001-482	Condenser, gasket material	Stockroom	10′	
102-9001-524	Microswitch	Stockroom	1	
102-9001-284	Switch, 24-6888	Stockroom	1	

PREVENTIVE MAINT. SCHEDULE

PLANT FORCES M		PLANT FORCES E		CONTRACT	
1	27	1	27	1	27
2	28	2	28	2	28
3	29	3	29	3	29
4	30	4	30	4	30
5 M	31	5	31 A	5	31
6	32	6	32	6	32
7	33	7	33	7	33
8	34	8	34	8	34
9 M	35 M	9 SA	35	9	35
10	36	10	36	10	36
11	37	11	37	11	37
12	38	12	38	12	38
13	39 M	13	39	13	39
14	40	14	40	14	40
15	41	15	41	15	41
16	42 A	16	42	16	42
17	43 M	17	43	17	43
18	44	18	44	18	44
19	45	19	45	19	45
20	46	20	46	20	46
21	47	21	47	21	47
22	48 M	22	48	22	48
23	49	23	49	23	49
24	50	24	50	24	50
25	51	25	51	25	51
26	52 M	26	52	26	52

Maint. Cycle	CODE	LABOR STANDARD PLANT FORCES	CONTRACT
Annual	A	41.0 E 32.0 M	
Semi-Annual	SA	8.0 .5	
Quarterly	Q		
Monthly	M	1.0	
Semi-Monthly	SM		
Weekly	W		

Figure 4–18. File card for historical equipment record.

Work Definition

The PM work to be performed must be clearly described. The preventive maintenance procedure outlined in the facilities maintenance manual indicates what is involved in performing PM on the chiller. There are a number of ways to transmit the required work content to the responsible worker. Fig. 4–20 is an example of a manual card system which calls out the work to be performed on the chiller for the programmed date. The card is given to the worker who performs the operation. He notes on the back of the card that the work has

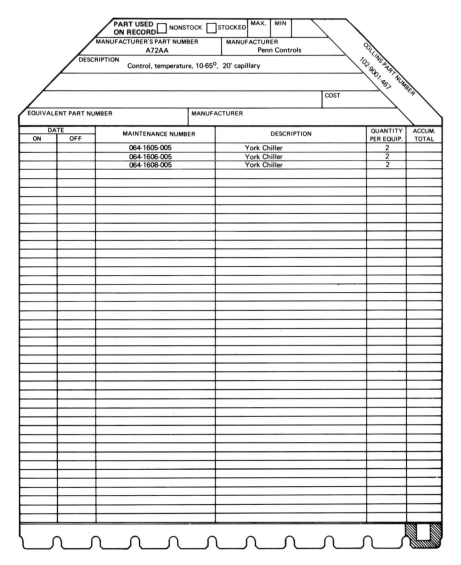

Figure 4-19. File card for equipment "part-used-on-record."

been done. Feedback is indispensable to a good system and provides the cost information that is necessary for evaluation. Card mutilation can be a problem if the card is not properly designed for handling.

A computer form for work definition on a more complex PM requirement is shown in Fig. 4-21. This particular example took the maintenance worker 7.5 hours to accomplish. The action taken was recorded on the printout form. It is important that the PM worker performs only the assigned task. Any

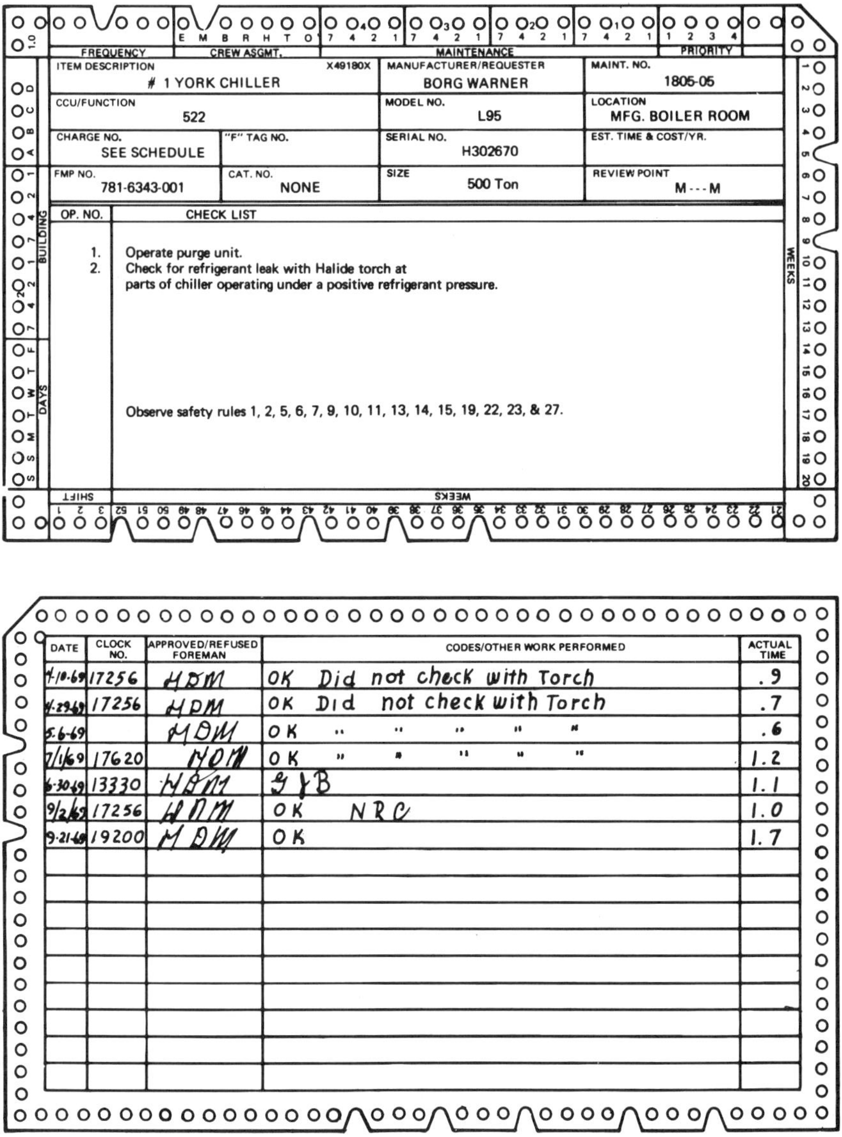

FREQUENCY | CREW ASGMT. | MAINTENANCE | PRIORITY

ITEM DESCRIPTION X49180X: # 1 YORK CHILLER		MANUFACTURER/REQUESTER: BORG WARNER	MAINT. NO.: 1805-05
CCU/FUNCTION: 522		MODEL NO.: L95	LOCATION: MFG. BOILER ROOM
CHARGE NO.: SEE SCHEDULE	"F" TAG NO.	SERIAL NO.: H302670	EST. TIME & COST/YR.
FMP NO.: 781-6343-001	CAT. NO.: NONE	SIZE: 500 Ton	REVIEW POINT: M---M

OP. NO.	CHECK LIST
1.	Operate purge unit.
2.	Check for refrigerant leak with Halide torch at parts of chiller operating under a positive refrigerant pressure.
	Observe safety rules 1, 2, 5, 6, 7, 9, 10, 11, 13, 14, 15, 19, 22, 23, & 27.

BUILDING · DAYS · SHIFT · WEEKS

DATE	CLOCK NO.	APPROVED/REFUSED FOREMAN	CODES/OTHER WORK PERFORMED	ACTUAL TIME
4-10-69	17256	HDM	OK Did not check with Torch	.9
4-29-69	17256	HDM	OK Did not check with Torch	.7
5-6-69		HDM	OK " " " " "	.6
7/1/69	17620	HDM	OK " " " " "	1.2
6-30-69	13330	HDM	GYB	1.1
9/2/69	17256	HDM	OK NRC	1.0
9-21-69	19200	HDM	OK	1.7

Figure 4–20. File card for programmed maintenance requirements.

additional corrective action required should be noted by the worker on the form and then reassigned at a later date. This procedure is necessary to ensure that the PM work is not confused with time-consuming corrective maintenance. A maintenance work order should be used for initiating the needed corrective action.

```
WO1117691247  CPN 061-0000-33A  PUNCH PRESS  WIEDEMANN  MODEL A-15  SERIAL 170    LOCODE 02AN18
EQUIP PRIORITY 0908  CHG NO 06-0838  WEEK SCHEDULED 0-19  PM CODE F5  LAST CAL 092469  STD MH 8.0  LIMITATION SHIFT 3 OR WKEND
SAFETY RULES 01, 02, 05, 06, 09, 10, 1, 26, 27
SPECIAL TOOLS +T1170066131, T1170025841, 11170065256, TEKSCOPE516, HICKOK539-8, TAPEREAD CK
MATERIALS 0574000071, 0061918010, 0061911010, 0574000067, 0061026010, 0574000068
SPARE PARTS    NONE
```

TASKS TO BE PERFORMED	CRAFT	ACTION – READING TAKEN – STATUS *
1. COAT BEAM WAYS W/TEXWAY LUBE D.	M	LUBED WAYS.
2. FILL OILCUPS OF INDEX PINLINK W/TEXWAY LUBE G.	M	FILLED CUPS.
3. CLEAN CABINET AIR FILTER.	M	CLEANED FILTER
4. CK AIRLINE LUBRICATOR FOR 10 TO 12 DROPS PER MINUTE.	M	TOO FAST – ADJUSTED FOR IO DROPS/M
5. LUBE TURRET DRIVE GEARS W/TEXMARFAK.2.	M	LUBED GEARS.
6. REMOVE + CLEAN AIR LINE FILTER.	M	CLEANED AIR FILTER IN U.S. DEGREASER.
7. CK ACCUMULATOR PRESSURE. IF BELOW 800 PSI, RECHARGE W/DRY NITROGEN	M	PRESSUR OK.
8. REMOVE MICRON FILTER. CLEAN W/SOLVENT + DRY LINTLESS CLOTH.	M	CLEANED FILTER
9. CK OIL PRESS SW LITE ILLUMS AT 400 PSI WHEN PRESS IS REDUCED. SET TO NORM.	M	OIL PRESSURE SWITCH O.K.
10. CK FOR SMALL LEAK AT HYD CYL HEAD ENDS. IF EXCESSIVE REPACK.	M	LEAKAGE NORMAL.
11. CK TURRET INDEX PIN FOR PLAY. SERVICE AS REQD.	M	PIN WORN – REPLACED PIN.
12. CK ROTARY STEP SW OPERATION. CLEAN, ADJUST, LUBE AS REQD.	M	CLEANED & LUBED SWITCH- OPERATES O.K.
13. LUBE PILLOW BLOCKS W/TEXMULTIFAK 2.	M	LUBED PILLOW BLOCKS
14. CK ALL HYD LINES + CONNECTIONS. REPAIR AS REQD.	M	LINES & CONNECTIONS OK.
15. CLEAN OIL COOLER SURFACES.	M	SURFACES DIRTY – CLEANED
16. CK TAPE READER. CLEAN + REPAIR AS REQD.	M	CLEANED LINT FROM READER HEADS.
17. LUBE READER CAMROLLER BRGS, PIVOTS, COMBS + POROUS RGS W/TEXRANDO HDA.	M	LUBED READER PARTS AS NOTED
18. LUBE READER DRIVE FEEDS, PAWLS, RATCHET WHEELS, DETENTS, CONTACT BAILS, SPRING-ENDS, + LATCHING SURFACES W/TEXMOLYTEX 2.		
19. CLEAN DUST FROM X + Y TABLE GEARS + RACKS W/SOFT BRISTLE BRUSH	M	CLEANED GEARS & RACKS.
20. CK X + Y AXES TACH GIBS FOR EXCESS PLAY. ADJUST AS REQD.	M	CAN NOT ADJUST EXCESS PLAY OUT - HOLD FOR CM *
21. LUBE X + Y AXES TACH GIBS LIGHTLY W/TEXRANDO HDA.	M	LUBED GIBS

MAINTENANCE MAN	CLOCK NO	HRS WKD	HRS WAIT*	TEST EQUIP USED	MATERIAL USED – QUANTITY	SPARES USED – QUANTITY
HEBRON, R.G.	26017	7.5	0.0	TAPE READER CHR.	057-4000-071 1 OZ.	102-9018-285 1 EA.
					005-1916-010 2 OZ.	
					057-1000-067 1 OZ.	
					035-1026-010 1/2 OZ.	
					037-4000-068 1 OZ.	

*EXPLAIN   ITEM 20 – DID NOT HAVE TIME TO CHECK FOR WORN PARTS.

REPORT NO XXXXX EQUIPMENT HISTORY RECORD FOR CALENDAR FROM 101869 TO 103169 AS NOTED BELOW

CPN 061-0000-338	WO NUMBER	EQUIP TYPE PUNCH PRESS	TYPE	MANUFACTURER WIEDEMANN	MODEL A-15	SERIAL NO 170	LOCODE 02AN18	LAST CAL DATE 092469	ACTUAL M–H
	WO NUMBER	TYPE	WORK ACCOMPLISHED						ACTUAL M–H
	WO101690916	CM	MACHINE OPERATING ERRONEOUSLY. FOUND TAPE WAS BAD, RPLD DRX						7.0
	WO101691426	CM	NO PWR TO UNIT. CLEANED CAM CONTACTS. ADJ ROR CAMS.						7.0
	WO102369742	CM	READER TROUBLE. ADJUSTED READER CLUTCH.						2.0
	WO102669815	CM	MACHINE OPERATING IN ERROR. ADJUSTED PROXIMITY AMP.						0.5
	WO102669929	CM	HANDWHEEL STICKING. ADJUSTED AIR PRESSURE + MICROSWITCH.						5.0
	WO103169837	CM	CLUTCH NOT OPERATING RIGHT. ADJ CLUTCH MICROSWITCH CAM.						0.5
	WO103169004	CM	OILER MALFUNCTIONING. REPAIRED OILER.						1.0
	WO103169201	CM	RAM NEEDS ADJUSTED. ADJUSTED RAM MICROSWITCH.						1.0
	WO103169646	CM	CHECK MACHINE OPERATION. CHECKED O.K.						1.0

Figure 4–21. Computer printout for preventive maintenance work requirements with worker's comments added.

Normally, the task definition for a preventive maintenance worker would include the following elements:
1) Routine inspection
2) Routine cleaning
3) Lubrication
4) Scheduled overhauls
5) Routine monitoring
6) Replacement of components
7) Routine adjustments
8) Condition reporting.

A task statement such as "Inspect and Repair as Necessary" is very detrimental to the PM objective. When this statement is used, a great deal of judgment is left to the worker. The scope of the work should be well defined to enable the worker to perform only the intended task. Loose definition of the elements of a task is one of the most common factors in the failure of a PM program.

The extension of the basic work definition elements is assumed to be corrective in nature and is normally brought about by condition reporting. This enlargement of scope includes such items as painting, repairs, or any corrective action to return the object to its original state. This part of the PM program should be generated by the information obtained during the PM inspection phase.

Scheduling

Scheduling and frequency determination are dependent upon each other. Normally the frequency determination is made during the engineering input phase. This information is then used to develop the schedule of PM activities. But the schedules must be reviewed on a continuous basis to check the accuracy and worth of the established frequency. Too-frequent activity will increase cost and too-infrequent activity will eventually have the same result. This relationship can be seen more clearly by examining Fig. 4–22. As the PM cost line

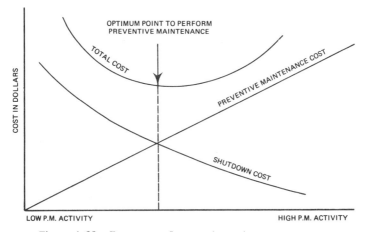

Figure 4–22. Frequency of preventive maintenance vs. cost.

increases, the shutdown cost line decreases. The point of intersection of the two lines is the optimum time to perform preventive maintenance. Of course, the real difficulty is in finding the optimum point. Sometimes much historical data must be gathered in order to verify initial assumptions.

The actual scheduling of the PM activity can be accomplished using the same scheduling technique used for other maintenance jobs. Fig. 4–6 showed PM activity worked in with other scheduled jobs. In a later part of this section, this scheduling method will be shown in a computerized schedule.

The PM engineer takes the information developed in the engineering input phase and converts the data into a format suitable for insertion into the computer (manual application will not be discussed but will be handled similarly). Fig. 4–23 is an example of a form which can be used to supply data to the key-

| P M NO. | CRAFT. | FREQ. | \multicolumn{13}{c}{CALL OUT} | STD. HRS. | DECIMAL POINT | CODE | DESCRIPTION |
			1	2	3	4	5	6	7	8	9	10	11	12	13				
4719-39	1	3	0	0	0	4	0	0	0	0	0	0	1	0	0	0 0 0	5	3	Wire Stripper
4720-39	1	3	0	0	0	4	0	0	0	0	0	0	1	0	0	0 0 0	5	3	'' ''
4721-39	1	3	0	0	0	4	0	0	0	0	0	0	1	0	0	0 0 0	5	3	'' ''
4722-39	1	3	0	0	0	4	0	0	0	0	0	0	1	0	0	0 0 0	5	3	'' ''
4723-39	1	3	0	0	0	4	0	0	0	0	0	0	1	0	0	0 0 0	5	3	'' ''
4724-39	1	3	0	0	0	4	0	0	0	0	0	0	1	0	0	0 0 0	5	3	'' ''
4725-39	1	3	0	0	0	4	0	0	0	0	0	0	1	0	0	0 0 0	5	3	'' ''
4726-39	1	3	0	0	0	4	0	0	0	0	0	0	1	0	0	0 0 0	5	3	'' ''
4727-39	1	3 .	0	0	0	4	0	0	0	0	0	0	1	0	0	0 0 0	5	3	'' ''
4731-39	1	3	0	0	0	4	0	0	0	0	0	0	1	0	0	0 0 0	5	3	'' ''
4732-39	1	3	0	0	0	4	0	0	0	0	0	0	1	0	0	0 0 0	5	3	'' ''
4738-39	1	3	0	0	0	4	0	0	0	0	0	0	1	0	0	0 0 0	5	3	'' ''
4741-39	1	3	0	0	0	4	0	0	0	0	0	0	1	0	0	0 0 0	5	3	'' ''
0118-08	2	1	3	3	3	3	3	3	3	3	3	3	3	3	3	0 0 0	4	3	Men's Restroom
0119-08	2	1	3	3	3	3	3	3	3	3	3	3	3	3	3	0 0 0	4	3	Women's Restroom
0120-11	2	1	3	3	3	3	3	3	3	3	3	3	3	3	3	0 0 0	2	3	Men's Restroom
0122-70	2	1	1	1	1	1	1	1	1	1	1	1	1	1	1	0 0 0	2	3	First Aid Restroom
2063-37	2	1	4	4	4	4	4	4	4	4	4	4	4	4	4	0 0 0	5	3	Fan Coil Unit
2221-11	2	3	0	0	0	3	0	0	0	0	0	4	0	0	0	0 0 0	8	3	Air Compressor

Figure 4–23. Form used for supplying scheduling data to key-punch operator.

punch operation for card punching. The form identifies the equipment and craft involved, states the type of frequency, calls out the activity by fiscal week, states hours to complete the task, and describes the unit. The callout section has 13 columns (four weeks per column). In the first line of the example, the semiannual frequency (Code 3) has been loaded into the fourth column as a 4 and into the eleventh column as a 1. The placement of the 4 represents the fourth week of that column, or fiscal week number 16.

It is important when scheduling PM work into fiscal weeks that manpower availability be considered and that a weekly balance be maintained. Fig. 4–24

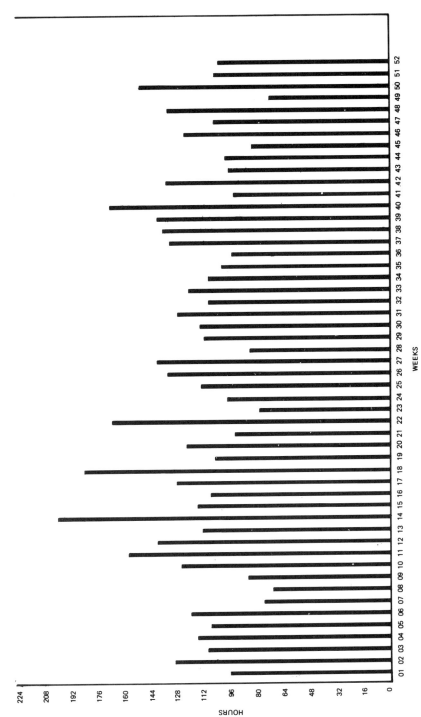

Figure 4–24. Weekly schedule of preventive maintenance activity.

shows a bar graph by week of the PM hours loaded. The scheduler attempts to build on the low bars wherever possible, as new requirements are added. It can readily be seen when overload conditions threaten, such as in fiscal week 14 in the example.

The information is keypunched and inserted into the computer. The computer prints out the weekly schedule of a particular fiscal week. Fig. 4–25 is an example of a printout of one page of electrical work for fiscal week number 27. The work definitions are generated for the scheduled tasks and the hours can be totalled for master scheduling input if desired. The specific example used is coded by week. The daily scheduling in this case would be performed by supervision. The selection of the period of scheduling depends primarily upon the type of production interface desired and the reaction time required. Because of the many variables which are unique to the individual plants, the scheduling period must be determined locally to meet specific conditions.

WEEK 27

BUILDING LOCATION	CRAFT	MACHINE NUMBER	DESCRIPTION	FREQUENCY	STD. TIME CODE	STD. HOURS
08	1	1225	4.16 UNDERGR. ELECT. DUCT.	1	3	10.0
09	1	1229	15KV SWITCHGEAR	1	3	4.0
20	1	1230	ITE LOAD CENTER	1	3	1.5
20	1	1231	ITE LOAD CENTER	1	3	1.5
05	1	2418	AHU	4	3	1.0
05	1	2421	AHU	4	3	1.0
05	1	2422	AHU	4	3	1.0
05	1	2423	AHU	4	3	1.0
05	1	2424	AHU	4	3	1.0
05	1	2425	AHU	4	3	1.0
05	1	2426	AHU	4	3	1.0
05	1	2427	AHU	4	3	1.0
05	1	2428	AHU	4	3	1.0
05	1	2429	AHU	4	3	1.0
05	1	2430	AHU	4	3	1.0
05	1	2432	AHU	4	3	1.0
05	1	2433	AHU	4	3	1.0
05	1	2433	AHU	4	3	1.0
05	1	2434	AHU	4	3	1.0
05	1	2435	AHU	4	3	1.0
05	1	2436	AHU	4	3	1.0
06	1	2437	AHU	4	3	1.0
06	1	2438	AHU	4	3	1.0
06	1	2439	AHU	4	3	1.0
20	1	2607	AIR CLEANER	4	4	1.0
20	1	2614	AIR CLEANER	4	3	1.0
20	1	2615	AIR CLEANER	4	3	1.0
05	1	2616	AIR CLEANER	4	3	1.0
05	1	2617	AIR CLEANER	4	3	1.0
05	1	2618	AIR CLEANER	4	3	1.0
05	1	2619	AIR CLEANER	4	3	1.0
05	1	2620	AIR CLEANER	4	3	1.0
21	1	2813	AIR INTAKE	1	3	.5
20	1	3928	HEATER	1	3	1.0
09	1	4274	TIME CLOCK	3	3	1.0
09	1	4275	TIME CLOCK	3	3	1.0
09	1	4276	TIME CLOCK	3	3	1.0
09	1	4277	TIME CLOCK	3	3	1.0
09	1	4278	TIME CLOCK	3	3	1.0
10	1	4279	TIME CLOCK	3	3	1.0
08	1	4280	TIME CLOCK	3	3	1.0
08	1	4289	TIME CLOCK	3	3	1.0
08	1	4699	MANLIFT	1	3	.3
08	1	4701	MANLIFT	1	3	.3
05	1	4809	EMERGENCY LITE	1	3	.3
080	1	4846	VERT A LIFT	1	3	.3
08	1	4868	MANLIFT	1	3	.2
08	1	4869	MANLIFT	1	3	.2
08	1	4870	MANLIFT	1	3	.2
08	1	4871	MANLIFT	1	3	.2
08	1	4872	MANLIFT	1	3	.2

Figure 4–25. Computer printout of one week's electrical preventive maintenance.

Evaluation and Follow Up

An effective PM program requires continuing reappraisal, analysis, and updating. The information collected and recorded must be reviewed and analyzed. Frequencies must be reviewed for meeting the economic test of established cost goals and must be changed or adapted to the current performance level of the equipment. Reports concerning cost, labor performance, breakdowns, downtime, corrective maintenance, equipment coverage, and other items should be compiled and issued. The reports should be concise and should be presented in both graphic and written form. The design of the reports is most important for persons who are involved in the evaluation and follow-up effort. The reports should clearly print out the significant information and highlight problem areas.

Close review of items which are responsible for the greatest amount of planned or unplanned downtime is necessary to determine whether equipment redesign or a PM adjustment could be economically used to reduce the downtime. Also, items of high-cost PM or repetitive-type failures would fall into the category for close scrutiny. As previously stated, the wealth of information accumulated must be reduced so these problem areas may be readily recognized.

The selling job of preventive maintenance must also continue. It is necessary to demonstrate the benefits of PM by including key production personnel on report distributions. They must be assured that their concurrence with a planned equipment shutdown was a sound decision. If the reports prove this point, the production department will be one of the strongest supporters of the program, and one of the greatest obstacles maintenance managers face will be overcome.

EDP APPLICATIONS

Electronic data processing is gaining momentum as the key factor in the current rapid technological change in industry. The computer has opened many doors with its ability to rapidly manipulate data. The machine will perform a task as directed, but is limited in application because of its lack of incentive. Management people must supply the incentive needed to cause this device to perform the required functions. The potential of EDP is tremendous, but this potential can only be realized if management will utilize the resources available to them.

Control Tool

The use of electronic data processing has previously been discussed with reference to its use in controlling and administering supplies. The use of EDP was briefly explained with reference to its use in making a preventive maintenance program more effective. EDP can also be used to make other maintenance functions, such as scheduling and cost control, more effective.

EDP provides an economical method for spotlighting any particular element of scheduling. This spotlighting of desired data can be accomplished by requesting a particular sort. When the basic data has been entered into the computer, it is only a matter of proper programming to economically obtain the output in the desired form. The scheduling output can be arranged by craft, priority, work request number, location of work, or one of several other ways. For example, the scheduling function may want the output by work request number, the area superintendent may like to have the schedule by location to cover all his activities, the craft foreman may only want to have his craft scheduled by job priority, and the stockroom may be sensitive to the job charge number and wish to have a printout in sequential order. An example of a computer schedule printout is shown in Fig. 4–26. This printout is similar in arrangement to the manual schedule shown previously in Fig. 4–6.

Many maintenance functions are required to provide such types of basic data as charge number, job estimate data, individual hours worked, and material charges without deriving any benefit from this data. In many cases control reports are available, but the maintenance function is unaware of their existence even though they have contributed data to the report. The accounting department uses the data for cost collection, proration, or tax information without being aware that it would be useful to the maintenance department. A survey of the computer reports being generated may provide the needed information.

Reports such as actual job cost versus standard cost, budget information, critical-path method analysis, personnel information and absenteeism, and labor efficiency are all good candidates for electronic data processing. The timeliness of the EDP reports will allow the manager to quickly spot his problem areas and implement solutions. The computerization approach to maintenance control is no longer new. It is now considered standard maintenance procedure.

Operating Tool

Electronic data processing is a means of keeping pace with the increasing intricacy of operation and repair of equipment. The maintenance of a machine which is operated and controlled by a maze of electronic devices must be performed by highly competent personnel who are knowledgeable concerning the design and construction of the unit. The need for locating faults by means of automatic programmed diagnostic tests would seem to be urgent for any sophisticated equipment that must provide uninterrupted on-line service. To have a computer-operated environmental system is the ideal for the maintenance manager. The headaches associated with manual operation are becoming more frequent as the equipment becomes more complicated and the demands of management, the union, and the workers for a better environment increase. This ideal is being approached in some areas with the use of electronic data processing.

With the use of digital or analog sensors and a well-developed program, the computer can actually control a building's environment within established tolerances; alert maintenance personnel to malfunctions or problem areas with an alarm sensor system; report data readings such as temperature, pressure, humidity, and kilowatts used; monitor water flow, air cleanliness, noise levels, and condition of effluents and liquids used in the operational system; optimize the system to gain maximum efficiency; and provide reports, both written and graphic. The computer will actually operate (start, modulate, or stop) the equipment which provides the changes in environment.

REPORT 19462   MAINTENANCE DEPARTMENT WORK SCHEDULE   PAGE 6

** MAINTENANCE AND OPERATIONS **

CAT	MAINT NO.	CHARGE NO.	DATE ENT.	BLDG NO.	DESCRIPTION OR CRAFT COMMENTS	CRAFT	IDENT	PR	HOURS SCHED	HOURS PLANNED	HOURS WORKED	HOURS BALANCE	P	C
2	002610	096962	0-24 SCHED	105 --	PAINT BOOTH SCHEDULE 0-23	MAINTENANCE-	31	X		37.5	54.9	17.4CR	COMPLETE	
2	002648	060563	0-24 SCHED	105 --	INST. NEW HOSE–SANDER	MAINTENANCE-	31	C	.	2.0	.	2.0		
2	002662	087928	0-24 SCHED / SCHED	105,133 --	PM WEEK =23	MAINTENANCE- / ELECTRICAL-	31 / 61	X / X	.	164.9 / 71.9	117.1 / 45.0	47.8 / 26.9	COMPLETE	
2	002663	087929	0-24 SCHED / SCHED	120,122 --	PM WEEK =23 / F/M	MAINTENANCE- / ELECTRICAL-	31 / 61	X / A+	10.0	29.2 / 17.0	24.0 / 7.0	5.2 / 10.0	X	X
2	002664	087930	0-24 SCHED / SCHED	130,181 --	PM WEEK =23	MAINTENANCE- / ELECTRICAL-	31 / 61	X / X	.	62.4 / 19.1	90.1 / .5	27.7CR / 18.6	COMPLETE	
2	002671	087933	0-24 SCHED	106 --	PAINT REST ROOM =20 + 21 / F/M	PAINTER-	41	A	24.0	43.8	8.0	35.8		
2	002672	060574	0-24 SCHED / SCHED / SCHED	120 -- --	RECOVER 2 ARM CHAIRS / STOCKROOM / SANDRY	MAINTENANCE- / OTHER- / OTHER-	31 / 71 / 72	C / C / C	.	1.0 / . / .	. / . / .	1.0 / .0 / .0		
2	002676	060573	0-24 SCHED	106 --	REPAINT 2 OFFICES	PAINTER-	41	X	.	10.2	10.0	.2	COMPLETE	
2	002713	087934	0-24 SCHED	120 --	REPL. BROKEN STAIR TREAD	CARPENTER-	21	C	.	2.0	.	2.0		
2	002742	096970	0-24 SCHED	105 --	PAINT SHOP SCHEDULE FW 0-24	MAINTENANCE-	31	X	.0	40.5	39.5	1.0	COMPLETE	
2	002743	096971	0-24 SCHED	105 --	DEGREASER SCHEDULE FW 0-24	MAINTENANCE-	31	X	.	8.3	6.5	1.8	COMPLETE	
2	002744	096972	0-24 SCHED	639 --	DEGREASER SCHEDULE FW 0-24	MAINTENANCE-	31	X	.	2.4	.	2.4	COMPLETE	
2	002745	096973	0-24 SCHED	137 --	DEGREASER SCHEDULE FW 0-24	MAINTENANCE-	31	X	.	1.5	1.5	.0	COMPLETE	
2	002746	096974	0-24 SCHED	138 --	DEGREASER SCHEDULE FW 0-24	MAINTENANCE-	31	X	.	2.4	2.5	.1CR	COMPLETE	
2	002747	096975	0-24 SCHED	109 --	DEGREASER SCHEDULE FW 0-24	MAINTENANCE-	31	X	.	2.4	2.5	.1CR	COMPLETE	

Figure 4-26. Computer printout of maintenance work schedule.

Certainly the use of EDP equipment will be necessary as an operating tool to meet the demands of the future. The maintenance manager should attempt to become educated in this area. If terms such as binary, disk file, bits, I/O, online, software, microsecond, FORTRAN, and COBOL are unfamiliar, then it is time to start the educational process.

PERSONNEL CONSIDERATIONS

The success or failure of a maintenance organization in accomplishing the task of properly maintaining facilities is directly related to the proper staffing of the organization and possession of the required skills by the personnel. A recent survey was conducted by Albert Raymond and Associates which revealed some very interesting information on maintenance staffing. The survey showed that the average ratio of maintenance hourly workers to supervisors was 11 to 1. Fig. 4–27 shows the worker-to-supervisor ratio for the ten largest industries reporting.

The ratio between workers and supervisors in maintenance is normally lower than ratios found elsewhere in industry. The low ratio is attributed to the highly mobile nature of maintenance which makes it virtually impossible for the supervisor to control the activities of a large number of workers. Also, many maintenance supervisors do not have support personnel, which requires them to plan, schedule, and procure materials themselves. This naturally detracts from their supervisory effectiveness.

The selection of a supervisor must be done with great care. The maintenance man who performs his work in an outstanding manner is not always the best candidate for a supervisory position. Ability to get along well with fellow workers is also important. Unless the new supervisor is well liked by his subordinates, problems will be encountered.

Certainly the technical aspect of maintenance is very important, and that importance will increase as technology advances. The supervisor must be knowledgeable in his area of responsibility. But the main worth of a supervisor is his decision-making ability; his capability to motivate his employees; his ability to direct the work in an efficient manner; and his sensitivity to differences in personalities.

Staffing — Skilled Trades

The Raymond survey indicated that on the average in the reporting industries the maintenance workers represented 6 percent of the plant employment. Fig. 4–28 shows this relationship for the industries which took part in the survey. The number and types of skills required by maintenance functions depend largely on the type of industry, the complexity of the equipment being maintained, the philosophy of reaction time, and other factors. Goals must be established which are consistent with management's philosophy with respect to maintenance. Manpower levels consistent with these goals must be established.

The demand for better-skilled personnel in the maintenance area has presented many maintenance functions with a manpower problem. The need for maintenance on equipment is being recognized by all segments of industry.

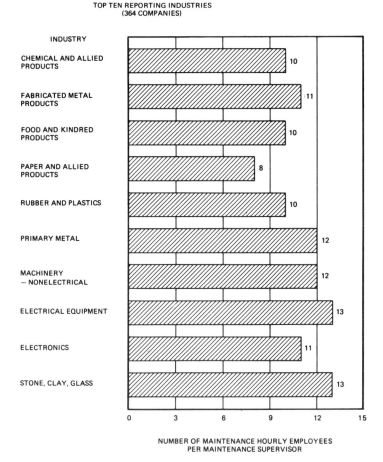

TOP TEN REPORTING INDUSTRIES
(364 COMPANIES)

Figure 4-27. Ratio of workers to supervisors in ten largest industries reporting.

Substantial expenditures are necessary to protect the large capital investment. Many maintenance workers currently on the payroll are relatively unproductive because of their lack of training. These factors have created a highly competitive market for qualified personnel.

As the mechanization of industry continues, the maintenance manpower levels will surge upward. Some production-minded managers will try to hold the maintenance manning levels down because they feel that this type of expenditure can be deferred.

Training

One of the most important elements in providing the skilled personnel to meet the coming "Age of Automation" will be the formal training program. The old method of on-the-job training will no longer suffice. Industry cannot

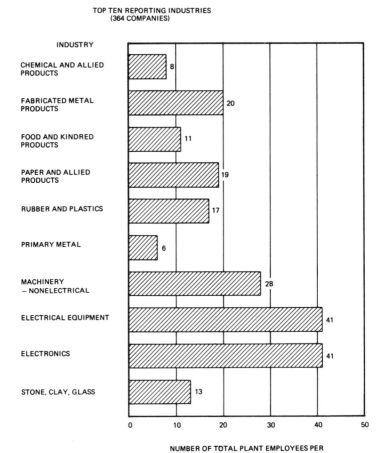

TOP TEN REPORTING INDUSTRIES
(364 COMPANIES)

NUMBER OF TOTAL PLANT EMPLOYEES PER
MAINTENANCE EMPLOYEE

Figure 4–28.   Ratio of plant employees to maintenance employees
in ten largest industries reporting.

continue to depend on training that can be picked up in the field and at the same
time hope that the individuals will not learn poor techniques.

Training can be accomplished in many ways. Some of the methods used are
as follows:

1) Apprenticeship programs
2) Company-sponsored courses
3) Outside educational institutions
4) Vendor schools
5) Correspondence courses

Apprenticeship Programs. Apprenticeship programs appear to be the most
widely used type of training. This approach combines practice with classroom work. The training schedule is usually established with a probationary
period, and the total program normally covers a span of from two to four

years. Age limits should be a factor in any apprentice training program because of the considerable investment by the company in training the individual.

The selection of individuals must be carefully conducted. Achievement and aptitude tests, along with formal or trade-school education, should be part of the selection procedure. If a union is involved, acceptance by the unit must be negotiated. Having high-caliber individuals enrolled will help ensure a successful training program.

The classroom work will introduce the individual to the techniques which he will apply in the field. The most common error in an apprentice program is the neglect of the classroom activities. Not having time to conduct the classes is normally the excuse. However, without the classroom work the supervisor will find that he has an inadequate on-the-job training situation. Information on apprentice training can be obtained from the Bureau of Apprenticeship and Training, U.S. Department of Labor, Washington, D.C.

Company-Sponsored Programs. Many companies have their own training staffs which conduct training programs or courses on a specialized basis. These courses are normally designed to cover specific subjects to quickly update or increase the knowledge of the maintenance employee. Even without a formal training staff, the maintenance organization should groom certain individuals as instructors. These instructors can teach or demonstrate improved maintenance techniques or give instruction in weak areas. Also, the development of training aids such as audiovisual simulators will greatly aid industry to train at the plant level. Training is basically a continuous process. As technology changes, a maintenance organization must be prepared through training to keep its employees abreast of these changes. Company-sponsored courses can be a great help in keeping employees up to date.

Outside Educational Institutions. There has been a tremendous growth of educational opportunities for the individual who is willing to attend classes in his spare time. The public institutions are offering subjects in the evenings and on weekends which are pertinent to the maintenance employee, and area vocation and trade schools are providing specialized training courses at an expanding rate. A maintenance organization can take advantage of this opportunity by encouraging a tuition refund program.

Vendor Schools. Many vendors offer excellent schools or instruction on their specific equipment or systems. They are normally staffed with well-qualified instructors and will hold the course at their own site or the client's site if required. The vendor schools are usually very productive, and the training is relatively inexpensive for the companies participating.

Correspondence Courses. Correspondence courses have been successfully used over the years as a training technique. The courses come in all shapes and forms. Most of them are designed to be taken by the individual who submits his completed questions back to the instructor for evaluation. However, some of the courses are designed to be taken in a group situation with a leader present. The great disadvantage of this type of training is the difficulty in motivating the employee to stick with the course. Normally, the course must be worked on at home where the atmosphere is not conducive to study.

Other methods of training are emerging. These include such techniques as programmed instruction wherein the trainee essentially teaches himself. He paces himself as he works the steps of a particular course and immediately checks to see if he has the right answer before going on to the next step. E. I. du Pont de Nemours & Company has extensively developed programmed instruction courses and has made them available to industry. The technical societies also offer these courses in a large number of fields.

Many more methods will undoubtedly be developed in the future to cope with the technological changes that are occurring. A maintenance manager must plan to train to obtain the skilled personnel he will need to solve the problems of the future. The labor market itself will not produce many such individuals. The trade-school graduate will move toward high-paying construction jobs. The responsibility for producing well-qualified employees falls upon the individual maintenance manager.

Chapter 5

Power and
Utilities Management

The power and utilities functions can best be described as the production and distribution of electrical power, steam, and compressed air and the distribution of water, oil, natural gas, and other gases used in the manufacturing process. The scope of these activities varies widely with the type of industry. In processing industries, power and utilities are generally classified as operating departments and will be out of the jurisdiction of the plant engineer. In manufacturing industries, the function may involve a power plant producing steam, electricity, and compressed air, or it may involve the purchase of electrical energy. In most cases, however, the function belongs within the plant engineer's scope of responsibility.

The production and distribution of the utilities must be continuous and uninterrupted. If electrical generating equipment is used, the plant engineer must have an alternate source of electrical power. Most companies have a link to the public utility in the area. Distribution lines should be so constructed that an area affected by a power failure can be isolated. The plant engineer is responsible for the economic operation of the power plant. During the past thirty years, oil and natural gas have replaced coal as the basic fuel for many power plants, but in many cases it is more economical to purchase power than to generate it. This is especially true if additional investment to replace generating equipment is required. Power plant operating cost reports should be prepared periodically by the plant engineer. The upkeep of power and utilities is generally provided by the plant maintenance department. The problems involved in startup of a new industrial power plant have been considered by Garay.[1] Routine and minor maintenance of boilers and generating equipment

---

[1] Paul N. Garay, "Train Your Operators Right for Your New Industrial Power Plant," *Power Engineering*, Vol. 61, No. 9 (Sept., 1957); "How to Set Up Operating Records for Your New Industrial Power Plant," *Power Engineering*, Vol. 61, No. 10 (Oct., 1957); "Tools and Stores You Need to Run that New Industrial Power Plant," *Power Engineering*, Vol. 61, No. 12 (Dec., 1957); "So You're Ready to Begin Operating that New Industrial Power Plant," *Power Engineering*, Vol. 62, No. 1 (Jan., 1958); "So You've Begun Operating that New Industrial Power Plant," *Power Engineering*, Vol. 62, No. 2 (Feb., 1958).

could be performed by the plant operating personnel during their regular shifts. The maintenance of distribution facilities is ordinarily performed by the electrical and pipefitting departments.

OPERATING RECORDS AND BUDGETING

In order to achieve full efficiency in the operation of the power plant, it is necessary to set up operating records. These records serve as the basis for the operating budget. In order to follow the budget guidelines, monthly reports should be prepared so that the plant engineer may take steps to meet his budget or, if the situation requires it, advise the comptroller of any changes required in his budget. Some of the records used are given in the following subsections.

Machinery Index

This type of record is generally kept in the plant engineer's office and in the power plant. This record is usually kept on a card and is a complete record of each item of equipment in the plant. It includes model, size, electrical information, power capacity, usage, and other types of pertinent, permanent information. Any information required on the mechanical details of items should also be included. Serial numbers and applicable drawing numbers are generally shown.

Machine History

This record should give a running account of all activity regarding a particular machine or piece of equipment and should be filed with the machinery index card.

Record of Service Parts for Machinery and Equipment

This record is generally in card form, and contains all the necessary information needed to purchase a particular part and accessories. It shows such activity as when parts were removed from the crib and when replacement parts were received. It is good practice to maintain an inventory record of all tools and equipment purchased by the company and issued to employees.

Operating records and analysis forms become a base on which operations can be judged. These are shift-by-shift records and should generally cover such information as materials received or used, the daily routine check-off lists, daily lubrication check-off lists, and feedwater treatment analysis results. Additionally, such boiler room operating information as lbs of steam delivered, Btu/lb of steam, pressure and temperature of steam, high and low water levels, feedwater used, feedwater pressures, condensate returned, fresh water used, electrical power delivered, kw hours generated, and average power factor should all be recorded. Most of the preceding items are records which should be maintained in the power plant. The plant engineer, in turn, should issue monthly power plant reports based on this information.

Year-by-year records of the plant demands for compressed air, electricity, and steam are shown in Figs. 5-1, 5-2 and 5-3. Installed capacity is indicated on the right side of the charts. The purpose of these records is to ensure that the

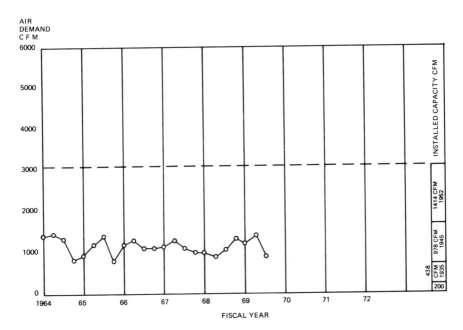

Figure 5-1. Plant demands for compressed air.

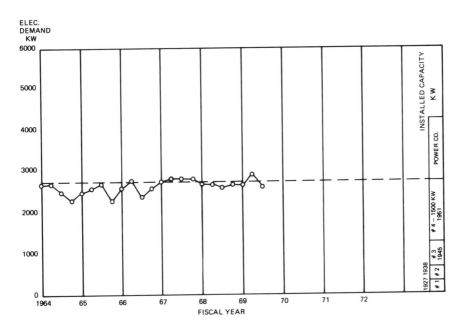

Figure 5-2. Plant demands for electricity.

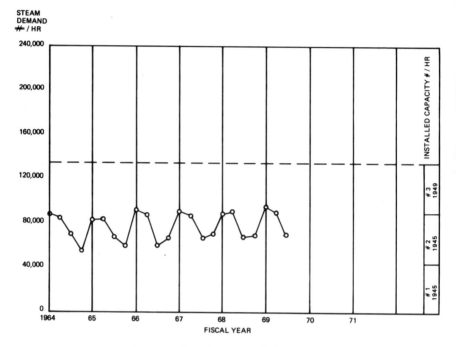

Figure 5–3. Plant demands for steam.

plant engineer is alert to peak demands relative to the installed capacity of these items.

Table V–1 shows a report on the operation of the power plant and the total factory utilities. This report is divided into three sections; factory requirements, power plant data, and power plant operating costs. Total utility requirements are not covered. Therefore, information cannot be compared from one month to the next.

Table V–1. Utilities and Fuels Report.

	Amount Provided	Cost	Maximum Demand
Factory Requirements			
Tons of finished products	4,397 tons		
Total power consumed	1,131,236 kwh		2,900 kw
Total compressed air	11,928 M cu ft		1,100 cfm
Total steam to factory	17,533.5 M lb		
City water	676,100 cu ft	$2,042.68	
Sewer rental		$375.00	
Total utilities		$36,219.29	
Raw water to factory	32,647.35 M lb		
Factory gas	34,834.9 therms	$1,792.65	

Table V–1. Utilities and Fuels Report *(Continued).*

Power Plant Requirements

Generated power	1,033,300 kwh	
Purchased power (energy)	97,936 kwh	$1,221.87
Purchased power (demand)	468 kw	$702.00
Purchased power total cost		$1,923.87
Compressed air (steam)	11,532 M cu ft	
Compressed air (electrical)	396 M cu ft	
Total steam produced	37,841 M lb	82 M lb/hr
Feedwater makeup	9,608.9 M lb	
Hp steam to factory	795 M lb	
Turbo-gen condensor returns	4,668.4 M lb	
Coal used	2,339.8 tons (8,561 Btu/lb)	
Gas used	169,019 therms	

Power Plant Costs	Engine Room			Boiler Room			Power House Total
	Labor	*Material*	*Total*	*Labor*	*Material*	*Total*	
Fuel – coal				$613.42	$10,739.68	$11,353.10	$11,353.10
Fuel – gas, oil					4,732.53	4,732.53	4,732.53
Engr. – firemen	$4,790.42		$4,790.42	4,828.90		4,828.90	9,619.32
Bldg. – grounds	5.00		5.00	5.00		5.00	10.00
Maintenance	295.09	$178.43	473.52	982.18	388.81	1,370.99	1,844.51
Supplies & exp.					516.17	516.17	516.17
Insurance		47.60	47.60		103.76	103.76	151.36
Depreciation		357.00	357.00		310.90	310.90	667.90
Property tax		678.40	678.40		511.80	511.80	1,190.20
Totals	$5,090.51	$1,261.43	$6,351.94	$6,429.50	$17,303.65	$23,733.15	$30,085.09

Table V–2 summarizes the costs of power plant operation, purchased utilities, and factory maintenance. A larger form could be used for the above information in order to provide space for dollar figures for each month of the year. Still another chart could be used to show the totals of these items by quarters or the totals for each year. In order for the plant engineer to obtain these figures, it is necessary that accounts be established in the accounting department to collect the various types of costs. Material requisitions should show the proper account number. Also the labor working orders should be written against a proper accounting number so that these costs may all be accumulated and published during the regular accounting department cost exhibits.

Each item shown in Table V–2 should be charged against special account numbers. The item power lines, lights and electrical equipment includes such items as labor and material for making repairs to all lighting facilities and power lines located throughout the factory. Equipment costs such as light fixtures, outlets, starter boxes, switchboards, and transformers should be included.

The last item in Table V–2 – heating, air conditioning, and gas and air systems – would include labor and material for making all repairs to heating facilities, air conditioning systems, gas lines, and air lines located throughout the

Table V-2. Summary of Utility Costs.

Power Plant Costs			
Fuel			
Coal 2,340 tons		$11,353.10	
Gas 169,019 therms		4,732.53	
Operators		9,619.32	
Maintenance & supplies		2,370.68	
Fixed charges			
Insurance	$ 151.36		
Taxes	667.90		
Depreciation	1,190.20		
Subtotal		2,009.46	
Total			$30,085.09
Purchased Utilities			
Electricity			
Energy	$1,221.87		
Demand	702.00		
Subtotal		1,923.87	
Water		2,042.68	
Sewer rental		375.00	
Natural gas — factory		1,792.65	
Total			6,104.20
Factory Maintenance			
Power lines, lights &		2,744.11	
electrical equipment			
Heating, air conditioning,			
gas and air systems		2,924.48	
Total			5,668.59
Total Cost of Utilities			$ 41,857.88
Cost of Product Finished			$4,860,795.00
Utility Cost as a Percent of Cost of			.84%
Product Finished			

factory. It also includes such items as air lines and blowers; hose or pipe; asbestos for covering pipe; gas lines; gas meters; gaskets for piping; oil burners; propane distribution systems; pumps of all types for water, naptha, brine, and oil; recording gages; refrigerator compressors; steam lines; and heating systems and unit heaters.

Tables V-3 and V-4 show a comparison of utility and fuel requirements and costs for two 1-year periods. This type of information is used by the plant engineer to evaluate the power plant and utility operation. Certainly, all of the items that are shown will not be applicable to every installation, but many will be.

CONSERVATION OF UTILITIES

In order to control the costs of power and utilities, an active program to conserve utilities is necessary. As in many areas of factory operations, employees

Table V–3. Comparison of Utility and Fuel Requirements and Costs.

| | | | Percentage Change | |
	1966	1965	Increase	Decrease
Production Requirements				
Factory production — tons	37,208	31,443	18.2	
Total electricity — kwh	11,032,746	10,548,556	4.6	
kwh/ton	297.0	335.0		11.4
Total compressed air —				
M cu ft	100,356	86,592	16.0	
M cu ft/ton	2.70	2.75		1.8
Domestic (city) water —				
M gal	44,000	42,450	3.9	
M gal/ton	1.18	1.35		12.6
Industrial process fuel —				
10⁶ Btu	50,118	43,485	15.5	
Process steam — 10⁶ Btu	44,000	37,500	17.4	
Total process fuel and				
steam — 10⁶ Btu	94,118	80,985	16.2	
Process fuel and steam —				
10⁶ Btu/ton	2.53	2.97		1.6
Heating steam — 10⁶ Btu	118,792	121,859		2.5
Total heating steam and				
gas — 10⁶ Btu	118,792	121,859		2.5
Heating steam and gas —				
10⁶ Btu/sq ft factory				
area	.116¢	.119¢		2.5
Cost of Utilities				
Net power plant	$285,300.21	$349,318.96		18.3
Purchased electricity	$20,476.03	$21,656.38		5.5
Purchased domestic water	$20,323.51	$18,533.72	9.6	
Firm process gas	$29,010.09	$25,852.74	12.1	
Total utility cost	$355,109.84	$415,361.80		14.6
Heating, electricity, and				
compressed air cost/ton	$8.22	$11.79		30.2
Domestic water and				
process fuel cost/ton	$1.33	$1.41		5.7
Total utility cost/ton	$9.55	$13.20		27.6
Industrial Fuel and Utility Purchases				
Electricity — kwh	1,036,246	1,162,656		11.0
Cost/kwh	1.92¢	1.86¢	5.9	
Domestic water — M gal	44,000	42,450	3.9	
Cost/M gal	46.20¢	43.70¢	5.8	
Firm process gas —				
10⁶ Btu	50,118	43,485	15.5	
Cost/10⁶ Btu	57.90¢	59.90¢		2.8

become accustomed to the day-to-day conditions in their areas; little thought is given to the dependable utilities around them. While many items of cost such as water leaks or lights left on may seem relatively small, the cost can be sizable when the total plant is considered.

It is recommended that the plant engineer develop a program for the con-

Table V–4. Comparison of Power Plant Performance and Costs.

	1966	1965	Percentage Change	
			Increase	*Decrease*
Power Plant Production				
Electricity – kwh	9,996,500	9,385,900	6.4	
Compressed air (steam)				
mcf	92,445	73,848	25.1	
Total equiv. power – kwh	10,181,390	9,533,596	6.8	
Aver. cost/kwh	0.715¢	0.978¢		27.0
Steam produced – 10⁶ Btu	321,350	305,920	5.0	
Coal – tons	10,598	21,583		50.8
Gas – 10⁶ Btu	242,886	55,532	328.0	
Total fuel consumed –				
10⁶ Btu	446,494	469,931		4.8
Average cost of				
fuel/10⁶ Btu	28.10¢	24.65¢	14.1	
Efficiency of				
combustion – %	71.9	65.2	10.0	
Efficiency of energy				
utilization – %	44.2	40.9	8.2	
Power Plant Costs				
Fuel	$125,417.75	$115,413.43	8.8	
Maintenance and				
materials	$27,837.62	$38,235.26		27.2
Operating labor	$98,539.59	$97,786.22	1.0	
Fixed charges	$33,505.25	$97,884.05		65.7
Total power plant costs	$285,300.21	$349,318.96		18.3
Boiler Room Costs				
Fuel cost/10⁶ Btu steam	39.10¢	37.78¢	3.6	
Maint. and mat. cost/10⁶				
Btu steam	5.65¢	7.97¢		29.2
Op. labor cost/10⁶				
Btu steam	14.55¢	16.10¢		9.6
Fixed cost/10⁶ Btu steam	4.72¢	14.80¢		68.1
Aver. cost/10⁶ Btu steam	64.02¢	76.65¢		16.5
Total boiler room costs	$205,442.56	$234,193.00		12.5
Engine Room Costs				
Maint. and mat. cost/				
equiv. kwh	.096¢	.145¢		33.8
Op. labor cost/equiv. kwh	.508¢	.511¢		0.7
Fixed cost/equiv. kwh	.180¢	.552¢		67.4
Aver. cost/equiv. kwh	.784¢	1.208¢		35.0
Total engine room costs	$79,847.65	$115,125.96		30.7

servation of utilities. Active participation in the program by production and maintenance supervisors can bring out a number of important projects.

The implementation of a utility conservation program can be divided into the following three phases:

Phase I

Review and analyze the utility rate structure and verify accuracy of utility billings. Rate schedules should be examined to determine the most advantageous schedule for each utility service. Such equipment as lighting, air conditioning, cooling systems, and air handling units should be reviewed for operating procedures, policies, and operating costs.

Phase II

Review production equipment associated with large utility consumption such as plating equipment, rinse tanks, degreasers, product washers and dryers, paint systems, process exhaust fans, direct-fired forge furnaces, and heat treating equipment.

Phase III

Provide a continuous review of all projects established in Phase I and Phase II. Utility conservation programs should be presented to production and maintenance supervision. Projects should be solicited from them and recognition should be given for conservation programs showing utility savings. Generally, production departments operate on a utility budget, and utility savings can be credited to the department supervision. Some items of savings to consider are listed below.

Electrical Power. Decrease the lighting level in unused areas. It is profitable to turn off a fluorescent or incandescent lamp if it will not be turned on again for an hour or more. Cleaning work can be done at a reduced light level (50 percent), and lights should be turned off in the area when janitors leave. Plant security guards can turn off unneeded lighting—inside and outside buildings. Light panels should be marked to indicate which can be turned off. Lighting circuits should be arranged for selective control. Use proper sizes of lamps; do not install a 200-watt bulb if a 100-watt bulb is sufficient.

Turn off process exhaust fans and building exhaust fans, especially in cold weather. Turn off snow-melter cables when not needed. Shut down cooling tower fans in cold weather. Operate paint system exhaust fans at required speed to meet codes. Turn off some unit heaters on weekends to reduce building temperature. Audit electric utility metering and invoices, and install recording demand and kilowatt-hour meters to back up and monitor power company's meter. Check and verify utility company billings.

Provide electrical power control equipment, and install capacitors to raise power factor above penalty point. A power factor of 85 percent is typical. Specify capacitors on all equipment using 15 hp or larger motors. Balance power load from utility by operation of on-site generating equipment.

Water. Leaks in the water system can occur almost anywhere; underground leaks are very common. Look for leaks in all employee facilities—washrooms, rest rooms, showers.

The most efficient use of water for cooling requires the water to remove the maximum amount of heat possible before being discharged into the sewer. The temperature rise of the water can be increased by controlling the temperature of the water that is allowed to discharge to the sewer. The best method for achieving this control is the use of a water recirculation system. When water thus recirculated reaches the desired discharge temperature, a temperature control valve opens and admits fresh water to the accumulating tank. This causes the warm water to overflow into the sewer. An additional benefit of using a recirculating system is that it eliminates problems caused by condensation in water-cooled equipment. Maintenance costs are reduced, especially for welders and transformers. The possibilities of using river water, pond water, or well water for water-cooling requirements should be explored.

Compressed Air. Promptly repair all air leaks. Select the proper size of equipment for the requirement. On off-shifts and weekends, operate only a minimum of equipment. Use the minimum air pressure for the application. If 20 psi will do the job, don't use 80 psi.

Heat. Determine building temperatures consistent with activities and set heat controls to the desired temperature. Reduce building heat on weekends and shutdown periods. Minimize heat loss caused by opening doors. Keep them closed on off shifts and weekends. Evaluate process heating for optimum operation and maintain the temperature. Minimize heat loss in winter months by controlling exhaust fans. Turn them off whenever possible. Establish a cleaning schedule for cleaning unit heaters and other types of heating equipment. Evaluate gas-fired heating furnaces for improper air supply or fuel supply. A Bailey heat prover should be used to determine the condition of firing and to maintain a combustion efficiency of 50 percent minimum.

POWER GENERATION

We live in a mechanical age. We are surrounded by a host of mechanical devices, many of which are operated by electrical energy. If we were denied the use of electrical power, our entire economy would collapse. Electrical power, therefore, must be provided constantly and in the quantities we need at all hours of the day. Industry must likewise be furnished electric power for the continuous operation of the manufacturing or processing facilities.

The two major requirements for the production of power are equipment which is able to produce power and an energy source or fuel for the equipment. Steam is the most common energy source for electric power generation, but gas and oil are also important. A good deal of electrical power is produced by hydroelectric plants. Generating stations owned and operated by industry use steam engines, steam turbines, gas turbines, or internal-combustion engines to drive generators. The discussion of generation of electricity will be limited to these types of engines.

Power Equipment

In a steam power plant, a fuel such as coal, oil, or gas is burned in a furnace, and the heat produced is used to change water into steam at a high pressure in a boiler. High-pressure steam is piped to the cylinder of a reciprocating steam engine where energy is expended in pushing a piston. In a steam turbine, the high-pressure steam strikes blades on a wheel to turn a drive shaft. The principal parts of a steam power plant are the following. A *furnace* is the part in which fuel is burned. If coal is used, a grate is used to hold the firebed. If gas or oil is used, burners are provided in place of grates. The furnace is connected to a chimney with breeching or a flue. The chimney provides draft so that the proper amount of air is available for combustion. The chimney also discharges gases produced by the combustion process. Draft is controlled by a damper placed in the breeching or flue leading to the chimney. Equipment may also be placed in this area to reinject particles of coal for more complete combustion as a part of air pollution control.

A *boiler* is a closed vessel which is filled about two-thirds full of water. The heat of combustion in the furnace is used to convert a portion of this water into steam. A water gage shows the height of the water level. Another gage shows the pressure of steam in the boiler. A safety valve is provided to release the steam pressure if it becomes too high.

A *setting* is the brickwork surrounding the boiler to provide the correct space for furnace, combustion chamber, and ashpit; to keep air from entering the furnace above the coal bed; and to minimize heat radiation.

A *feed pump* delivers water to the boiler as required.

Fuel Source

The principal fuels used in steam power plants are coal, oil, and natural gas. The heating value of a fuel is based upon the amount of heat emitted by the complete combustion of one unit of solid or liquid fuel or of one unit of volume of gaseous fuel.

The heating value of the fuel is measured in heat units — British thermal units (Btu's). This heating value can be determined by chemical analysis or by an instrument called a calorimeter. The heating value of a fuel is very important in estimating its commercial value. However, other properties must also be considered. These properties are the amount of moisture, volatile matter, fixed carbon, and ash and sulphur the fuel contains.

Coal has powered the industrial revolution and given impetus to the modern machine age. We are now on the threshold of a new plateau of technology and progress — the atomic era. With nuclear power plants actually being constructed and with scientific knowledge of the atom daily taking giant strides, it may appear that coal will become obsolete in a few decades. Although there are some individuals who believe that the role of coal as a major power fuel is about to be ended, such a view is premature because coal will continue to be an important energy factor throughout our lifetime. However, coal available for steam plant use will decline in quality as higher grades are mined out. This process is occurring now and will increase progressively in the years to come. As coal grades decline in quality, the problems of safe storage increase, but the techniques of successful storage and handling developed in recent years make it entirely safe and practical to stockpile bituminous coal of all grades.

To the plant engineer, the most important facts about coal are its price, its performance in the furnace, and its storage characteristics. Every user must weigh each of these three factors in relation to their importance and use and arrive at an equation that solves his particular problem. In regard to storage of coal, the most important properties of a given coal are its content of natural moisture, oxygen, and sulphur. Each of these contributes to the rate of oxidation, and the oxidation rate of coal determines its tendency to ignite spontaneously. A good basic rule to follow in storing coal is either to (1) insure complete and continuous ventilation, or (2) seal the coal mass airtight.

It would appear that the best coal to buy, whenever storage is a consideration, is high-rank, double-screened bituminous, low in sulphur and moisture content and not subject to slaking (picking up moisture). There are some situations where this practice is economically feasible, but usually a compromise must be effected among mine price, freight rates, and coal characteristics. If it should appear advantageous to compromise on coal quality because of availability or price structure, another cost factor must be considered. It may be necessary to provide mechanical equipment to do the coal handling job. This, of course, entails capital investment and maintenance expense which become a part of the overall cost of the coal and cannot be neglected in predicting fuel expense.

It is impossible to give estimates here of what the cost of such equipment expense might be for, let us say, an average coal-burning plant. There really is no average plant; every coal user has his own unique set of conditions. Organizations which do not have personnel familiar with these problems would do well to consult recognized professional fuel engineers. These men not only know the complicated structure of freight rates and coal prices, but can also recommend the type of storage and mechanical equipment best suited to each particular situation. Regardless of the size of the boiler plant, reasonable mechanization of coal handling from delivery to storage and from storage to furnace hoppers will usually effect an overall savings. A well-equipped boiler room that does not require the continuous manning of a coal scoop to keep it operating will attract a better type of man who can devote more time to watching his fire and maintaining it at peak efficiency. Chutes or inexpensive portable conveyors will move coal into storage from either trucks or railcars. Coal hoppers can be loaded with monorail buckets or bin-to-hopper conveyors. In some cases, a lift truck or a front end loader may be used.

Reserve coal for emergency should be stored on the ground where possible. A 45-day supply is considered to be standard. It is not necessary to invest in heavy equipment to lay down a stockpile of this kind. The equipment and labor can be contracted on those rare occasions when it will be needed. Correct methods should be used in building the coal pile to ensure safe storage. It is likely that a certain amount of degradation will take place to create fines during working and handling of the coal, and unless compaction is thorough, trouble may arise later. Bituminous coal should not be stored in a pile greater than 10 feet in height. Once a batch of coal has shown advanced signs of heating, it cannot be relied upon to remain safe. It is advisable to burn such coal as soon as possible.

The plant engineer should know how much coal the plant has in storage at all times. Coal in storage is an inventory item that has dollar value which is important for financial and tax purposes. It is an essential part of production costs, and it is vital to know the quantity in reserve in the event of stoppages of transportation or supply. For these and other reasons, records must be kept of the number of tons in storage. These records should be kept up to date on a daily basis.

Oil is used as a fuel in steam generation in the Midwestern and Western states where the cost of oil is less than that of coal or natural gas. The advantages of oil over coal are reduced handling costs, less labor in firing, better combustion, and the elimination of smoke after combustion. The following characteristics are important in the selection of a fuel oil: flash point, viscosity, specific gravity, moisture, sulphur, content of sediment, and heating value.

Natural gas, which up until a few years ago was used only in areas near gas-producing wells, is now becoming an important fuel for steam generation. Pipeline extensions have made this possible. Many installations use natural gas during warm weather at reduced rates and coal during the domestic heating season. The changeover from gas to coal in boiler furnaces can be accomplished in a short time by boiler-room operators.

Auxiliary Equipment

In order to offset unequal expansion and contraction caused by feeding cold water into a boiler, equipment is generally added to heat the feedwater used in the boiler. Most plants are provided with feedwater heaters which heat the water by exhaust steam. This, of course, increases the economy of the power plant, using exhaust steam which would otherwise be wasted. Heating feedwater outside the boiler also purifies the water before it enters the boiler. Feedwater can also be heated by waste chimney gases. Heaters can be constructed so that exhaust steam and water come into direct contact and the steam gives up its heat by condensation. Such heaters are called open feedwater heaters. Closed feedwater heaters are sometimes used, but are more expensive than the open types. A feedwater heater using heat from flue gases as they leave the boiler is called an *economizer*. This equipment increases the capacity of the boiler plant and provides a means of storing larger quantities of hot water. Generally, one economizer is provided for each boiler.

A great deal of heat escapes from a boiler plant through the flue gas. Preheating the air prior to combustion raises the efficiency of the boiler because the amount of heat required to raise the temperature of the air after it enters the furnace is decreased.

A chimney carries off gases formed during the process of combustion. The chimney discharges these gases at an elevation where these gases do not create a problem in the fresh air. The chimney also, of course, creates a draft so that fresh air passing through the fuel bed can produce continuous combustion. Most installations depend on chimneys for draft. The draft is produced in a chimney as a result of hot gases inside the chimney being lighter than the outside cold air. The intensity of the draft depends on the chimney height. The higher the chimney, the greater the draft. Chimney draft is measured in inches of water. This means that the draft is strong enough to support a column of water at a given height. Draft produced by chimneys is generally from $\frac{1}{2}$ to $\frac{3}{4}$ in. of water. In some cases, chimney draft is insufficient and some artificial method of creating draft has to be used. Artificial draft can be produced by a fan and may have a large range of pressures.

Feedpumps and injectors force water into steam boilers. A pump is used for hot water and an injector is used only when the water is cold. Direct-acting steam pumps are commonly used for feeding small, stationary boilers. Their speed can be regulated to meet the feedwater requirements of the boiler. Centrifugal pumps are used in large power plants and are generally driven by steam turbines or electric motors.

Steam Engines

The simplest type of steam engine consists of a piston and cylinder with valves to admit and exhaust steam, a governor for regulating the speed, lubrication for reducing friction, and stuffing boxes for preventing loss of steam. Steam from the boiler enters the steam chest of the engine and is admitted alternately through ports to either end of the cylinder. This valve also releases and exhausts the steam which moves the piston in both directions in the cylinder. The shaft can be connected directly to the equipment which is to be driven, or it can be connected by belts or chains. A flywheel is mounted on the shaft in order to make the rate of rotation uniform and to carry the engine over dead center at either end of the piston stroke. The flywheel also is used occasionally to drive a pulley. An eccentric rotating with the shaft provides a reciprocating motion to the valve through the eccentric rod and valve stem. The main steam pressure losses in a steam engine are the following:

1) Loss occurring as steam is moved from the boiler to the engine cylinder because of the action of the steam pipe and ports. Steam loses part of its energy overcoming friction as it passes through a small port.

2) Loss due to leakage past the piston and valves. These losses are generally small and may be kept small by proper maintenance.

3) Loss resulting from condensation in the cylinder which has been cooled by the exhaust steam which previously filled the cylinder.

4) Loss associated with the exhaust. More than 75 percent of the heat available in the steam is carried away in the exhaust.

This exhaust steam can be used for heating feedwater, for heating buildings or in connection with various manufacturing processes. Noncondensing engines exhaust steam directly into the atmosphere, into heating coils, or into feedwater heaters where the heat from the exhaust steam is used to heat feedwater or buildings or is used in manufacturing processes in the factory. Exhaust steam from a condensing engine escapes from the engine cylinder into a condenser where it is cooled and condensed to water. This produces a reduction in back pressure. The reduction in back pressure increases the work done in the cylinder. Because of this lower back pressure, a condensing engine will use about 25 percent less steam than a noncondensing engine of the same size.

Valve Settings. The purposes of setting valves on a steam engine is to equalize the work performed on both ends of the piston. The methods used for setting valves vary with the type of valve, but the general principles applying to plain side valves are most easily understood. The first step is to determine dead center for both ends of the engine. To set the valve for equal lead on both ends, set the engine on dead center on one end and measure the lead at that end. Move the engine to the other dead center and measure the lead again. If the lead is not the same, the difference can be corrected by moving the valve on the valve stem. The same procedure is then followed for setting equal cut-off on the valve.

Steam Engine Governors. The function of a governor is to control the speed of rotation of a motor regardless of the power which is developed. In a steam engine, the governor maintains a uniform speed of rotation by varying the initial pressure of steam applied or by changing the point of cutoff and hence the portion of the stroke during which the steam is admitted. Throttling governors regulate the speed of an engine by varying the initial pressure of the steam supplied to the engine. In high-speed automatic engines, throttling is accomplished by a form of flywheel or shaft governor which controls the point of cutoff by changing the position of the eccentric. The centrifugal force which causes movement of the governor weight also changes the point of cutoff.

Steam Turbines

The steam turbine produces rotary motion on its shaft directly without any reciprocating parts as are found in the steam engine or internal combustion engine. The simple turbine is a bladed wheel to which rotary motion is imparted by means of a steam jet impinging on the blades. In one type of steam turbine, steam emitted from a fixed expanding nozzle is directed on the curved blades. The expansion of the steam occurs in the nozzle, resulting in a steam jet of high velocity. This is called the impulse type of steam turbine. In a reaction turbine, steam is expanded within the stationary and the moving blades of the machine. Work is partially produced by the reaction of expanding steam as it flows from moving blades to stationary or guide blades. Commercial steam turbines utilize both the impulse of the steam against the blades and the reaction of the steam as it leaves the blades.

The history of the steam turbine goes back to the second century B.C. Hero of Alexandria designed a steam motor which consisted of a hollow, spherical vessel rotating on two supports. Steam was delivered to the vessel through one of the supports and the steam was allowed to escape by means of two right-angled exhausts bent in opposite directions. Rotation of the sphere was produced by the reaction of the steam escaping from the exhausts. The steam turbine did not become commercially successful until the end of the nineteenth century.

The DeLaval steam turbine was the first successful simple-impulse turbine. Though this design is now obsolete, its principle of operation is used in today's commercial turbines. In 1889 Dr. DeLaval designed the expanding nozzle used in this turbine. In this design, steam enters a steam chest where it is distributed to one or more nozzles and is expanded to exhaust pressure and strikes the blades on the turbine wheel. Nozzles are fitted with stop valves so that when the turbine is lightly loaded one or more nozzles can be blocked off. After performing its work, the steam passes through an exhaust pipe into the open air or into a condenser. Since the total expansion of the steam takes place in one set of nozzles, the velocity of the turbine wheel in this type of design is high and must be reduced by the provision of gearing. A throttling governor is used for speed regulation.

The reaction steam turbine is a multipressure-stage design and differs from the impulse turbine in that stationary blades are substituted for nozzles. The blades are shaped so that they can perform the functions both of nozzles and of the blades of impulse turbines. The reaction turbine has many stages. Each stage consists of a set of stationary and rotating blades. Part of the expansion of the steam takes place in the moving blades and part in the stationary blades. Reaction-type turbines are controlled by an indirect type of governor. The governor allows the main steam admission valve to remain open for longer or shorter periods of time depending upon the load carried by the machine.

Whenever an application requires a high and constant rotative speed where a high starting effort is not required and where there is no need for reversing, the steam turbine is the ideal selection. Thus, the steam turbine is well suited for use in electrical generating stations. In power plants where exhaust steam is used for heating or manufacturing purposes, a bleeder turbine or a reciprocating engine should be selected. Steam turbines are also used for boiler feed pumps, hot well pumps, circulating pumps, and in ship propulsion.

Engine and Turbine Auxiliaries

Condensers. The advantage of using condensers is that they reduce the back pressure against which the engine exhausts. In the case of the steam turbine, the available energy in the steam can be more than doubled by carrying a high vacuum, as compared with the noncondensing operation. The gain in economy depends upon the size of engine or turbine and also on the type of machine.

Steam can be readily condensed, and in the form of water it occupies a much smaller volume. If exhaust steam from an engine is placed into a vessel and is condensed before being discharged, the work required to maintain the vacuum is greatly reduced because the work of the condenser pump is limited to removing a small volume of water. In the operation of condensers, steam temperature must be below that corresponding to the vacuum to be carried. The condenser is never free from air, and the temperature of the condensed steam is several degrees below that corresponding to the vacuum carried. Air enters with the boiler feedwater and also leaks into the condenser through piping and valves. Air mixed with the steam destroys the vacuum and raises the pressure in the condenser above that theoretically required. It must be continuously removed if the vacuum is to be maintained.

Condensers are of two types—jet and surface. Jet condensers produce condensation by the mixing of exhaust steam and circulating water. This mixture then leaves the condenser at the same temperature. In the surface condenser, exhaust steam and circulating water are separated by tubes. The heat transfer between the steam and the circulating water takes place by conduction through the tubes. The surface condenser is more commonly used in large power plants. Surface condensers are used where the condensed steam is returned to the boiler and where the cooling water is not suitable for the making of steam.

In a condenser operation, a wet-air pump and a circulating pump are both required. A dry-air pump is used to maintain a high vacuum and is used in addition to a hot-well pump and a water-circulating pump. Wet-air pumps are used to remove the condensed steam, the noncondensable vapors, and the cooling water. Dry-air pumps remove only the noncondensable vapors and are, therefore, used in steam turbine installations where a high vacuum is required. Hot-well or condensate pumps are those that remove condensate from surface condensers. A circulating pump is used to move cooling water through the condenser.

Cooling Ponds and Cooling Devices. From 30 to 70 pounds of water are required to condense a single pound of steam. In some localities it may be economical to discharge the water which has passed through the condenser. However, in most areas plants cannot afford to simply discharge such a high volume of water. The means for reclaiming water depends upon the cooling effect derived from the evaporation of water. Air has the property of evaporating and absorbing water. The rate of evaporation depends upon the velocity and degree of contact between air and water, and the amount of water absorbed by the air depends upon the condition of the air.

There are three principal systems used for reclaiming condenser circulating water: cooling ponds, spray ponds, and cooling towers. Cooling ponds obtain their cooling effect upon the exposure of a large area of water to the air. Cooling by this method is principally by evaporation. Surface area is most important, so generally ponds used for this purpose are relatively shallow but have a large surface area. Since cooling ponds may freeze in the winter, continuous use of this method may not be feasible.

In a spray pond system, hot water from the condensers is cooled by spraying the water into the air so that it falls in a thin mist onto the surface of the pond. In this method a large amount of water surface is exposed to the air and thus a substantial cooling effect is achieved in a comparatively small space. Water is forced under pressure through nozzles in this type of system. In order to obtain the same cooling effect from a cooling pond as a spray pond, the cooling pond would have to be 50 times as large.

A cooling tower is a structure of wood, sheet iron, or concrete that is filled with mats of steel wire, wood, or tile. Water from the condenser is released at the top of the tower and distributed over the top surface. As the water falls to the ground level, it is retarded and broken up by the mats and thus brought into contact with the air that ascends through the tower. The cooling towers are so constructed that all sides admit air freely. Cooling towers of this design and those of the forced draft design (commonly used in smaller installations) can be used throughout the year and provide a dependable means for cooling condensate.

Steam Plant Testing

In order to operate a steam power plant efficiently, it must be equipped with suitable instrumentation. This instrumentation includes steam pressure gages; thermometers for measuring temperatures of feedwater, flue gases, and steam (if steam is superheated); equipment to measure weight of feedwater; a means of metering steam generated by boilers; steam calorimeters to determine the quality of saturated steam and draft gases; instruments for analyzing flue gases; electrical instruments; and other instruments applicable to a particular installation. The test of the power plant is a test of each of the principal parts. It is a combined test of the steam boiler, the steam engine or turbine, and of other power plant equipment. Determining that the plant is operating satisfactorily may be done by reading various instruments periodically or by using recording instruments. Recording instruments give a continuous record which is often highly desirable in studying the daily operation of the plant. In a boiler operation, the amount of coal used gives a direct measure of the heat supplied. To find the energy transformed, it is necessary to measure the weight of the water evaporated, the quality of steam generated, the boiler pressure, and the feedwater temperature. To determine losses in a boiler plant, it is necessary to know the temperature of flue gases, draft at various points of the boiler, and the analysis of the flue gas.

Prior to making a test, a thorough examination should be made of all equipment, piping, valves, etc., and any defects should be corrected. If a plant is operating continuously, the test period of a boiler should follow the regular period of cleaning the fires. The starting time should be noted as well as the thickness of the coal bed, the water level, and the steam pressure. At the end of the test, the fires should again be burned low so that conditions are the same as observed at the beginning—water level and steam pressure also being the same—and the elapsed time should be recorded. Care should be taken when weighing the test fuel so that accurate measurements are obtained. Procedures for making this measurement will vary widely with the size of the power plant installation.

The most satisfactory method for weighing feedwater consists of the use of one or more tanks each placed on platform scales. These are raised a certain distance above the floor in order to empty into a receiving tank which, in turn, is connected to the boiler feed pump. Additionally, many commercial types of feedwater meters are available. Calibration of the meter before and after the test is recommended.

Various gages are available to determine the draft at different points of a boiler setting. The simplest form of a draft gage is a U-tube or manometer. A tube is filled with water and connected by means of a piece of tubing to the point where the pressure is to be measured. Pressure is measured by the level of the liquid and is generally presented in inches of water. For the measurement of low pressures, an inclined tube is used.

Temperatures are measured by the use of thermometers, electrical-resistance thermometers, mechanical pyrometers, and thermoelectric pyrometers. Below 500° F, temperatures are measured with an ordinary mercury-filled glass thermometer. Above 500° F, a special nitrogen-filled glass thermometer is employed.

Platform scales and surface condensers are the most satisfactory method of weighing the amount of steam used by engines or turbines. This method uses two scales and two tanks which are alternately filled with condensed steam from the condenser. Many forms of steam meters are used for measuring steam, and such meters should be properly calibrated according to the conditions in which they will be operating. A Bailey boiler meter measures and records the amount of steam the boiler is making, the amount of air used to burn the fuel, the firebox draft, and the flue gas temperature.

Gas Turbines

The gas turbine, practically unknown to the electric utility industry ten years ago, has recently become an important part of the industry for "peak-load" generation. The gas turbine's capital cost is low, it is easy to install, it starts fast—5 to 30 minutes—and it requires little maintenance. Following the 1965 East Coast blackout, utilities turned to the gas turbine for additional generating capacity because the equipment could be delivered in 12 months and installed in one month. High fuel costs for gas or distillate and relatively inefficient operation are the principal disadvantages of the gas turbine. Most installations use the gas turbine as back-up for steam generation equipment and for peak-load requirements operating between 500 and 1,000 hours per year.

The development of the gas turbine led to development of the first jet propulsion aircraft engine in 1936. Applications which followed were power for stationary power plants, industrial processes, locomotives, and ships. A simple gas turbine plant includes a *compressor*, a *combustor*, and a turbine. It can also include heat exchangers, additional compressors with intercoolers, and additional turbines with auxiliary combustors. Gas turbines generally do not exceed 25,000 kw generation.

Industrial applications for the simple gas turbine are found in oil refineries and chemical processes. Available by-product hot compressed gases can be readily used in the turbine. In turn, the turbine can be used to supply compressed air for the process and power for electrical generation. In the steel industry, blast furnace gases can be used. Again, the excess compressed air can be used in the blast furnace operation. Turbine exhaust can be used to produce process steam or hot water. Most gas turbines in use today are of the simple open-cycle design. Ambient air enters a compressor and, after compression, passes through a combustion chamber where the gas temperature is raised by fuel combustion. The gas is then expanded back to the atmosphere through a turbine. If the exhaust energy can be used for process heating, the net operating costs will be reduced.

A closed-cycle gas turbine permits the use of any gas as a working substance and almost any fuel as the energy source. After the gas has been compressed, it passes through a heat exchanger, is then expanded through the turbine, and returns through a "precooler." This turbine is restricted to power shaft applications. Installations are large in size because of the heat exchangers. Installations in the United States are of the open-cycle design because of the availability of natural gas as a fuel. In Europe, the closed-cycle design is most frequently used.

Components. The *air compressor* is as important to the gas turbine power plant as is the turbine. The net output of the plant is the difference between the turbine output and the compressor input.

The turbine and the compressor must be properly matched. A single-stage centrifugal compressor is selected when the operating pressure ratio does not exceed 4:1. Most of its applications are in jet aircraft power plants. The axial-flow, multistaged compressor is used to handle large quantities of air. This compressor is used in stationary power plants and aircraft turbine plants.

A *combustor* is a direct-fired air heater. In the open-cycle gas turbine, fuel is burned under pressure to heat the air to arrive at a specific temperature at the turbine. Inlet temperature varies from 250° to 750° F. With generation, temperatures are as high as 1100° F. Outlet temperatures vary from 1200° to 1450° F for industrial turbine installations. Basic combustor design provides for injection of atomized fuel into an area where ignition and flame mix with incoming air. It is easy to achieve a 98 percent combustion efficiency with a static pressure loss of less than five percent. As a result, the combustion process receives little attention as compared to the expansion, compression, and heat-transfer processes involved in the turbine operation.

Starting equipment becomes highly important when a gas turbine is used for emergency "black-plant" startup. If the turbine's main auxiliaries are driven from the turbine shaft, only a small diesel turning-gear motor and an emergency lubricating pump motor need be operated by battery. Once running, the generator can start the larger power plant motors. The generator and its exciter must be designed to minimize voltage dips during startup of large motors. The largest motor should be started first to reduce the danger of stalling smaller motors.

Fuels. Fuels for industrial gas turbines are natural gas, propane, butane, petroleum distillates, refinery and chemical plant gases, and liquids and residual fuel oil. It is important that fuels are purchased to meet specifications required for each application. Power plant life and output can be greatly affected by the fuel used. Combustor design must be compatible with the fuel used. Coal-fired gas turbines have not yet been successful.

Future Developments. Since steam industrial power plants are smaller and operate at lower pressures, they are less efficient than the public utilities. A gas turbine can be installed at less cost than a steam plant. Utility power plants have established a trend toward large plants with higher-pressure steam. The ability to accept load swings is thereby decreased. Nuclear plants operate at high load factors. As generating capacity is increased by nuclear and high-pressure steam units, the lower-pressure steam plants will become a smaller part of the total. Provisions must be made to quickly and frequently cover peak loads. Gas turbines are ideally suited for this type of operation and should gain further acceptance for this application.

Internal-Combustion Engines

The four-stroke cycle, internal-combustion engine was made practical by Nicholas Otto in 1878. Otto engines require two complete revolutions of the crankshaft, or four strokes of the piston, to produce one power stroke. This cycle can be modified so that the work carried out in the four-stroke engine can be performed by only two strokes of the piston or one revolution of the crankshaft. Large, two-stroke cycle engines are often made double-acting and have the same number of power impulses per revolution as a single-cylinder steam engine. Fuel and air are delivered to each end of the piston at the correct time by auxiliary pumps. An intake valve is provided at each end of the cylinder. Exhaust is through ports near the middle of the cylinder which are uncovered by the piston at the end of each working stroke.

The Diesel engine cycle has the same events as the Otto engine; that is, intake, compression, ignition, expansion, and exhaust. In the Otto engine, air is mixed with fuel in definite proportions and the mixture is compressed. In the Diesel engine, only air is admitted to the cylinder prior to compression. Compression pressures as high as desired are possible without danger from preignition, and they vary from 450 to 500 lb/sq in. At the end of the compression stroke, fuel oil is injected into the cylinder. It enters as a fine spray, mixes with the highly compressed air and is ignited and burned at nearly constant pressure. The duration of the oil injection is controlled by the load on the engine.

Internal-combustion engines installed in power plants should be governed by the same general requirements as those applying to steam engines. Adequate space must be provided around the engines so that any part may be reached to facilitate starting, oiling, inspection, and repair. Fuel tanks should be installed outside of buildings and should be lower than the pipe by which they are connected to the engine room. Foundations for Diesel engines should be very substantial. Foundations should be separated from the walls of the building in order that the structure will not be affected by the vibrations of the engine.

ELECTRIC POWER SOURCES

Generators produce either alternating current or direct current. Direct current for industrial applications is most often obtained from a rectified alternating current or from d-c generators driven by a-c motors. Both single-phase and three-phase generation of alternating current is provided by factory power plants and major power companies.

Factory-Generated Power

The method of generating alternating electric current can be most simply described by a single loop of wire (the armature) and a horseshoe magnet (the poles). If the loop is rotated within the magnetic field between the two poles of the magnet, an electric current will begin to be generated in the loop. As the loop approaches the center of the magnetic field, the current will increase and will reach its maximum at the center of the field. As the loop rotates out of the magnetic field, the current gradually diminishes until it drops off entirely. By continued rotation of the loop, the current flow will begin again in the opposite direction. Instead of a positive flow, as in the first 180 deg of rotation, a negative flow is obtained. This alternating current flow can be represented graphically by showing the first half of the rotation, which represents the positive flow of electricity, above a zero-current line and the last 180 deg of the cycle below the zero line. This type of alternating current is called single-phase current; it is shown graphically in Fig. 5–4.

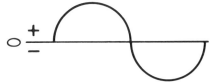

Figure 5–4. Single-phase alternating current.

In order to establish a stronger magnetic field, an electromagnet is used instead of a permanent horseshoe magnet in most large a-c generators. The electromagnet, and the addition of many more loops of wire to the armature, greatly increases the amount of current flow.

There are many uses for electrical power where heavy loads require greater energy to start and keep those loads moving. Three-phase current is used for these applications. The graphic representation of this three-phase current is shown in Fig. 5–5.

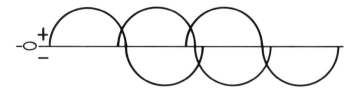

Figure 5–5.   Three-phase alternating current.

Purchased Power

The generation of electrical energy develops great quantities of waste heat. This waste heat can be used for factory heating and for processes requiring low-pressure steam. If such needs are not very large, it is probably more economical to purchase power than to generate it. An analysis should be made for additions and expansions to existing facilities to determine if the increased needs will justify on-site generation. There can also be economic factors which would make it desirable for a plant to install its own generating equipment.

A number of companies have determined that the return on capital can be greater if it is applied toward machinery and equipment used in the manufacture of their product as opposed to additional or replacement machinery for electrical power generation. Many companies with normal demands up to 20,000 kva purchase all of their electrical energy. Switching gear for companies that purchase power is split almost equally between manual and automatic. Many companies use alternate feeders to their plants. Substations are owned by nearly one-half of the companies that use purchased power. It is necessary for the plant engineer to be knowledgeable of the amount of reserve transformer capacity. He should be alert to providing expansion of incoming power switch-gear.

Even plants and companies who provide on-site generation for electrical energy should probably provide a means of purchasing power in the event that plant generating equipment should break down. It is possible that a purchase of power during certain periods of the year or on weekends could be an economical solution. Where it is necessary to replace existing power generators, consideration should be given to gas turbine sets, a relatively new and highly efficient form of power generation.

Power Distribution

The complexity of the power distribution network is related to the plant's requirements and size. Not all facilities will have the same type of network. A process industry will have a more complex transmission and distribution network than a warehouse. In addition, a decision must be made whether to run the feeders overhead or underground. Each method has certain requirements to be met. These will be detailed in the local code governing electrical installations.

Radial distribution systems are preferred by a vast majority of companies because of their economy and simplicity. Selective system advocates find that flexibility offsets the added cost. Transformer sizes in load center substations vary from 100 to 7500 kva. A radial arrangement of secondary distribution is virtually universal, although some use a form of secondary selective circuiting in part of their systems. Bus duct is the favored method of distributing low-voltage power by about one-half of the manufacturers surveyed. The balance use cable in conduit, in trays, or in raceways.

Some provision for future expansion of low-voltage systems is made by most companies. These provisions range from leaving room in substations for extra transformers to installing oversize or spare conduits or buying equipment sized for future loads. The proper selection of primary and secondary power distribution equipment is a function of the plant engineers' departments and, of course, must be based on the electrical code requirements in the areas in which the company is located.

It is quite common to use load center distribution systems. This, however, has increased the demand for transformers. Some installations require transformers to be installed in vaults to make them self-cooling. Others are installed close to the load center in buildings. The particular application will determine the type and location of the transformer. In general, the load center substations are located amid the equipment they serve. Some locations may be indoors. An understanding of the National Electrical Manufacturers Association (NEMA) standards will help the designer recognize the capabilities and limitations of various motors. These standards are perhaps the most helpful guide available in the selection of the correct motor in any application.

The recommended lighting level for offices is about 100 footcandles. The lighting needs vary widely for production areas but can be as low as 15 footcandles or a very brilliant 300 footcandles. A good average is approximately 75 footcandles. An average warehouse illumination is approximately 30 footcandles. Fluorescent lighting is used in most plants. Mercury vapor units are used for many new installations.

UTILITIES

A utility is one of the vital services essential to manufacturing. Usually, utilities are thought of as basic services—provision of water and steam, compressed air and other compressed gases, and natural gas and other petroleum gases. However, these utilities should also be considered as systems; they are the pipes, valves, fittings, and routings and other methods used to efficiently deliver these services where they are needed.

Water

The uses of water in industry fall into five convenient categories. Water is a means for converting energy. Utility companies and individual plants in the United States in 1955 had an installed capacity of 138,000,000 kw, of which nearly 110,000,000 kw were in central steam stations. Water can readily be used for cooling or for heating. Approximately 85 percent of the water used by industry is used for cooling. It is a convenient fluid for transporting and processing many materials. For instance, water helped produce 30,000,000 tons of paper and paperboard in 1955. Water also becomes a part of many products of industry. In 1955, for example, 90,000,000 barrels of beer were processed. Finally, water has been our standard economical means of passing along our domestic and industrial wastes for someone else to worry about. Details of these five categories of industrial uses for water are given below.

Water for Converting Energy. In electric power production using steam turbines or engines, we must use water in the boiler operations to make the steam required. The chemical energy of the fuel and the oxygen of the air are released as heat in the furnace. Steam from the boiler expands through the spinning turbine, and the heat energy becomes mechanical energy. Only a very small amount of water is actually consumed by the boilers in a steam generator plant. Most of the water is recycled from the condenser back to the boilers. The only water consumed in the generating cycle is that which is lost unintentionally. Some steam from the industrial power plant may go out to process operations from which it never returns. The quality of water evaporated in boilers has changed greatly over the past years. There have also been a great many improvements in the treatment of boiler feedwater. These include the following efforts:

1) To more efficiently process the water in order to remove not only the small particles of solids carried in suspension but also the calcium, magnesium, silica, and oxygen present in the solution.

2) To keep the condensate and feedwater from dissolving and carrying to the boiler iron, copper, and other metals from which the condenser, pumps, heaters, and connecting lines are made.

3) To control chemically the conditions in the boiler itself so that chemicals not wanted in the water can be isolated before they cause trouble.

4) To keep the boiler water in the boiler instead of allowing some of it to escape as steam.

Water for Cooling. In an industrial power plant, steam withdrawn from the turbine at one or more stages may be condensed in heat exchangers in order to give up latent heat to materials being processed.

Much of the water used by industry is returned to its source several degrees hotter after making one pass through a condenser, a cooling jacket on a furnace, a heat exchanger, a still, or a chemical process operation. Treatment of this once-through water is usually prohibitively expensive. However, if the water carries so much limestone in the solution that it rapidly coats the condenser tubes with a scale of calcium carbonate, it may be less expensive to add polyphosphate than to clean the tubes at frequent intervals. Water used once in condensers is chlorinated intermittently to kill simple forms of plant and animal life. These proliferate on the comfortably warm tube surfaces to form slimes which promote corrosion as well as interfere with the transfer of heat.

When the water is recirculated in a cooling tower, chemical conditioning becomes economically justifiable. New water enters the system only as makeup for the amount lost by evaporation and windage and for that deliberately blown down to keep dissolved solids from accumulating beyond a desirable level. Control of alkalinity to keep the pH of the recirculating water below 8 for the protection of the wood is comparable to the protection of steel in a cooling system by the addition of polyphosphate. Control of chlorine to kill slime organisms without leaving a residue sufficiently high to damage the wood is more of a problem. This, together with the hope that the development of fungi can also be controlled, has caused a number of materials to be offered as biocides. While some of these are being used to condition cooling water, chlorine remains the first choice.

Water as a Constituent of a Product. Specifications for water incorporated in the products of industry are as varied as the products themselves. Obviously, something less than perfectly pure water will do for soup. Taste, odor, color, hardness, alkalinity, or small amounts of iron or manganese all become critical, however, in some products.

Water for Transporting and Processing Material. Industry has always moved raw material and finished products whenever it could by ship and barge. These materials include ores, clays, and other minerals; precipitated filters and pigments; and sand and gravel dredged out of riverbeds. Industrial materials processed in water, although not necessarily transported in it, are common. Textiles from the original (natural or synthetic) fiber through to the final dyed or printed fabric move from one washing or rinsing to another. The attractively finished metal surfaces in automobiles, dishwashers, stoves, toasters, or other household appliances are subjected to processing in one or more aqueous solutions as they are cleaned, rinsed, plated, or painted.

Water as a Means for Waste Disposal. Flushing the waste products of civilization into rivers is a disposal method long favored by the human race. The progressive control of pollution so that our available water may be reused the optimum number of times on its way to the oceans is our greatest water problem. It is far cheaper to keep industrial wastes from getting into the water than it is to remove them once they are in. Good management of water within a plant, therefore, seeks continually to accumulate the maximum amount of wastes in the minimum amount of water. The wastes from the chemical treatment of water can themselves add to the overall problem. In the removal of dissolved salts by ion exchange resins, regeneration of the resins will add more pounds of dissolved substances than were initially present. If the waste water is discharged into the river, the cost of similar treatment in the next plant downsteam goes up.

Water actually is a very important raw material for industry. As a nation, we have a plentiful supply; but it is not as well distributed as we should like. To keep ourselves provided with adequate water where and when we want it will cost us progressively more in human effort. Our greatest problem is to control the pollution of water by domestic and industrial wastes. The concept of trying to flush our wastes away by maximum dilution is no longer feasible. We must try to confine contamination at each point in an industrial plant to the smallest practical amount of water, and treat each waste stream in whatever way may be necessary.

Steam

Throughout the United States, no power operation is more important or widespread than making steam. Despite the number of large hydroelectric installations in recent years, generating equipment operated by steam produces far more kilowatt hours than all others combined. Steam is also used extensively for process heating and for space heating in industries. Even though an industry may not have electrical power generation equipment, it may still have steam-producing equipment. Process steam is generated by nearly one-half of the industrial companies in the United States. Process steam is used in manufacturing to heat products, water, or other media to assist in washing, painting, or drying products. Service steam is used for space heating. In those industries generating their own electrical power, the steam used for processes and space heating is generally low-pressure or exhaust steam from engines and turbines used for generating electricity.

The production of steam has been covered earlier under "Power Generation." The distribution of steam from the powerhouse to all areas of the factory is normally done in either overhead lines or underground installations. In either case, the steam lines must be well insulated. Local codes and plant practice will dictate certain steam line requirements such as types of hangers, anchors, expansion loops, or ball drop joints.

Compressed Air

Compressed air powers a growing number of tools and devices, operates delicate instruments, agitates and atomizes liquids, blows out soot, and conveys materials. It is hard to find a plant where this versatile power service isn't put to use. The control of compressed air equipment and its distribution is generally a responsibility of the plant engineer.

In addition to an air compressor, there are a number of auxiliary devices that are needed. Some of these are included as a part of the compressor, and others usually come separately. Intake air filters prevent dust and other atmospheric impurities from entering the compressor. An intercooler is used to remove water and oil vapors by cooling between stages in a multistage compressor. Aftercoolers reduce temperatures and moisture content of the air after it leaves the compressor's final stage. These coolers may be water-cooled or evaporative. Separators are used between aftercoolers and receivers to remove moisture and oil in proportion to their ability to lower air temperature. Traps are used at separators, drain pockets, and in the distribution lines to discharge condensed moisture. Since much air may be lost through traps discharging continuously, and since condensation in air lines is not as rapid as in steam lines, intermittent discharge traps are usually recommended for air service. Receivers dampen pulsations or pressure waves in compressor discharge and act as reservoirs, and they precipitate any moisture that may be carried forward from aftercoolers.

The plant engineer will undoubtedly be more involved with the distribution of the compressed air system than with the air compressing equipment. There are two general types of installations. The first consists of one large compressor in a central location with supply piping in the form of a loop with runs leading to the areas which are using the compressed air. The low investment cost per unit of capacity, the lower unit power cost, and the minimum of electrical equipment are the principal advantages of the central system. The second type of system, the unit system, consists of individual compressors located in the areas where the compressed air is used. In this type of installation each compressor serves the area in which it is located with only emergency connections between the different areas. Advantages for the unit system consist of low initial investment, less pressure loss in piping, reduced engineering and planning, simpler installation, greater flexibility, and unlimited expansion possibilities.

The plant engineer should insure that the distribution system has been well designed. Important design features of the system include the following:

1) The intake pipe should be at least as large as the air compressor intake opening. For each 10 ft of run from the compressor, the line should be 1 in. larger in diameter.

2) The discharge line should be at least as large as the compressor outlet opening. A valve drain should be provided for the lowest point in the discharge line and in any pockets formed by the piping. The line to the point of use should be large enough so that pressure loss is reasonably low. A loss of less than 5 pounds per square inch is ideal.

3) Outlets for drops to air-operated equipment should be placed on the top of the pipe in such a manner that moisture won't drain from the main end of the hose.

4) Next to low pressure, moisture and solids are the worst enemies of a good air-tool operation. Full use should be made of separators, strainers, traps, and drop legs.

The best guide to compressor operation and maintenance is the manual supplied by the manufacturer of the equipment. By carefully following the instructions in such manuals, the plant engineer should be able to insure top-notch performance of compressed air equipment.

CO_2 Gas

CO_2 gas is frequently used as a fire extinguishing agent, or as a shielding medium for arc welding operations. Under most circumstances, CO_2 is purchased in 220-cu-ft bottles. Some industries make extensive use of CO_2 gas, and a central distribution system for the bulk gas may be economically feasible. CO_2 is also a very effective means of fire protection in the powerhouse. It can quite easily be distributed through pipe lines to a generator, exciter, switchgear, or other electrical equipment. The residue from the use of CO_2 for fire fighting can usually be wiped or brushed away. There are generally no adverse effects on electrical windings, contacts, or movable components.

Argon Gas

Argon gas is primarily used in the steel fabricating industry for use in welding operations. The semiautomatic gas–metal-arc process uses argon as a shielding gas. This gas can be purchased in 220-cu-ft tanks, in a rack of six or more such tanks, or in bulk. Again, the economic situation determines the distribution method to be used. A central system includes a storage tank and the necessary controls to meter and add a small amount of oxygen to the gas and to change the liquid argon to a gas for distribution. The piping used in distribution is pressure welded.

Natural Gas

A gas meter and pressure reducing equipment are installed at the point where the gas line enters the plant property. Normal pressures used in the plant or factory vary from a few ounces through 30 psig. Because of the fire hazard of the product, special precautions are necessary. Piping for natural gas installations is of the welded type, and the valves and fittings used have been constructed specifically for gas service. The gas pipelines in the plant should be painted a distinctive color so that they can easily be identified by employees.

Liquified Petroleum Gas

Liquified petroleum gas (LPG) can be delivered to the plant either in 40-lb bottles or in bulk. This gas is generally propane or butane. It is widely used as a fuel for boilers, furnaces, and drying ovens and for operation of material-handling equipment such as forklift trucks and pull tractors. It may be used as a substitute for natural gas. The latter may not be available at an attractive price at all times of the year. LPG is heavier than air and thus settles into low places. It can be a hazard if there are basement areas in the vicinity of LPG installations. With proper precautions, the gas can be used safely.

MAINTENANCE OF POWER EQUIPMENT

In order to provide continuous electrical power, steam, and compressed air, the maintenance of power generation equipment is of vital importance. The generating facility must be continuously maintained. Since most power plant operations are on a 24-hours-per-day, 7-days-per-week basis, routine maintanance becomes more of a problem. Only a few power plants are equipped with sufficient standby equipment to perform these services at any time. It is, therefore, of prime importance to preschedule preventive maintenance. Again, the plant engineer should follow the manufacturer's recommendations on lubrication and preventive maintenance.

Maintenance of Power Generation Equipment[2]

In designing a maintenance program for power generation equipment, the following categories of servicing should be covered:
1) Breakdown maintenance
2) Preventive maintenance on a regularly scheduled basis, including routine lubrication and inspection
3) Corrective maintenance which is performed because of conditions which may become apparent during routine inspection.

The plant engineer should establish a policy for the maintenance of each item of equipment. Breakdown maintenance is usually applied only to those units which will not cause shutdowns or dangerous conditions upon failure. Small items such as sump pumps, blowers, etc., are not serviced beyond occasional lubrication and casual inspection.

Preventive maintenance may include routine lubrication and major lubrication (which require disassembly or oil change). It may also include repacking, testing, and adjustment of bearings cleaning and adjusting of linkages and control accessories; and other items as recommended by the manufacturer. Work of this type can be scheduled according to the manpower available and the amount of spare equipment to cover the necessary outages.

Corrective maintenance is performed to repair faults which are found dur-

---

[2]Most of the information in this section is from Garay, "Maintenance of Power Generation Equipment," *Power Engineering*, Vol. 62, No. 2 (Feb., 1958).

ing inspection. Generally, major disassembly should not be performed to discover the faults. This type of fault will generally become apparent by noise, vibration, overheating, loss of performance, leakage, or excessive current drain. These external symptoms should be closely watched as a part of routine operating procedure. A clamp-on ammeter will show the operating current of a drive motor and will not require disassembly of the unit. If the motor load is normal, it doesn't necessarily mean that the machine is all right. However, a motor which is using overload current is a good indication there may be a problem.

Checking performance figures is another good way to spot trouble. A pump which fails to deliver rated shutoff head or a turbine that fails to come up to speed at its rated steam pressure and pump output pressure is probably in need of closer inspection. When pump or turbine casings are opened, examine the condition of the shafts. Inspect turbine wheels and impellers closely for cracks, especially at points of stress concentration. When disassembling or assembling machinery, follow the manufacturer's instruction book.

A complete inventory of spare parts for all equipment is not practical. A stock of spare parts means a costly inventory which provides no return on investment. Spare parts should be limited to those items that require replacement regularly or cannot be readily obtained in case of a breakdown.

Specialized tools and equipment such as valve reseating machinery, cylinder bores, etc., should be on hand only if the cost can be justified. In some cases it is possible to rebuild equipment at a considerable savings over replacement. This can be accomplished by powerhouse maintenance personnel or, preferably, by specialists in equipment rebuilding.

In addition to setting up lubrication programs and oil changing programs, other preventive maintenance is recommended in accordance with manufacturer's maintenance instruction books. It is a good practice to assign daily tests and inspections by a set of standing orders for the plant. The plant engineer should study the instructions for each piece of machinery and set up a list of work which must be performed once a week, once a month or once or twice a year. This list should then be worked into the master maintenance schedule. It can be made up on large sheets, one for each time period.

Other items of maintenance which may not generally be found in maintenance instruction books include the following:

1) Filling of fuel tanks twice a year to the overflow in order to coat the inside of the tank thoroughly
2) Draining or pumping water out of the bottom of the oil storage tanks once a year
3) Lifting the safeties each time steam is raised but not until the boiler reaches 75 percent of normal pressure
4) Testing of safeties twice a year and reseting as necessary
5) Blowing down all metering lines once a month
6) Blowing down CO_2 recording system piping weekly and cleaning the unit thoroughly
7) Operating all valves in every machine in the power plant at least once every two or three months
8) Cleaning out the dirt legs on steam lines twice a year
9) Blowing down water tanks every three months until clean water flows

10) Inspecting furnace flues and uptakes every month and cleaning out as necessary
11) Cleaning the deposits from induced draft fans every three months or more often if they are subject to rainwater drips
12) Blowing out soot at least once every night
13) Inspecting and oiling the ladder rungs, cables, pulleys and handrails around the smokestack every two months
14) Inspecting the power plant for locations which may collect unwanted deposits that can corrode, stick, or seize.

Maintenance of instruments should be performed with a minimum of disassembly. Routine care should include blowing down the lines leading to the instruments, occasional bleeding of the air releases on the instruments, and changing pins and charts. Instruments that are exposed to corrosive conditions, such as CO_2 recorders in boiler rooms, will require regular cleaning, watering, filter changing, and calibrating with a master instrument. The pipes leading to the boiler from this instrument are also a source of difficulty due to corrosion. If an instrument appears to be off, reference should be made to the instruction manual on the instrument for probable causes of trouble. If the connections, piping, wiring, etc., prove to be in order, and the instrument has been properly bled, then the manufacturer's serviceman should be called in.

Draft gages are generally free of trouble. The most common malfunction occurs as a result of a leak or blockage in the lines leading to the boiler. The second malfunction occurs as a result of an operator blowing into the piping to clean it out. This may result in ruptured diaphragms or broken linkages. Pressure gages do not require care after initial calibration against a test gage. A pressure gage which vibrates excessively should be fitted with a snubber or vibration damper, because continuous vibration will quickly wear out linkage. Water glasses should be kept clean and blown down. On boilers of 250 psi and up, it may be necessary to replace glasses at least once each year because of the etching effect of the boiler water.

With regular maintenance, smoke indicators are generally accurate. As parts of the instrument become soiled, they may require calibration. The sensing elements in the stack must be kept clean and properly aligned. Flow meters and temperature recorders are complex but usually dependable. Unless a good precision mechanic or instrument man is the maintenance man, instruments should be serviced only by manufacturer's personnel. Flame failure safety devices should be checked each time a boiler is fired. Otherwise it should be checked bimonthly. The test should include all units in the shutdown circuit and should cover all the conditions to which such a device will respond.

If low-water cutouts are fitted to the boilers (and they should be), they should be tested at least monthly. The units are dependable, but sediment, corrosion, scale, or other conditions may cause them not to operate when needed.

Maintenance of Power Distribution Equipment

Power distribution equipment such as conductors, raceways, cables, and conduit, when properly sized for the loads encountered and installed in conformity with electrical codes, require very little maintenance. Switchgear should be cleaned and lubricated on a regular basis. Generally, this maintenance can be on a yearly basis unless unusual operating conditions are encountered.

Maintenance of Heating, Ventilating, and Air-Conditioning Equipment

The maintenance of heating, ventilating, and air-conditioning systems varies greatly with the types of installations in the particular plant and location. Air-conditioning equipment is found in almost 100 percent of the offices in industry. Approximately six out of ten plants have some air-conditioning in production areas. This again varies with the type of industry. Hot-air duct heating is used in nearly one-half of the installations, and it is usually a part of the overall heating and air-conditioning system. Nearly one-third of all plants and industries make use of unit heaters in shop production areas. These generally include ventilating equipment. During the heating season or air conditioning season, preventive maintenance will generally consist of lubrication of motors, shafts, etc. Maintenance work is scheduled during the off-season. At that point, the equipment should be carefully inspected so that worn parts may be replaced before failure. Unless there is an unusual amount of dust and pollution in the air where unit heaters are operating, once-a-year cleaning of the equipment should be adequate. This again would be performed during the off-season. The schedule of preventive maintenance should be set up on the basis of the manufacturer's recommended operating and maintenance instructions. There may be problems with equipment that cannot be handled by factory maintenance personnel. The plant engineer should contact manufacturers for services of field engineers for this equipment.

PERSONNEL CONSIDERATIONS

Depending upon the classifications of personnel that are needed, the plant engineer should expect the power plant and utility maintenance staff to display the following characteristics:

1) The ability to adapt to newer, more technical operating and maintenance techniques
2) The willingness and intelligence to increase their knowledge of the power plant operation by subscribing to periodical magazines or by participating in study courses
3) The desire to obtain the education necessary to perform the work expected of them
4) The ability to handle operation, maintenance, paperwork, and performance analysis within the limits of the job requirements.

The classifications of work generally used in the powerhouse and utilities areas are powerhouse operator and/or maintenance man; boiler room operator; powerhouse helper; crane operator or bulldozer operator—for coal handling; electrician; and pipe fitter, heating, and ventilating maintenance man.

Tables V–5, V–6, and V–7 show a typical training schedule for training employees in the classifications of powerhouse operator and/or maintenance man, pipe fitter and ventilating maintenance man, and electrician. Helpers who show an interest in and demonstrate capabilities in powerhouse operation should be considered for the boiler room operator's classification. In turn, the

Table V–5. Training Program — Power House Operator and/or Maintenance Man.

Training Subject	Hours
Boiler room operations	648
Chemistry	54
Electrical department	216
Grinders (external or surface)	36
Lathes	36
Machine maintenance	216
Milling machines	36
Pipefitting, heating, ventilating	216
Power house maintenance	648
Shapers or planers	36
Steam turbines and auxiliary equipment operations	648
Switchboards and power house records and reports	860
Related classroom study	350
Total	4,000

Table V–6. Training Program — Pipe Fitting, Heating, and Ventilating Maintenance Man.

Training Subject	Hours
Pipe fabrication	216
Installation and maintenance of high and low pressure process piping, including air, oil, gas, paint, steam, water, acid, and ammonia	1,266
Installation and maintenance of steam and hot water heating systems with high and low pressure	1,266
Installation of piping for waste, soil, sewage, vent, and leaders	432
Installation and connection of fixtures used in plumbing and drainage system	288
Installation and maintenance of piping on air conditioning and refrigeration systems	144
Repairing of valves, steam traps, air vents, and radiators	180
Related classroom study	208
Total	4,000

boiler room operator's classification could be a good source of employees to be placed in the powerhouse and/or maintenance man classification.

When the supervisor of powerhouse employees assigns duties to his men, he should avoid indefinite responsibilities. If a task is assigned to a particular shift, it may become a neglected assignment, since each man has different ideas of how to do the job or when to do it. Operators generally have parallel duties relating to operation and the daily or shift maintenance connected with it. Unless some employees are doing only maintenance work, the manager may find that it will pay him to assign definite responsibilities for specific equipment to the man best suited to the work.

Table V-7. Apprenticeship for Electrician.

Training Subject	Hours
Electrical construction (including power house, substations, power supplies, machines, and lighting)	2,448
Electrical design	288
Machine maintenance (hydraulics)	216
Maintenance and repair (including machine controls, welders, heat treating equipment, power supplies, transformers, motors, motor repair, generators, hoists, cranes, elevators, and power tools)	4,348
Related classroom study	700
Total	8,000

Lubrication, water testing, chemical feeding, blowdowns, checking of operating conditions, inspections, and many necessary routine functions must be handled on a shift-to-shift or daily basis and must be done by personnel on duty at the time. Multiple-responsibility assignments should be avoided if the best performance is to be obtained from personnel. A schedule of duties should be prepared detailing what should be done by each operator. This is in addition to the maintenance schedule which is worked out for equipment items for each man. The list of duties should be prepared from manufacturers' instruction guides, from information in the plant operating manuals, and from experience gained when something has been omitted.

Chapter 6

Waste and Pollution Control

The 1962 decision by a major steel company to construct an integrated steel plant in northeast Indiana caused many of the residents to wonder, "Will our area be turned into a Gary–East Chicago?" As an indication of the company's determination to avoid this stigma, the second purchase order on the project was placed with a waste-water consulting engineer. To combat pollution, the company uses exhaust treatment systems for the furnaces. They also inject waste pickle liquors and waste ammonia liquors some 4,000 feet below the surface of the ground, and they treat every drop of contaminated effluent prior to discharge. The residents are now reassured. It is clear to them that their environment is not being altered and their property values are not being jeopardized.

But pollution problems are not so easily resolved for existing manufacturing facilities. A new plant can easily by planned, developed, engineered, and operated to meet present regulatory practices with additional capacity to meet more stringent criteria. However, consider the dilemma of a manager of a 20-year-old plant, a marginally profitable operation, which has nothing in the way of treatment facilities – not even separate sewers for toxic wastes – and yet is expected to conform to the same criteria as the new plant.

"Conform to what?" the plant manager may well ask. Every state has individual rules and regulations based in general on the Federal Air and Water Quality Acts. These acts establish criteria for the concentration of contaminants, pH, suspended solids, oils, temperature, and quantity of waste water discharged by plants. Normally, the basis of these criteria is the capacity of the receiving media to assimilate the waste discharges. However, with the growth of our population and industry, this ability to assimilate waste is decreasing rapidly. Cities have regulations for waste-water discharges from manufacturing facilities into their sewage treatment plants based on the amenability of the raw or pretreated waste water to their treatment process. The states bordering the Ohio River have agreed that the plants in the valley will conform to criteria established by the Ohio River Valley Sanitation Commission (ORSANCO).

State regulations along this river vary, and without the ORSANCO regulations two plants of the same corporation on opposite banks of the river would have widely different criteria to conform to.

To complicate the problem still further, there are local effluent standards in some places and river quality standards in others. From the engineering point of view, effluent standards are preferred since they eliminate the need for extremely expensive equipment to determine the assimilative capacity of streams. Another complication is the problem of air pollution. We may have a plant that is discharging SO_2 into the atmosphere. We know the amount discharged, but how can we determine how much this is affecting adjacent areas?

To show the approach taken by one engineer, the following paragraph was used by him in his report to a large midwestern regulatory agency.[1] In the absence of specific standards, the engineer defined the expected effluent characteristics and requested approval for discharge as follows:

Certain criteria have been developed by the Stream Pollution Control Board which are contained in their "Report of Water Quality Criteria and Plan for Implementation." These regulations establish quality requirements for discharge to the receiving streams.

To meet these requirements, the effluents from the plant should contain the following limiting concentrations, etc., based on a 24-hour period except for cyanides which test is based on any single value.

1) Floating solids   — Not objectionable
2) Color   — Not objectionable
3) pH   — 6 to 10
4) Temperature   — Not to exceed 93 F
5) Suspended solids — Not to exceed 25 mg/l
6) Oils   — Not to exceed 5 mg/l above influent
7) BOD   — Not to exceed 15 mg/l
8) Chromes   — Not to exceed 1.0 mg/l
9) Fluorides   — Not to exceed 1.5 mg/l
10) Cyanides   — Not to exceed 0.1 mg/l

All effluent from the plant will meet or be better than the above stipulated requirements.

WATER POLLUTION ABATEMENT

Historically, treatment of water dates back to Biblical times. People 4,000 years ago used the desert sand to filter their drinking water. The treatment of industrial waste waters, however, is quite a recent practice. The paper, petroleum, and steel industries each claim to be the pioneer in developing wastewater treatment facilities. It is a moot question as to who actually was the first. Civil, chemical, and plating engineers are all involved in the design of waste disposal and recovery systems.[2]

[1] *Planning and Making Industrial Waste Surveys* (Cincinnati: Ohio River Valley Water Sanitation Commission, Apr., 1952).

[2] Thomas R. Camp, "Sedimentation and the Design of Settling Tanks," *Transactions of the American Society of Civil Engineers*, Vol. 3 (1946), 895–958; Myron Ceresa and Leslie E. Lancy, "Metal Finishing Waste Disposal," *Metal Finishing*, Vol. 66, No. 4 (Apr., 1968), 56–62; No. 5 (May, 1968), 60–65; No. 6 (June, 1968), 112–18; R. Pinner, "Integrated Recovery Systems in Finishing Department," *Metal Finishing Journal*, Vol. 13, No. 154 (Oct., 1967), 334–39; G. Mattock, "Modern Trends in Effluent Control," *Metal Finishing Journal*, Vol. 14, No. 161 (May, 1968), 168–70; 172–75.

Due to industry and population growth, the ability of our streams and lakes to assimilate waste has reached the vanishing point. These bodies of water are polluted physically, chemically, biologically, and thermally. The physical contamination is caused by solids and oils in the waste water; chemical contamination is caused by dissolved materials, acids, toxics, or nutrients in the discharge; biological contamination is caused by algae, fungi, viruses, bacteria, and other living organisms; thermal pollution is a result of cooling processes required by either furnaces or by ancillary equipment such as heat exchangers, air compressors, air conditioners, etc. Some discharges contain two, three, or more contaminants. Selection of the treatment process depends upon the type and nature of the contaminant carried by the fluid waste water.

The five basic approaches for waste-water treatment are: (1) segregation, (2) separation, (3) alteration, (4) combination, and (5) elimination. One case which illustrates these basics is the plating manufacturer who segregated his storm and industrial water, recirculated cyanide-bearing waste water, treated only the blowdown with his alkaline and acid rinse waters, neutralized his concentrated pickling water, and recirculated uncontaminated cooling waters. All other contaminated process waters were combined and treated prior to discharge to the receiving stream.

The five approaches are defined as follows:

1) *Segregation* is actually not a treatment process. It is the construction of individual piping systems to keep the storm, sanitary, and industrial sewage in separate systems.

2) *Separation* is the process for removing materials or oils by means of lagoons, settling tanks, filters, or flotation units.

3) *Alteration* is the addition of substances to the waste-water stream which either reduce, destroy, render the contaminants harmless, or form a precipitate. Usually alteration is followed by separation.

4) *Combination* is the mixing of more than one waste stream to form a more treatable waste water. This also may be followed by separation. An example is mixing of an acid-bearing water with an alkali waste water.

5) *Elimination* is the destruction or complete removal of the contaminant. It is accomplished by a change in the process, deep-well injection, disinfection, oxidation, evaporation, or incineration.

It must be realized that there are no real criteria for capital investments in waste-water treatment facilities. Segregation in an existing manufacturing plant may be economically impossible. A contaminant in the plant's water supply may make a treatment facility mandatory. Sufficient area may not be available for the use of a lagoon. Therefore, it is essential to acknowledge that each manufacturing plant, no matter what the layout, the product, or the type of operation, is a unique problem. A tabulation of typical water-treatment facility installation costs is shown in Table VI-1.

The only significant facts we can conclude from this Table VI-1 are that equipment costs represent only about 25 percent of the total and that the civil engineering work, etc., is the highest percentage. To safely estimate the cost of facilities for a plant, a complete study with general arrangements, layouts, and other plans is required by qualified engineering personnel.

Table VI–1. Typical Waste-Water Treatment Facility Installation Costs.

	Application		
	*Existing Aluminum Plant**	*New Steel Plant†*	*Plating Works‡*
Cost Area	*1,200 gpm flow*	*46,000 gpm flow*	*700 gpm flow*
Civil, structural and architectural engineering	$410,000	$3,000,000	$165,000
Mechanical and electrical equipment	160,000	3,000,000	55,000
Equipment installation	60,000	1,250,000	25,000
Engineering	70,000	650,000	50,000
Total	$700,000	$7,900,000	$295,000

*Total waste water treatment.
†One major treatment facility; three others not included.
‡One major facility; two others are included.

Major Treatment Methods

Four of the most widely accepted treatment processes are: physical, chemical, biological, and thermal. Most treatment methods consist of a combination of these processes.

Physical treatment is the simplest and least expensive method for the removal of suspended and floating materials from a stream. It relies on the variation in densities of the waste solids or liquids in the carrier. Heat or air may be introduced to accelerate the removal process. Fig. 6–1 shows a flow diagram for the simplest treatment process.

Chemical treatment normally adds one step to the physical process. Generally, one or more coagulants (chemical additives) are introduced into the

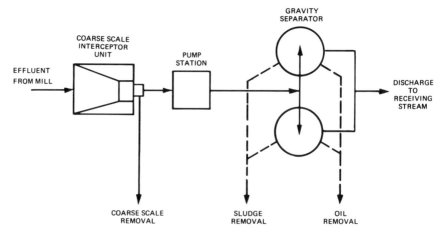

Figure 6–1. Simple physical waste treatment process in a typical steel plant.

stream which react with the fine suspended, dissolved, or colloidal contaminants. When adding these chemicals, a chemical reaction occurs which permits separation by the density variation principle.

Also included in this process is the neutralization of alkaline or acidic waste waters. Depending upon the amounts and types of chemicals present, precipitates may or may not be formed. In most cases, coagulation and flocculation are combined with precipitation. The precipitants are removed by the density principle. The resultant effluent may contain undesirable residual chemicals, either unaffected by the process or possibly formed by chemical reaction. Removal of these contaminants can only be accomplished by elimination, the most costly process. Fig. 6–2 shows a typical flow diagram for chemical treatment.

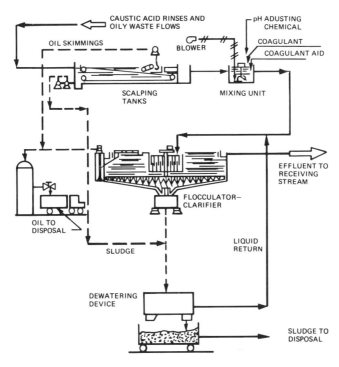

Figure 6-2. Chemical treatment and separation processes in a typical steel plant.

In the biological treatment process, microorganisms convert the waste water contaminants to volatile, separable, or disposable material. It is essential that the environment be maintained fairly uniformly. The process takes place in the presence (aerobic) or complete lack of oxygen (anaerobic). This process is applied to waste waters containing colloidal and dissolved organics. It is also used to concentrate waste waters containing solid organic matter.

In either the aerobic or anaerobic atmosphere, the key element is oxygen. In the former, oxygen is added to reduce the contaminants to the harmless elements nitrogen, carbon dioxide, and water. A fairly recent development in this field is the application of nearly pure oxygen in lieu of air which contains only about 21 percent oxygen. No final results as to the efficiency of the use of pure oxygen for this purpose are available as yet. In the anaerobic process, the bacteria obtain energy by reducing complex organics to simple acids. A second stage of decomposition occurs by the reduction of volatile acids to hydrogen sulfide, carbon dioxide, and methane. Fig. 6–3 shows a flow diagram of a typical biological treatment system.

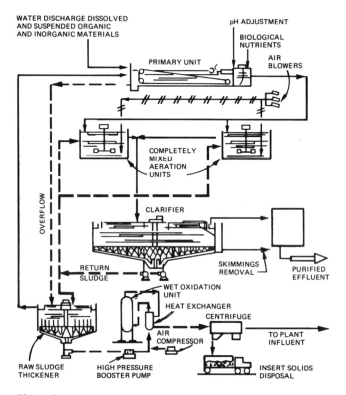

Figure 6–3. Typical biological treatment process in a paper mill.

A new process, which is gaining wide acceptance, is the use of cooling towers for aerating water. Chemicals should be added to prevent solids buildup, to stabilize the water, and to eliminate algae. The cooling tower process may be used with untreated, treated, or cooled water.

Power houses use huge quantities of cooling water in the generation of electricity. Many inland facilities are equipped with closed water recirculation systems. However, the plants located along oceans or lakes are generally once-through systems. These companies have long resisted the imposition of temperature discharge limits. It is virtually certain that regulations will be enacted to control this situation.

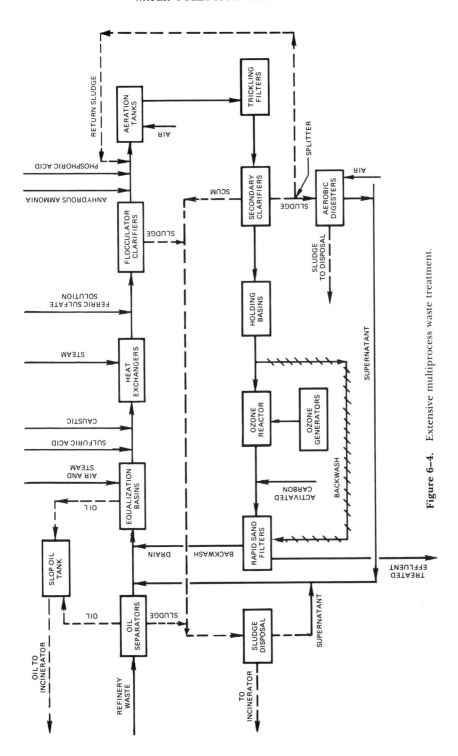

Figure 6-4. Extensive multiprocess waste treatment.

Other Treatment Methods

There are several ways for removing dissolved chemicals besides that of precipitation. These methods include adsorption, ion exchange, and oxidation. Adsorbents such as activated carbon, silica gel, and alumina clays remove the solubles as adsorbed layers. In the ion exchange process, a nonobjectionable ion is exchanged for an objectionable one by attaching itself to the exchange medium. Oxidation by incineration, ozone, and chlorine are other processes of complete destruction. Dialysis, electrodialysis, and reverse osmosis employ selective membranes, which, when combined with driving forces, separate the contaminants from the waste stream. Other complete removal or destruction processes are deep-well injection, regeneration of acids or alkalies, and some patented processes used in connection with the disposition of pickling or plating wastes. All are expensive and leave much to be desired from an operating point of view.

An example of an extensive multiprocess treatment is shown in Fig. 6–4. An examination of this illustration indicates that a combination of methods of treatment is required. In the future, plant engineers will have to consider such combinations in obtaining a satisfactory effluent.

AIR POLLUTION ABATEMENT

Around the fourteenth century, legend has it, King Edward I of England found a blacksmith discharging a noxious black smoke from a fire in his establishment. After lecturing the man, Edward had him executed. The problem of noxious smoke is still with us, but the solution today is not as simple as it was for a fourteenth-century king.

Air pollution is defined as a negative variation from the atmospheric norm. Nowever, the norm has undergone great qualitative changes over the years and is still changing. Emissions into the air are classified as either primary or secondary. The primary types include (1) solids, (2) organic compounds, and (3) sulfur, halogens, or radioactive compounds. Secondary pollutants are more complex. They are the products created by combining two or more primary emissions or the reaction of the primary emissions with the atmosphere and sunlight. Their effects include (1) visibility reduction, (2) material or agricultural damage, (3) physiological effect on man or domestic animals, and (4) psychological effect.

How would you clean up air pollutants? The answer to this question is simply to use devices that will eliminate emissions and provide high stacks to disperse offensive substances. A plant manager may protest that this will cost a great deal of money, but this is not necessarily true. Technology can achieve a good deal even with limited financial resources. The following data represents guideline air pollution abatement costs.

Representative Costs

The only industry to publish rule-of-thumb costs for typical air pollution abatement facilities is the steel industry. A tabulation of these costs is given in Table VI-2. The cost variations shown in this table indicate that estimating ranges from very difficult to next to impossible; thus, plant engineers definitely require outside assistance from consultants or suppliers.

Table VI–2. Typical Costs for Air Pollution Abatement Facilities.

Type of Collector	Equipment Cost ($/cfm)	Erection Cost ($/cfm)	Yearly Maintenance and Repair Cost ($/cfm)
Mechanical collector	.07– .25	.03–.12	.005–.02
Electrostatic precipitator	.25–1.00	.12–.50	.01 –.025
Fabric filter	.35–1.25	.25–.50	.02 –.08
Wet scrubber	.10– .40	.04–.16	.02 –.05

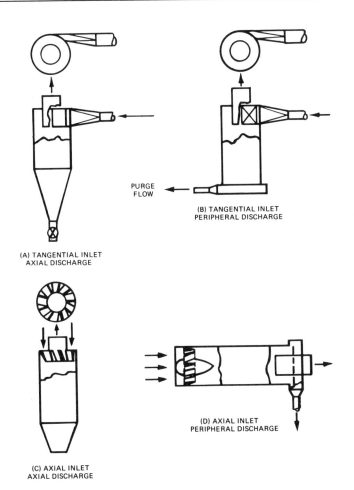

(A) TANGENTIAL INLET AXIAL DISCHARGE

PURGE FLOW

(B) TANGENTIAL INLET PERIPHERAL DISCHARGE

(C) AXIAL INLET AXIAL DISCHARGE

(D) AXIAL INLET PERIPHERAL DISCHARGE

Figure 6–5. Four types of centrifugal separators or cyclones for air emission control.

Control Systems

Source control is the preferred method of treatment of air pollutants. The five best known methods are: (1) centrifugal force, (2) filtration, (3) electrostatic precipitation, (4) liquid scrubbing, and (5) gas-solid adsorption.

Centrifugal Force. This is the primary mechanism for collecting particles in a vertical separator. In other separation equipment, such as filters, liquid scrubbers, etc., the force is significant but is not of primary consequence in the method. The cyclone or centrifugal separator is the least costly and has the lowest collection efficiency of all the air pollution control systems. In general, the efficiency of such units is directly proportional to the particle size; the larger the particles the greater the efficiency. Design factors for cyclones include body diameter/height ratio, cone design, inlet design, dust discharge, gas outlet design, and effect of internal roughness. Probably the most troublesome part of the operation of the cyclone is the erosion that occurs as a result of dust particles impacting on the cyclone wall. Four popular cyclone designs are shown in Fig. 6–5.

Filters. Filtration is the most efficient and desirable method for removing particulates from gases. Filters generally operate at satisfactory efficiency with moderate power consumption. However, the lowest operation cost occurs with the highest initial expenditure. A typical bag filter is shown in Fig. 6–6. This design employs reverse flow and mechanical shaking for cleaning.

Industrial installations usually employ fabric-type filters to recover valuable material. These filters commonly consist of a tubular bag or envelope on top of a wire frame. Gases pass from the outside inward, and the material is collected and removed periodically. The frequency of material removal is based on the

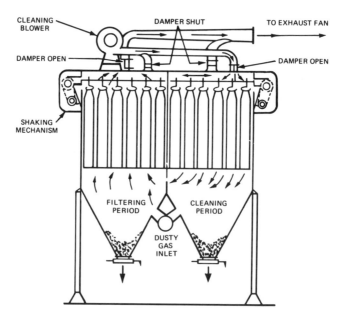

Figure 6–6. Typical emission particle bag filter.

increase in differential pressure across the medium. Methods of cleaning vary according to manufacture, material, and installation. Quite often the change of the filter medium is an important factor. Other filter or substrate materials used are paper for radioactive materials or bacterial particulates, fibrous mats for air conditioning or ventilation systems, and aggregate bed filters for coke plants. Cleaning of these filters is quite complicated and costs are high.

Electrostatic Precipitation. This removal process is accomplished by passing the gas between a pair of electrodes—one being a discharge electrode at a high potential and the other an electronically grounded electrode. The potential difference must be high enough so that a corona discharge surrounds the discharge electrode. A tube-type electrostatic precipitator is shown is Fig. 6–7. The operating efficiency of these devices has been estimated at 95 percent or

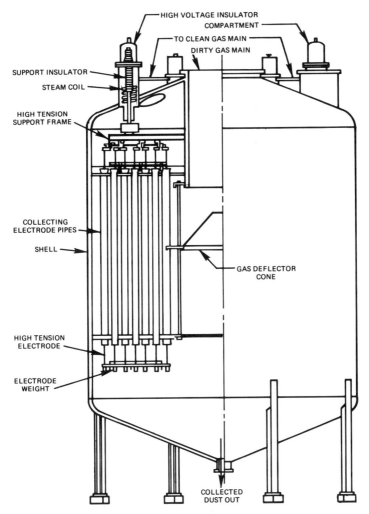

Figure 6–7. Tube-type electrostatic air emission precipitator.

higher. The major factor accounting for these high efficiencies is that the energy applied is directed to the particles to be removed. The disadvantages are the high initial cost, spark problems, and consequent explosion hazards if either particles or gas are combustible.

Liquid Scrubbing. When water is used as the liquid cleaning medium, the problem of air pollution is replaced by that of water pollution. However, this difficulty can be eliminated if the final effluent from the liquid scrubbing operation meets the water quality standards. When oils or other substances are used as the liquid cleaning medium, the solids may be removed by coagulation, sedimentation, filtration, or other methods and the liquid recirculated.

The liquid scrubbing method is effective for both particle removal and gas absorption. For the former, the number and variety of designs of scrubbers available are bewildering; however, the basic mechanisms for removal are few. Inertial force is the dominant feature, while electrostatic attraction, diffusion, thermal forces, and sedimentation are also effective. Typical liquid scrubbing devices are shown in Fig. 6–8.

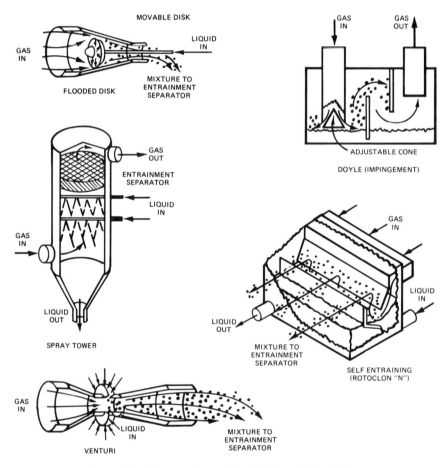

Figure 6–8. Spray and atomizing liquid scrubbing devices.

An example of the use of liquid scrubbing for gas absorption is the removal of SO_2 from a gas by passing it through a $Na(HO)_3$ solution. The sodium combines with the SO_2 to form a sodium sulfate precipitate. The rate of absorption of the gas is affected by the rate at which the reactant can be added to replace itself and the speed of the chemical reaction. Intermixing is usually accomplished between the gas and the reactant by (1) the dispersion of the gas, (2) the use of agitation, (3) the addition of packing elements, (4) the type of suspension used, or (5) the speed of removal of the residue.

Gas-solid Adsorption. This process uses the tendency of a gas or vapor to adhere to a solid. The most widely used solids are activated carbon, siliceous oxides, and metallic oxides. Adsorption depends upon many factors, including concentration, size, shape, temperature, and chemical nature. Disposal is by concentration, destruction, or solvent recovery. A typical flow diagram for a solvent recovery system is shown in Fig. 6–9.

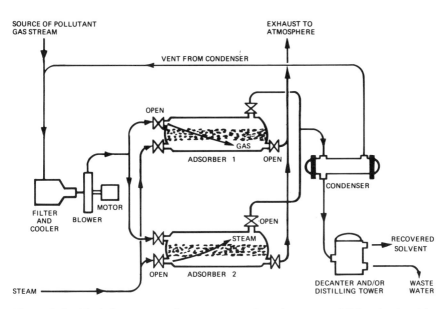

Figure 6–9. Typical two-stage solvent-recovery adsorption system. While adsorber 1 is adsorbing, adsorber 2 is being steamed. After the first adsorber is saturated and number 2 is cleaned, their functions are reversed.

Ultimate costs are the key to process selection. Some variables, used to determine cost in a chemical plant are the following:

1) Current delivered equipment costs.
2) Installed equipment costs. This is taken from the manufacturer's literature or is calculated at 1.5 times the delivered cost.
3) Process piping. This is estimated to be 30 to 60 percent of the installed cost.
4) Instrumentation. This is estimated to be 3 to 20 percent of the installed cost, depending upon the amount of automatic control.
5) Buildings and site preparation. This is estimated to be 10 to 30 percent of

installed cost for outdoor and 60 to 100 percent for indoor facilities.

6) Auxiliaries. This is estimated at 0 to 5 percent of installed cost for minor additions and from 25 to 100 percent for new facilities.

7) Outside lines not integral with the process. These are estimated at 5 to 15 percent of installed cost for intermediate cases.

DEVELOPING THE PROGRAM FOR IMPLEMENTATION

Generally, the implementation of a waste pollution abatement program is divided into the following five phases:

Phase I   — Initiate the program by selecting the engineering consultant.

Phase II   — Define the problem, analyze the wastes, conduct treatability tests during operation or on a similar facility (for a new addition), prepare the design report, and establish a budget cost.

Phase III — Design engineer, prepare specifications, solicit bids, purchase equipment and/or construction services.

Phase IV — Construct the facilities.

Phase V   — Start up the equipment and assure that it meets the specifications and the design requirements.

Phase I — Select the Consultant

There are three alternatives to follow in initiating the program: either an "in-house expert" is used, a vendor is consulted, or a professional engineer specializing in this field is retained. The use of a plant's engineering staff has generally been found to be unsuccessful, since its technical knowledge is slanted toward production and its time is limited. Vendors are primarily interested in selling their products and thus cannot be objective in their recommendations. Limited or complete use of the consulting engineers (alone or in conjunction with the contractor) is considered to be the most satisfactory method.

In recent years, professional pollution control consulting engineers are being used with greater frequency. Spurred on by industry's demands to complete this work economically, these consultants either design or review the selection of the required control equipment, or assist the companies' own in-house specialists. In fact, in 1967 a total of 2,000 companies completed treatment facilities, many designed by consultants. An excellent treatise on this subject, from the March, 1969, edition of *Modern Manufacturing*, emphasizes the following considerations in choosing the consulting engineer:

1) Prepare a list of prequalified engineering concerns with similar installations, after discussions with authorities, including the state regulatory agency.

2) Mail to each selected concern details of your waste problems and request examples of similar installations they have designed.

3) Check their references concerning their previously completed plant's operation, startup of the designed facilities, etc.

4) Invite three or four to an interview for a more comprehensive discussion.

5) Select the individual engineer to complete the study. Remember engi-

neering is "people oriented," and it is essential that their proposed project manager be interviewed.

6) During their study to ascertain the nature of the problem, decide whether the engineering department, the selected engineer, or another engineer will be chosen to complete the detailed design.

It is essential that the waste discharges for the entire plant's operational cycle be reviewed, the effluent's contaminants be acknowledged, and no data or discharge covered up.

Phase II — Prepare a Design Report

The end result of the study program is the design report. It should include the following as a minimum:

1) The recommended treatment process, including descriptions of the modifications to existing facilities and the required new facilities. A background of the other alternatives investigated with the reasons for not recommending their adoption should be included.

2) Organization of the report so that portions can be abstracted and submitted to regulatory agencies to assure that the work is under way and the end results will comply with the requirements of the agency.

3) Drawings which show equipment arrangement and engineering details to indicate how the proposed facilities will fit into the plant.

4) A detailed study to establish operating costs and capital expenditures required for the new facilities. These costs should be given in sufficient detail that questions from management can be answered.

5) A phased construction program which will permit the establishment of a budget.

Phase III — Prepare the Specifications

Each plant will have specific design engineering requirements for this phase. In some cases the work will be performed with in-house personnel. In other cases the company will allow the contractors to purchase and install the equipment to their own standards. Still other firms will have plant standards to which the contractors must conform. It is the plant engineer's responsibility to establish the drawing and specification requirements prior to obtaining proposals for engineering services. A copy of a typical bid inquiry for these services is given as follows:

Bid Inquiry Data

The engineer shall provide the services described below for the facilities indicated in our Design Report attached to this inquiry. These services shall include at least the following:

1) Providing detailed specifications for mechanical equipment, instrumentation and controls, and electrical equipment utilizing applicable plant standards.

2) Preparing construction engineering drawings, bills of material for foundations, embedded steel, mechanical equipment, piping, civil work, instrumentation, and electrical work for new facilities and modifications to existing facilities. (Design engineering drawings are required only for building superstructures, tankage, and appurtenances.)

3) Completing detailed construction estimates based on the construction engineering drawings.

4) Preparing a final report, a portion of which can be used for transmittal to appropriate regulatory agencies.
5) Comparing bidder's proposals with recommendations to purchase.
6) Reviewing and approving all equipment suppliers' certified drawings and shop fabrication drawings.
7) Conducting field observations and consultations during construction, at mutually agreed stages, on a per diem basis.
8) Preparing operation manuals for the designed facilities.

Phase IV — Construct the Facilities

Overseeing the construction of the facilities is the responsibility of the plant engineer. Additionally, normal plant operations must be maintained during the period of construction of the new facilities. Several important points to be kept in mind are the need for progress reporting, including comparison with the original construction schedule; field superintendence (with one man in charge) to make on-the-spot decisions; parking and storage facilities for personnel and equipment; coordination between other contractors or production personnel; issuance of written or oral field orders; and revision of drawings to bring them up to date to make sure there is an as-built set for operations.

Phase V — Startup of the Equipment

Startup services is an example of the problem of who does what. Some maintain it should be the job of the operations people, and others say the contractor. Both groups are undermanned and usually do not have the expertise. So lately, plant engineers are choosing the phase III engineer to complete these services. He knows the process, is familiar with the intent of the specifications and the total operation. However, the operations people, who will be responsible ultimately, should be on the site during this period to both observe and function.

After the facilities are operating and have been "de-bugged," there is normally a one-year guarantee on the operation of the equipment. The process responsibility should have been assigned previously to the phase III engineer. The operations personnel then take over, and a program should be established for periodic monitoring to report to either state or local authorities. Typical examples of the monitoring data which should be prepared during this stage are shown in Tables VI–3 and VI–4, an example of a monthly pollution control report submitted to a midwestern state.

FUTURE DEVELOPMENTS

The residues from water and air pollution control devices are major dilemmas for each plant installing abatement facilities. A simple treatment process such as neutralization of an acid or alkali often creates as difficult a problem as it solves. When sulfuric acid pickle liquor is neutralized in a steel plant, a gelatinous hydroxide sludge is formed and the treated effluent contains suspended solids with a high iron salt content. The resultant sludge can be thickened and dewatered on vacuum filters, centrifuges, or drying beds. The reduction in water content is limited by these means. Further reduction is possible by means of an incinerator. (Note the use of the word *possible* — no one has built an operable unit at this time.) After drying, the residues could be used for land fill.

Table VI-3. Waste-Water Pollution Abatement Summary.

Description	Origin	Characteristic or Composition	Basic Treatment Process
Steel Industry			
Flue dust	Blast or basic oxygen furnace and other gas washer systems	Iron oxides and coke	Physical or physical-chemical
Waste ammonia liquor	Coke plant	Phenol, cyanide, and light oils	Biological-physical or deep well
Mill scale	Hot-rolling mills	Iron oxides	Physical or chemical-physical
Oil bearing waste-water	Cold-rolling mills	Suspended solids and oils	Chemical-physical
Pickling waters	Cold mills	Dissolved acid and bases, and suspended solids	Chemical-physical or deep well
Cooling water	All facilities	Temperature	Thermal
Pulp and Paper Industry			
Rinses	Bleaching, thickening, de-inking, defiltering	Dissolved chemical dyes, oils, and fiber	Biological, physical
Wash waters	Pulp washers	Suspended pulp, dissolved chemicals	Biological, physical or chemical-physical
White waters	Paper machines	Fibers, dye	Physical or chemical-physical
Digester liquor	Chemical and mechanical digestion	Concentrated organics, suspended pulp, sulfates and sulfides	Biological, chemical-physical
Oil Refineries and Petrochemical Industry			
Oil emulsions	Distillation units	Oils, organics and suspended inorganics	Chemical-physical or biological
Scrubber discharges and solvents	Process units	Sulfur compounds, acids and alkalis, phenols	Physical or chemical-physical
Sludges	Recovery units	Insoluble sulfur compounds, tars	Physical

Table VI-3. Wastewater Pollution Abatement Summary (*Continued*).

Description	Origin	Characteristic of Composition	Basic Treatment Process
Oil Refineries and Petrochemical Industry (*Continued*)			
Miscellaneous	Oil tanks	Brines, suspended material, lead compounds	Physical or chemical-physical
Cooling water	Recirculation system blowdowns	Temperature	Thermal
Chemical and Pharmaceutical Industry			
Wash products	Soap and detergent	Dissolved chemicals	Chemical-physical
Solvents	Explosives manufacture, insecticides	Dissolved organic solvents	Chemical-physical
Solvents, acids, bases, and salts	Organic chemicals production	Suspended and dissolved complexes	Physical, chemical
Acids, bases, salts	Acid and caustic production, fertilizer plants, inorganics	Dissolved salts, sulfates, chlorides, nitrates, phosphates	Physical, chemical
Spent wastes	Antibiotics, medicines	Dissolved inorganics, organics, fungi, bacteria, suspended materials	Physical, biological, chemical
Mines and Ore Dressing Industry			
Mine drainage	Ground water	Acid water	Chemical-physical
Tailings, gangue	Ore beneficiation	Suspended solids, dissolved salts	Physical, chemical

Table VI-3. Wastewater Pollution Abatement Summary (*Continued*).

Description	Origin	Characteristic of Composition	Basic Treatment Process
Textile Industry			
Wash waters	Dyeing, oiling, washing, sizing, fulling	Dissolved chemicals, soaps	Chemical-physical
Scour waste	Scouring	Greases, dissolved and suspended solids	Physical, chemical
Food Processing Industry			
Organic washes	Agricultural chemicals	Suspended and dissolved materials, oils, starch pulp, organic sugars	Biological, physical, or chemical
Rinsing and wash waters	Cleaning raw products	Suspended colloidal and dissolved organic materials	Biological, physical, or chemical
Liquid and solid residues	Vegetables processing Fruit – hulls, trimmings; Meat – blood, manure, tankwater, slimes	Suspended colloidal and dissolved organic materials	Biological, physical, or chemical
Cleaning waters	Equipment, packaging and washdown	Suspended colloidal and dissolved organic materials	Biological, physical, or chemical

Table VI–4. Air Pollution Abatement Summary.

Source	Availability of Technology	Remarks
Electrical Generating or Industrial Heating Plants		
Coal fired	Removal of particles, smoke, and CO; none for SO and NO	Control of particulate during soot blowing required
Oil fired	Removal of smoke and CO, particulates, see note below; none for SO	Partial control of NO is possible
Gas fired	Particles and smoke not applicable, removal of CO	Partial control of NO is possible
Industrial Incinerators		
Single chamber	None for particles, CO, smoke, or organics	Eliminate single-chamber type from air pollution standpoint
Multiple chamber	Removal of particles, smoke, CO, organics	More effective control of particulate emissions required
Steel Industry		
Coke plants	Removal of ammonia, benzol, and organics; none for particles, SO, or odors	Old ovens impossible to control, emissions while charging and discharging difficult to control
Blast furnace	Removal of particles, SO; none for NO	Some furnaces use CO as fuel
Sinter plant	Removal of particles, SO, CO, and fluorides; none for NO	Control extremely difficult for older plants
Open hearths	See note below	Being phased out for production purposes; old plants cannot afford new devices
Basic oxygen furnace	Removal of particles and CO; none for NO	Control during blows has caused many local pollution problems
Electric furnaces	Removal of particles; none for NO	Control during filling and charging not controlled
Scarfing in many mill applications	For particle removal in many older facilities, see note below	

NO – Nitrogen oxides.
CO – Carbon monoxide.
SO – Sulfur oxides.
Note – Emission control feasible, but uneconomical in relation to capital investment, cost of finished product, or ability of operator to control in relationship to costs.

Table VI–4. Air Pollution Abatement Summary (*Continued*).

Source	Availability of Technology	Remarks
Aluminum Industry Primary reduction	Removal of particles and fluorides; none for carbonaceous matter	Fluoride control poor in Soderburg furnaces
Secondary processes	Removal of particles and chlorine	
Ore Smelting and Refining Lead, zinc, and copper smelting	Removal of particles and SO; none for NO	
Zinc, brass, and taconite refinery	Removal of particles; none for NO	Small scrap reclaiming operations consider control extremely burdensome
Petroleum Industry Refining	Removal of hydrocarbons and hydrogen sulfide	Control is difficult for obnoxious odors in refineries
Cracking, reforming, and treating	Removal of particles, CO, hydrogen sulfide, and odors	Odors often very noticeable
Solvents and Paints Paint spraying	Removal of particles; none for solvents	Solvent removal, see note below
Degreasing and oven	Removal of solvent; none for water vapor and NO	Europeans have process for water vapor removal
Paper Industry Digesters	Removal of sulfur compounds	Older facilities have problems
Smelt tanks and lime kilns	Removal of particles and sulfur compounds; none for NO	
Recovery furnace	Removal of particles and CO; none for SO, NO, and sulfur compounds	Odorous sulfur–compound odors usually very poor
Evaporators	None for sulfur compounds and odors	

NO—Nitrogen oxides.
CO—Carbon monoxide.
SO—Sulfur oxides.
Note—Emission control feasible, but uneconomical in relation to capital investment, cost of finished product, or ability of operator to control in relationship to costs.

Table VI-4. Air Pollution Abatement Summary (*Continued*)

Source	Availability of Technology	Remarks
Chemical Industry		
Sulfuric acid	Removal of mist and SO; none for NO	Better control required for SO
Other acids	Removal of solvents and mists	Chlorine and fluoride control often difficult; particulates cause problems in some cases
Synthetic ammonia	Removal of organic base ammonia	Technology well developed for large plants
Ammonia soda ash	Removal of ammonia soda and gas	
Lime	Removal of particles and NO	
Caustic soda	Removal of hydrocarbons, hydrochloric acid, and vinyl chloride compounds	Requires extremely tight process' control
Alum	Removal of particles and mists	Control difficult in older plants
Miscellaneous: rubber, formaldehyde, etc.	Removal of particles, mist, etc., possible	Odor control is poor and tight system required
Food Processing		
General	Removal of particles and odors possible	Smoke, odor control, chlorides are often unsatisfactory

NO—Nitrogen oxides.
CO—Carbon monoxide.
SO—Sulfur oxides.
Note—Emission control feasible, but uneconomical in relation to capital investment, cost of finished product, or ability of operator to control in relationship to costs.

Organic sludges generated in biological treatment plants can be digested to reduce their volatile matter. The remaining residues have been used successfully for fertilizer in some areas. However, residues from other biological processes, such as from coke or oil refineries, can only be incinerated, and this process creates an air pollution problem.

Oils and skimmings can be removed from waste waters, but at high costs. When removal requires the addition of metal salts for cracking, the operating costs increase greatly and the same sludge problems described above are then present. As sanitary-fill areas for waste disposal become increasingly difficult to find, increased attention will be given to the problem of disposing of these sludges.

All those in this young field of pollution abatement believe the key to the problem is recirculation. In fact, one steel company is attempting to recirculate waste gases. An auto manufacturer is considering treatment and recirculation of all industrial water used with tertiary treatment by reverse osmosis of the blowdown. In many plants, attempts are being made to reconstitute sludge and incinerate the remainder. Removed oils and greases are being employed in the incineration of all the burnable rubbish in one plant. To reduce the size and cost of waste treatment facilities, some industries pretreat their wastes and discharge them to city sewage treatment plants for final treatment.

The above are the challenges facing engineering, research, and development. The answer to them is simple — develop the most economically feasible solution to meet the present problems with the ability to modify them in the future.

Chapter 7

Safety and
Plant Protection

Safety and plant protection are undoubtedly the most important of the secondary responsibilities of the plant engineer. When safety and plant protection are not under the plant engineering department, they are usually found under the personnel department. This is particularly true when the plant is engaged in sensitive government work and security clearances, document accountability, and arrangements for classified visitors are major activities.

SAFETY

The old saying, Accidents don't just happen; they are caused! is still true today. Proper selection of equipment, adequate training, and careful supervision of personnel are essential to trouble-free operation. Accidents seriously affect the efficiency of a company through injuries to personnel and damage to equipment and materials. Additionally, workmen's compensation insurance premiums are higher for a company with a poor safety record.

Safety is primarily a management concern. A worker is rarely disciplined for having hurt himself on the job unless the injury occurred as a result of gross neglect of the rules, jeopardizing others as well as himself. Top management's attitude toward accident prevention in a company is almost invariably reflected in the attitude of the supervisory force. Similarly, the worker's attitude is usually the same as that of his supervisor. If top management is not genuinely interested in preventing accidents and injuries, no one else is likely to be. An accident prevention program must have the demonstrated support of management if employee cooperation and participation are to be obtained.

A company or plant that attempts to curb accidents without a definite guiding policy — one which is planned, publicized, and promoted — will always be simply "putting out fires." The details for carrying out an accident prevention program may be assigned, but the responsibility for the basic policy cannot be delegated. At the beginning of such a program, a considerable amount of high-level attention is necessary because safety is often a new activity and involves unfamiliar procedures. Consequently, the overall policy should state clearly the objectives to be achieved.

To initiate the safety program, top management must issue a statement of policy for the guidance of managers, supervisors, and employees. Such a statement of policy will indicate management's point of view and should cover in general the basic elements of the policy. Organizations like the National Safety Council and the large insurance carriers are very interested in safety and can provide a great deal of information in this area. However, management should avoid the verbatim use of advice from such sources. If employees are to be impressed by the seriousness of management's interest in safety, then they must be addressed in simple, matter-of-fact terms without the use of generalities and clichés which give the program a specious "window-dressing" appearance.

Top management's responsibility for the safety program does not end with the establishment of the safety organization and approval of its activities. Executives must take the initiative in keeping interest alive. Safety departments or activities, like any other phase of business, must have leadership and guidance. It is essential that management assign full responsibility for safety activities to a single individual. The decision concerning placement of the responsibility will be based on the size of the company and the nature of its operations.

Safety Program

The man responsible for the safety program may be known as the safety engineer, the supervisor of safety, or the director of safety, depending upon the size of the organization, the nature of the duties assigned, his personal qualifications, and the kind of assistance given him. Whatever his title, the safety man will be responsible for solving two principal problems—how to remove physical hazards from the plant, and how to substitute safe practices for unsafe practices.

Accident prevention must deal with both of these problems. A good safety program will be wasted if it is not accompanied by successful training and motivation of employees. Similarly, the most impressive employee relations program will fall flat if employees suspect that management is interested in reducing the number of accidents only if this can be accomplished at a very modest cost. Safety personnel, therefore, must be selected so that both the engineering and training aspects of the job are well handled.

The duties of the safety engineer include:

1) Formulating, administering, and making necessary changes in the program
2) Submitting weekly or monthly reports to management
3) Acting in an advisory capacity on all safety matters
4) Maintaining an accident record system, personally investigating and reporting on all major accidents, supervising the investigations made by his staff, reviewing the accident reports filed by supervisors, and checking the corrective action taken by the supervisor
5) Cooperating with the education department in the safety training of all employees
6) Cooperating with the medical department to ensure proper selection and placement of employees
7) Making personal inspections and supervising inspections made by his

staff and by special employee committees for the purpose of discovering and correcting unsafe conditions

8) Maintaining outside professional contacts to exchange information with other safety people and to keep the safety program up to date

9) Making certain that federal, state, and local laws, ordinances, etc., bearing on safety matters are complied with

10) Securing necessary advice from state labor departments or insurance carriers on matters pertaining to safety and health

11) Controlling or supervising fire prevention or fire-fighting activities where these are not the responsibility of other departments

12) Approving designs of new equipment and reviewing the safety aspects of new construction and remodeling.

The amount of assistance needed by the safety engineer in dealing with these requirements depends upon his degree of responsibility, the size of the company, its operating policies, and the type of operation.

Hazardous Areas

There are certain areas of the plant to which the safety engineer should give particular attention. These include those locations where welding, plating, and solvent cleaning are being performed. When welding operations are performed on a small scale, it is satisfactory to secure the gas directly from cylinders. If the welding production is larger, the gas supplies may be centralized by means of manifolds. A separate manifold should be used for each gas. When cylinders are used they should be securely fastened to a post or other upright structure, or mounted in a special cart. Unfastened cylinders are easily knocked over and can cause injuries.

Both oxygen and acetylene are supplied in high-pressure cylinders that are manufactured, tested, and maintained in accordance with the regulations of the Interstate Commerce Commission. They are shipped in a high-pressure state to permit economical transportation. Therefore, users must not tamper with, alter, or otherwise change these cylinders in any respect. Should anything unusual develop in connection with a compressed gas cylinder, it should be moved outdoors away from any possible source of ignition, and the supplier should be notified immediately. Follow his instructions on handling and disposal.

In plating operations, large quantities of toxic and corrosive substances are handled. However, the operations can be conducted so there is no danger to the health of the workers. The hazardous substances include the cyanides, chromates, and heavy metals such as lead and zinc. Additionally, hydrochloric, sulfuric, and hydrofluoric acids are used.

Some of the measures to be observed in dealing with these substances consist of training in safe handling procedures, adequate ventilation, and protective equipment. Protective equipment includes a U.S. Bureau of Mines–approved toxic dust respirator, a face shield or goggles, rubber gloves, and protective apron and trousers. Any spilled material should be flushed away. Drench showers should be provided to cope with splashes on personnel.

In solvent cleaning operations it has always been assumed that fire was the principal hazard. However, in recent years there has been a trend toward the use of the nonflammable chlorinated hydrocarbons, such as trichlorethylene or perchlorethylene. The solvent cleaning procedure consists of immersing parts in tanks of solvent to dissolve oil or grease. The solvent is sometimes heated and agitated but is usually at room temperature. Other types of cleaning are frequently used in conjunction with the solvent cleaning.

In vapor degreasing, a refinement of the solvent cleaning method, the parts to be cleaned are suspended in the solvent vapor which condenses on the parts and drains off with the dissolved oil and grease. Adequate ventilation is extremely important in both vapor degreasing and solvent cleaning operations. No degreaser should be installed near open flames, high-temperature surfaces (750° F or above), or welding operations. High temperature breaks down the solvent, causing the release of highly toxic gases.

The great danger in solvent cleaning is the flammability of the solvents. Of the 50 most commonly used solvents, only a few are nonflammable—carbon tetrachloride, chloroform, methyl chloroform, methyl chloride, perchlorethylene, tetrachlorethane, trichlorethylene, and the fluorinated hydrocarbons. All of the other commonly used solvents are flammable, some much more so than others. While most solvents have flash points well above ordinary room temperatures, others do not and are very easily ignited.

Areas in which flammable vapors are present are designated as Class I in Article 500 of the *National Electric Code.* In many locations the local fire department will have rules or codes which regulate construction, electrical equipment, storage, transfer, and other factors relative to the use and handling of flammable liquids. In other locations, labor department or health department rules may provide control. In the absence of specific rules, or even if such rules exist but are less rigid, the *National Electric Code* provisions should be followed to ensure an adequate level of safety for the operation.

PLANT PROTECTION

The three major aspects of plant protection are fire prevention, fire protection, and plant security. Fire prevention is the program which guards against or prevents fires. Fire protection is the program for combatting or checking a fire once it has started. Plant security is the program for safeguarding the facilities against intruders, sabotage, and theft. The best practice appears to be to have these three activities under a single chief or supervisor, with guards doubling as firemen when a fire does break out.

Fire Prevention

Fire prevention is a program, like safety, which requires proper instruction, adequate training, careful supervision of personnel, and management support. Unless employees, supervision, and management act as a supportive group for the program, any effort directed toward fire prevention cannot be effective. It is difficult to overemphasize the importance of fire prevention. A fire is probably the fastest possible way to put a company out of business and people out of work.

The best time to stop a fire is before it starts. Even though buildings are properly designed and provided with protective devices and fire-safety features, only regular periodic inspections can ensure their full value. In addition to inspections made by insurance companies, the fire protection bureaus of fire departments, and state agencies, every industrial plant should include periodic self-inspections in its fire prevention program.

In many plants the responsibility for locating and reporting fire hazards is entrusted to the fire brigade or one of its members. The function of these brigades is to inspect for common fire causes such as poor housekeeping, improper storage of flammable materials, smoking violations, and excessive accumulation of dust or flammable material. Regardless of the size of the plant, fire hazards can be detected and eliminated through frequent inspections. Fire-fighting equipment should be checked regularly to make sure that it is ready for any emergency.

The inspector, fire chief, or other individual in charge of fire prevention should have a complete list of all the equipment that should be inspected at regular intervals. If fire brigade members are assigned to this duty, they should receive special instructions. It is best to have men alternate on inspections. Fire equipment inspection should cover the following checklist:

    1) Control valves on fire protection systems are open and sealed
    2) Hydrants are operative and water pressure is adequate
    3) Fire pump is functioning properly
    4) Hose and hose-house equipment is in good condition
    5) Sprinkler system reserve tank is full
    6) Special types of protection (carbon dioxide, foam, or other automatic systems) are operative
    7) Fire alarm system is operative
    8) Extinguishers, masks, resuscitators, etc., are all in good condition
    9) Fire doors, fire escapes, and access ladders are all in good repair

In addition to fire equipment, electrical equipment, and machinery and processing equipment, housekeeping conditions should be checked at regular intervals. In some high-hazard occupancies, daily inspections are required. Otherwise, thorough weekly or monthly inspections are satisfactory, especially if the plant safety committee inspects for simple fire causes.

Special inspections may be required following alterations to the plant. A complete check, early enough in the season for replacement or repair, should be made of equipment that was exposed to freezing temperatures. For the greatest benefit, a written record should be kept as shown in Fig. 7–1. It should be a form that is drawn up specifically for the conditions of the individual plant. This form will assist the inspector in making comments and bringing recommendations to the attention of those responsible.

Careless smoking is probably the most common cause of industrial fires. Although it might be desirable to eliminate smoking completely in a plant, such a rule is difficult to enforce. It is better to allow smoking at specified times and in safe places where supervision can be maintained than to have it done surreptitiously in out-of-the-way places. "No Smoking" areas should be marked with conspicuous signs. The rule should be rigorously enforced. Everyone, including visitors and management, should adhere to the regulation. It may be necessary to use more than signs to draw attention to the "No Smoking" areas. Colored lines on the floor and illuminated barriers have been effective around high-hazard areas. Even in plants where there is little fire hazard, employees

SPRINKLER VALVES		Open	Shut	Sealed
	AREA CONTROLLED			
1.	P. I. V. # 1 – N. W. Section			
2.	P. I. V. # 2 – S. W. Section			
3.	City Pit – S. W. Corner – Bldg. 105			
4.	S. C. V. # 1			
5.	S. C. V. # 2			
6.	P. I. V. # 3 – Center N to S			
7.	S. C. V. # 3			
8.	S. C. V. # 4			
9.	P. I. V. # 4 – S. E. Section			
10.	P. I. V. # 5 – N. E. Section			
11.	East S. C. V. # 5 – S. & E. of P. I. V. # 5			
12.	East S. C. V. # 6 – to Engineering Bldg.			
13.	East S. C. V. # 7 – P. I. V.'s # 6, # 7, # 8			
14.	P. I. V. # 6 – MBA # 1 South 1/3			
15.	P. I. V. # 7 – MBA # 1 Mid 1/3			
16.	P. I. V. # 8 – MBA # 1 North 1/3			
17.	East S. C. V. # 8			
18.	P. I. V. # 11 – MBA # 3 S. E. 1/2 Section			
19.	P. I. V. # 12 – MBA # 3 N. E. 1/2 Section			
20.	S. C. V. # 9 – MBA # 3 N. E.			
21.	P. I. V. # 13 – N. E. Bldg. 108			
22.	P. I. V. # 14 – N. E. Bldg. 108			
23.	P. I. V. # 15 – N. E. Center Bldg. 108			
24.	S. C. V. # 10 – North P. I. V. # 15 Bldg. 108			
25.	P. I. V. # 16 – North Center Bldg. 108			
26.	P. I. V. # 17 – West Center Bldg. 108			

Date_____

Buildings 105, 106, 107, 108, 109, 110, 111, 112

WATER PRESSURE: _____ lb. at yard level.

FIRE PUMP: Turned over and found in good condition? _____

Suction reservoir full? _____ Heating system in use? _____

Temperature at cold water return _____ Circulation good? _____

HYDRANTS AND HOSE EQUIPMENT: In good condition? _____

AUTOMATIC SPRINKLERS: Any heads missing? _____

Disconnected? _____ Obstructed by high-piled stock? _____

Any rooms not sufficiently heated to prevent freezing? _____

How many extra heads available? _____

SPRINKLER ALARMS: Tested? _____ In good condition? _____

Do not test hydraulic alarms when temperatures are below freezing.

EXTINGUISHERS, SMALL HOSE: In good condition? _____

FIRE DOORS: All inspected? _____ In good order? _____

ELECTRICAL EQUIPMENT: Any defects noted? _____

_____

HOUSEKEEPING: Good throughout? _____

Combustible waste removed before night? _____

SPRINKLERS: If sprinklers were closed since last weekly inspection, were red tags used? _____

Were valves reopened wide and sealed? _____

Was good full-flow drain test made after each valve was reopened? _____

REMARKS: On other matters relating to fire hazard _____

_____

_____

_____

_____

Inspector_____

Figure 7–1. Weekly record of fire equipment inspection.

should be encouraged to deposit matches and smoking materials in safe containers rather than on the floor.

Spontaneous combustion results from a chemical reaction in which there is a slow generation of heat from the oxidation of organic compounds. Under certain conditions, the reaction is accelerated until the ignition temperature of the material has been reached. This occurs where there is sufficient air for oxidation but not enough ventilation to carry away the heat as fast as it is generated. It is a condition usually found in quantities of bulk material packed loosely enough for a large amount of surface to be exposed to oxidation. High temperature increases the tendency toward spontaneous combustion.

The presence of moisture also can help to cause spontaneous combustion unless the material is wet beyond a certain point. Materials like unslaked lime and sodium chlorate promote spontaneous combustion, especially when wet. Such chemicals should be stored in a cool, dry place away from combustible material. The best preventives are either total exclusion of air or good ventilation. With small amounts of material, the former method is practical. With large quantities of material, such as piles of bituminous coal, both methods have been used with success. Fires in iron, nickel, aluminum, magnesium, and other finely divided metal powders are sometimes attributed to spontaneous ignition believed to result from the oxidation of cutting or lubricating oils or possibly from chemical impurities.

Collection and Storage of Combustibles

Many industrial fires are the result of accumulations of oil-soaked and paint-saturated clothing, rags, waste, excelsior, and other combustible refuse. Such material should be deposited in noncombustible receptables, having self-closing covers, that are provided specifically for this purpose and are removed daily.

Effective exhaust systems will remove gases, vapors, dusts, and other airborne contaminants, many of which can be fire hazards. Exhaust systems and machine enclosures will help to prevent accumulation of flammable materials on floors or on machine parts. Such materials are most hazardous when airborne, rather than when they have settled.

Clean waste, though not as dangerous as oil-soaked waste, is readily combustible and should be kept in metal cans or bins with self-closing covers. Excelsior, cotton, kapok, jute, and other highly combustible fibrous material should be stored in covered noncombustible containers and, if large quantities are kept on hand, in fire-resistant rooms equipped with fire doors and automatic sprinklers. Portable extinguishers, hose lines, or other types of extinguishing equipment for Class A fires should be available for use at such storage places. A schedule for collection of all combustible waste and rubbish should be a part of the fire prevention program.

Accumulations of dust should be cleaned at regular intervals from overhead pipes, beams, and machines, particularly from bearings and other heated surfaces. All organic and many of the inorganic materials, if ground finely enough, will burn and propagate flame. Roofs should be kept free from sawdust, shavings, and other combustible refuse. Such cleaning preferably should be done by means of a vacuum cleaner. No combustible material should be allowed to accumulate or be stored in air, elevator, or stair shafts or tunnels; in out-of-the-way corners; near electric motors or machinery or steam pipes; or within 10 feet of any stove, furnace, or boiler.

Rubbish Disposal

Fires are often caused by burning rubbish in plant yards too near combustible buildings, sheds, lumber piles, fences, and grass or other combustible material. Burning of rubbish outdoors, either in a wire basket type of burner or in an improvised steel drum, must be handled with great care. Holes in these containers are usually so large that they do not contain sparks; thus they must be used in cleared open areas free of weeds and other combustible materials. They should not be allowed to burn unattended.

It is much better for smaller companies, especially those in congested areas, to have rubbish collected. If refuse must be burned, the best and safest way is with a well-designed incinerator of masonry or steel, equipped with spark-arresting devices. Local ordinances and codes should be referred to prior to making any decision on rubbish disposal. Wind and weather conditions should be suitable before fires are lighted. Only controllable amounts should be burned at one time. No fire should be started on a windy day when there is any possibility of its spreading to combustible material. It is always advisable to have a fire hose or other fire fighting equipment available.

To prevent flashbacks or explosions in the burner, special precautions should be taken with sawdust or shavings soaked with oils or flammable solvents. Volatile drippings should be allowed to vaporize in the open if there is no danger of their traveling along the ground and being ignited, or only very small quantities of the material should be burned at any one time and then only in open containers or pits.

Outdoor housekeeping is just as important as that within the plant. Combustible rubbish, weeds, and grass should not be allowed to accumulate in plant yards, particularly near buildings, other combustible materials, or storage tanks of flammable liquids. Waste chemicals, especially heat-producing (oxidizing) compounds, should be removed to a safe area.

Where space permits, a permanent area should be established for the disposal and burning of waste products. This area should have a standby water supply, should be kept clean and free of weeds, and may include a pit where flammable liquid products are burned. Some plants segregate waste products into drums that are transported to a burning ground. The drum is placed on a rack and connected to a burner a safe distance away. The burner is surrounded by checkered brickwork to confine the flame. Those chemicals which cannot be burned can be buried in a location where they will not be disturbed until they have dissipated or become neutralized. Care must be taken not to contaminate any water supplies. Where substantial amounts of these materials must be disposed of—more than a few barrels a year—a specialist firm should be consulted.

Locker Rooms

Lockers in which oil-soaked clothing, waste, or newspapers are kept are always a serious fire hazard. Every precaution should be taken to provide fire-safe lockers and to prevent such flammable accumulations. Lockers should be made of metal and should have solid, fire-resistant sides and backs, but doors should have some openwork for ventilation. Lockers should be large enough so that air can circulate freely. The employees should not be allowed to leave oil- or paint-saturated clothing in the lockers. Where automatic sprinkler systems are used in the locker rooms, locker tops should be covered with screening or should be made of perforated metal so that water can reach the burning contents. Lockers which have sloping tops and stand flat on the floor will prevent the accumulation of rubbish both above and below.

Dust Hazards

An explosion hazard exists wherever material that will burn or oxidize readily is reduced to powder form and wherever dust is produced or handled in the manufacture or processing of such materials. There are two ways to prevent dust explosions: (1) prevent the formation of explosive mixtures of dust and air, and (2) prevent the ignition of such mixtures if their formation cannot be prevented.

Extraordinary precautions, if such are necessary, should be taken to avoid accumulations of dust which may build up to explosive proportions. Extensive use of local exhaust and frequent cleaning will do much to minimize the hazards. Where possible, dusty operations should be segregated, and dust producing equipment should be totally enclosed and exhausted to prevent leakage of dust into the general work area.

Gases and Flammable Vapors

Gases and vapors which are flammable and which produce flammable mixtures with air or oxygen are common in industry. Some such gases are acetylene, propane, hydrogen, carbon monoxide, methane, natural gas, manufactured gas, and ammonia. Highly volatile liquids which have flammable vapors include those such as gasoline, benzene, naptha, and methyl alcohol. Vapors of kerosene, turpentine, Stoddard solvent, and other liquids with flash points above 100° F are also flammable, but these liquids must generally be heated above room temperature to form flammable concentrations.

When flammable liquids, including those with flash points above 100° F, must be handled and used, only minimum amounts, in safety containers, should be allowed in work areas. In addition to its flammability with air or oxygen, acetylene is an unstable gas. Under pressure, it may dissociate with violence when subjected to high temperatures. For that reason, its generation and distribution through piping systems is limited to a maximum pressure of 15 psi. This pressure limitation does not apply to acetylene contained in Interstate Commerce Commission specification cylinders, as they contain a stabilizing agent.

There are a number of precautions to be taken to prevent the development of explosive mixtures. Equipment for the handling and storage of flammable gases should be so constructed, inspected, and maintained that the danger of leakage and explosive mixture formation is reduced to a minimum. The design should comply with existing codes and regulations. Equipment should be inspected at regular intervals by qualified individuals either from the plant staff or from an outside source.

Ventilation will usually prevent excessive accumulation of gases and vapors. The method of ventilation necessary varies with the nature of the gas or vapor to be removed and depends upon whether it is heavier or lighter than air at the point of removal. Inasmuch as heating or cooling of the gas or vapor may change its density, the ventilation or exhaust system, or both, should be designed for operating conditions and should not be based on the nominal density figures.

Natural draft ventilation may be through openings near the floor, near the ceiling, or in both locations. The best method, however, is a positive local exhaust system, using explosion-proof electrical equipment and moving air from as close to the source of a vapor or gas as possible. A nonexplosion-proof exhaust fan motor may be used if it is installed outside the ductwork.

In general, industrial gases such as acetylene, carbon monoxide, hydrogen, and natural gas are lighter than air. The vapors of flammable liquids are generally heavier than air; these include such substances as gasoline, naptha, kerosene, amyl acetate, and carbon disulfide. This is logical, because gas or vapor density is proportional to molecular weight, and the compounds which are normally liquids at room temperature have higher molecular weights than those which are gases.

Inert gases are sometimes used to prevent explosions of gases, vapors, and dusts. Their function is to keep the concentration of oxygen below the point at which it will support combustion. High-fire-hazard commercial processes, such as lacquer manufacturing, are sometimes flooded with carbon dioxide, nitrogen, or other inert gases. Inert gases are also sometimes used as a means of transferring flammable liquids, for flooding storage tanks of volatile flammable liquids, and for purging gas holders or pipelines. Inert gases, since they dilute the oxygen in the air, also have widespread use for standby emergency fire extinguishing.

Unburned gases or flammable vapors in the combustion chambers of unit heaters; boilers; furnaces; and enameling, drying, and baking ovens may form an explosive mixture with air. Interruption of the gas feed pressure or extinguishing of the flame or pilot light may cause accumulation of unburned fuel. A number of safety devices have been developed to overcome this hazard. Most of them are automatic in operation and provide for ventilation and for the control and interlocking of gas and air supplies, which guarantees freedom from explosive mixtures.

Means should be provided on gas- and oil-fired equipment to ventilate or purge the combustion zone thoroughly in case of flame failure. The operators in charge of firing these devices should know the ventilating or purging time required in the event of flame failure. In the event of flame failure, the program controller should take over, forcing the operator to go through the interlocked startup procedure which includes a timed preignition purge cycle. It is advisable to check the atmosphere inside large industrial equipment with a combustible gas indicator before relighting.

Gas-fired equipment, including controls, should be inspected and tested at regular intervals. It should be kept in good repair in accordance with the manufacturer's recommendations, and only trained personnel should be allowed to operate it. Gas valves should be inspected frequently for leaks. If a leak is detected, ventilation is needed immediately, and the condition must be corrected before the equipment is used. The recommendations of the manufacturer of the equipment and the gas company should be followed.

Under certain conditions a suppression system may be used to reduce the force of an explosion. This type of system is designed to detect an explosion as it is starting and to actuate devices that suppress, vent, or take other action to prevent the full explosive impact, as an explosion is not an instantaneous occurrence but a wave-type phenomenon which takes a definite time for the development of destructive pressures. Such a system requires split-second timing. The mechanism for dispersal of the suppression agent must operate at extremely high speed to fill the enclosure completely within milliseconds. The suppression agent must be dispersed from the suppressors in the form of a very fine mist at a rapid speed. This is normally accomplished through the use of a small secondary explosive force. The suppression agent is usually a noncombustible liquid compatible with the combustion process to be suppressed.

In an effort to establish some control over operations that use open flames or produce sparks, many firms have instituted hot-work permit programs. These programs require that authorization be secured before equipment capable of igniting combustible materials is used outside of normal work areas. The first step in inaugurating a hot-work program is the development of a policy statement by management. Some of the major features of this program are:

1) Inspection of the area where work is to be done
2) Establishment of a fire watch
3) Provision of fire extinguishing equipment
4) Communication with and coordination of all departments concerned
5) Isolation of combustibles from sources of ignition
6) Limitation of unauthorized use of flame- or spark-producing equipment.

A hot-work permit or tag is generally used to administer the program (see Fig. 7–2). Although standard forms are available from insurance companies, many plants develop special forms peculiar to their operation. It is desirable to

CUTTING & WELDING IS HAZARDOUS!

CAN IT BE AVOIDED?
IS THERE A SAFER WAY?

PERMIT

APPLIES ONLY TO AREA SPECIFIED BELOW

Date _____

Building _____ Floor _____

Nature of the job _____

_____

_____

The above location has been examined. The precautions checked on reverse of card have been taken to prevent fire. Permission is granted for this work.

Permit expires: _____
                          Date   Time

Signed _____
                          Fire Safety Supervisor

Time started _____ Time finished _____

FINAL CHECK–UP

Work area and all adjacent areas to which sparks and heat might have spread (such as floors above and below and on opposite side of walls) were inspected for at least 30 minutes after the work was completed and were found fire safe.

Signed _____

After signing, return permit to person who issued it.

Figure 7–2. Hot-work permit tag.

have the tag a distinctive color, so that it cannot be confused with a conventional routing or shipping tag.

Fires and other emergency situations often involve chemicals that have varying degrees of flammability, toxicity, and reactivity (or stability). Information on these hazards must be readily available to those confronted with such emergencies if safety, fire prevention, and effective fire control are to be achieved.

A system for the rapid identification of hazardous properties of chemicals was adopted in 1961 by the National Fire Protection Association. For uniformity, this system recommends the use of a diamond shaped symbol and numerals indicating the degree of hazard (see Fig. 7–3). The three categories of hazards are identified for each material; these are for health, flammability, and reactivity. The order of severity in each category is indicated numerically by five divisions ranging from 4, which indicates a severe hazard, to 0, which indicates that no special hazard is involved. Colors are used to better identify each category; blue for health, red for flammability, and yellow for reactivity. At the bottom of the three-part diagram is an open space. This space may be used to indicate such information as radioactivity, proper fire extinguishing agent, skin hazard, unusual reactivity with water, pressurized container, or protective handling equipment required.

When small-scale operations are being performed which may result in explosions, it is desirable, if possible, to confine these to special cells. The cells should be of very rugged construction on all but one side, which is an outside wall. Should an explosion occur, it will blow out the light-weight wall of the cell, protecting the workers inside of the plant from the effects. An earth wall or other obstruction is constructed opposite the light, outside wall so that debris will not be carried a great distance. When the likelihood of such explosions is high, it may be desirable to use remote handling apparatus to minimize the danger to operating personnel.

The use of radioactive materials imposes extremely special requirements that are beyond the scope of this book. It should be noted that explosions of radioactive materials are possible but are extremely unlikely if the proper procedures are followed. The regulations of the Atomic Energy Commission and the procedures of the Department of Commerce in this area should be checked before attempting to use radioactive substances.

Fire Protection

For maximum protection, many companies provide a fire alarm system in their plants or in particular areas of the plants. These systems are preferably tied into a central annunciator, which indicates the location of the fire. In any plant in which there is a burglar alarm system which sounds an alarm at an independent company remote from the plant, the actuation of a sprinkler head can also be made to sound an alarm.

Alarm Systems. There are several types of automatic alarm systems available; some common ones are the following:

1) Automatic heat detectors—These can be either low-melting-point metal types or bimetallic strips of a design similar to that of a conventional heating thermostat. If the detectors use low-melting-point metals, it is good practice to send at least two out of a hundred to a testing facility

REMEMBER THIS LABEL

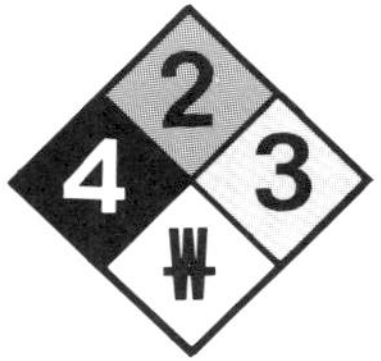

IT COULD SAVE YOU FROM SERIOUS INJURY

Many chemicals have inherent characteristics which place them into one of the following hazard categories: HEALTH, FIRE, REACTIVITY. The above label has been designed to aid you in identifying the potential hazard of a particular chemical. As shown in the table, the color indicates the type of hazard; the number indicates the severity. The white space is for special instructions. For Example: ~~W~~ means, "Don't put water on chemical."

SIGNAL	Identification of Health Hazard Color Code: BLUE	SIGNAL	Identification of Flammability Color Code: RED	SIGNAL	Identification of Reactivity (Stability) Color Code: YELLOW
	Type of Possible Injury		Susceptibility of Materials to Burning		Susceptibility to Release of Energy
4	Materials which on very short exposure could cause death or major residual injury even though prompt medical treatment were given.	4	Materials which will rapidly or completely vaporize at atmospheric pressure and normal ambient temperature, or which are readily dispersed in air and which will burn readily.	4	Materials which are readily capable of detonation or of explosive decomposition or reaction at normal temperatures and pressures.
3	Materials which on short exposure could cause serious temporary or residual injury even though prompt medical treatment were given.	3	Liquids and solids that can be ignited under almost all ambient temperature conditions.	3	Materials which are capable of detonation but require a strong initiating source and which must be heated under confinement before initiation.
2	Materials which on intense or continued exposure could cause temporary incapacitation of possible residual injury unless prompt medical treatment is given.	2	Materials that must be moderately heated or exposed to relatively high ambient temperatures before ignition can occur.	2	Materials which readily undergo violent chemical change.
1	Materials which on exposure would cause irritation but only minor residual injury even if no treatment is given.	1	Materials that must be preheated before ignition can occur.	1	Materials which are normally stable but which can become unstable in combination with other common materials or at elevated temperatures and pressures.
0	Materials which on exposure under fire conditions would offer no hazard beyond that of ordinary combustible materials.	0	Materials that will not burn.	0	Materials which are normally stable.

PLEASE RETAIN THIS CARD FOR YOUR PERSONAL REFERENCE

Figure 7–3. Hazardous-chemicals identification label.

on a yearly basis. The bimetallic detectors can be checked while installed on the ceiling by holding a 60–75-watt lamp within an inch of the unit.

2) Automatic smoke detectors—These are usually photoelectric cells and light-beam arrangements similar to conventional door-opening devices. The light source and the cell must be kept clean and the light bulb replaced periodically. The 5,000-hr light bulb should be replaced at least twice a year. At the same time, the mechanism should be actuated by blowing smoke towards it. The ionization type of fire detector will also require periodic cleaning and checking. This type of detector will sense fires when the combustion consists chiefly of flame rather than smoke.

3) Sprinkler flow detectors. Typically, sprinkler heads are actuated by the melting of a fusible plug. The flow of the water is detected by a flow sensing device. This device can be checked by opening the "inspector's test valve." Connections to the flow sensing device should be checked at least once a year. Some water-flow detectors are actuated by a reduction in pressure. These detectors are connected to the upper chamber of the main sprinkler valve. They are checked by first closing the main valve and then opening the inspector's test valve, thereby releasing the trapped pressure in the sprinkler piping. Paddle-type water flow detectors can be checked by opening the inspector's test valve at the highest point in the sprinkler system piping.

In addition to the automatic alarm systems, there are also the manual fire alarm stations. These consist of noncode stations which sound an alarm at a central station, or of coded stations which sound a coded alarm based on the location of the pulled box. The maintenance of the noncode manual stations consists of periodic operation tests, replacement of the "break-glass" windows or rods, and checking of terminal connections for looseness or corrosion. Operation of at least one station a month is recommended, and a log should be kept of these tests. Generally speaking, these manual fire stations should not be located in positions outside the plant where they are accessible to the public at large. False alarms are an extremely difficult problem for many municipal fire departments and are causing many cities to consider abandoning such systems in favor of telephone notification systems.

The maintenance of selectively coded alarm stations is similar to the maintenance of the noncode stations. Additionally, the coding clockwork mechanisms should be cleaned and oiled with watch-grade oil every five years, and their operation should be checked at least every two years. A log should be kept of these checks.

Relays used in fire alarm equipment will normally require adjustments after many months of service. Contact cleaning should be done only with a contact burnishing tool, although a fine steel file may be used if there is excessive pitting. If small d-c motors are used, the brushes must be replaced when they become worn. Fuses should be checked for good contact and freedom from corrosion.

Sprinkler Systems. Sprinkler systems are frequently used in storage areas where a fire could break out and remain undetected for a substantial period of time. However, they should be used with considerable discretion, as water damage after a fire is often a great problem. Sprinkler systems are usually so designed that when a single sprinkler head is actuated, every sprinkler head in the area starts spraying.

In areas where oils, solvents, or gasoline are stored, sprinkler systems would not be appropriate. Here, carbon dioxide or foam systems would be more effective, although sprinklers may be used in adjacent areas. Solvents and oils are usually lighter than water; thus, the flaming oil would float on top of the water, carrying the fire to other areas.

The level of pressure in the sprinkler system is normally monitored at a remote location. If the water pressure falls off due to a failure in the system or the accidental closing of a valve an alarm signal is triggered. Also, a signal would be sounded if the sprinkler water started to flow, as was mentioned earlier under "Alarm Systems."

Fire Brigade. A fire brigade of employees is an important adjunct to any fire protection program. These employees should be trained in first aid as well as fire-fighting techniques. It is not sufficient to simply designate certain employees as members of the brigade. A thorough training program as well as periodic refresher courses should be instituted. The fire brigade should have two types of activities—emergency and general.

The emergency activities would consist of telephoning the location of the fire to the plant or municipal fire department or pulling the alarm box. Then other employees would be moved out of the area. Finally, the brigade would start fighting the fire. Employee firemen have the advantage in that they are on the scene and are familiar with plant equipment and hazards. They can also assist the plant or municipal firemen when they arrive at the fire and be ready to apply first aid to any employees who may have been injured or overcome by smoke.

There should be several employees in each department familiar with the overall evacuation plan. Advance assignments should be made with respect to shutting doors and windows to close off drafts to prevent the fire from spreading. Additional responsibilities include turning off fans, motors, and other equipment and removing important records and documents. The general activities of the fire brigade include warning other employees of poor housekeeping and providing training, etc., as described earlier under "Fire Prevention."

Security

Security is often one of the responsibilities of the plant engineer, but it is usually a subject of which he has little knowledge. It is a highly specialized field in which many companies have found that the best approach is to rely upon outside contracting organization. Some of the major areas of security are a uniformed guard force, a burglar alarm system, and investigative agencies. Fig. 7–4 is a schematic representation of the objectives of a typical industrial security department.

Guard Force. The guards may be either company employees or may be provided by an outside agency. When plant security is provided by a company guard force, this should not be a separate organization from the watchmen. Some firms consider it desirable to have uniformed, physically fit guards at the entrances but believe that the watchmen can be elderly retainers marking time

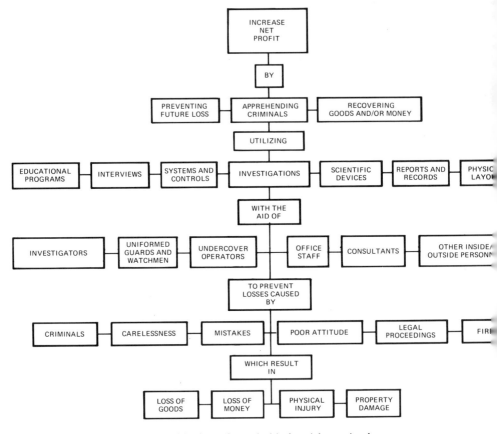

Figure 7–4. Objectives of a typical industrial security department.

until retirement. This may be good employee relations, but it is poor security. Uniformed guards do not feel insulted when asked to punch a recording clock. This is a routine procedure they follow in many plants.

When recruiting new employees as guards, a serious effort should be made to check references. Former policemen are particularly good candidates, and they can readily be checked out with their previous supervisors. If a candidate has had many changes in employment, and there are gaps between jobs, he may be only a drifter who will not stay long with any firm, or he may have been discharged for suspicions that were not strong enough for legal action. Reference checks by telephone will produce better results than those by correspondence. The former supervisors will be more candid over the telephone than they would be in a letter. However, letters should be obtained whenever possible to supplement the telephone conversation.

The contracting of an outside guard service is an excellent way to reduce administrative costs. The outside service will handle all employee relations with the guards and be in a position to run a very thorough security check on new applicants. The outside guards will be rotated periodically from one plant to another, preventing friendships from building up with employees and eliminating the possibility of collusion for theft. Whenever classified government work is being performed, the outside service can provide guards with the necessary clearances in a short period of time. It would take many months for a plant to clear its own employees for this type of work, and those employees could leave after a plant has undergone the expense of having them cleared.

Burglar Alarm System. There is a wide variety of burglar alarm systems available. Most companies in the field have particular types which they recommend, and any individual who is unfamiliar with the different systems is apt to become confused. The systems include infrared sensors, ultrasonics, capacitance change detectors, and many other types. Here, the problem may consist of the temptation to purchase hardware rather than an integrated system. If a plant is small, a relatively simple system maintained by the employees may be sufficient. In the case of a larger plant, it is probably better to sign a contract with a specialist firm which will periodically inspect the system and check to see that it is operating properly. No burglar alarm system that simply sounds a local alarm is adequate; there must be a central station at which an annunciator indicates the location of an attempted intrusion. This station must be manned 24 hours a day by sufficient personnel so that it is not necessary for the monitoring guard to leave his post. In large plants, it may be desirable to have individual guards equipped with walkie-talkies so that they can be alerted by the monitor. Lightweight paging units are also available which signal the guard to call in on the nearest telephone.

Investigative Agencies. There are a number of reasons for hiring investigative agencies. They may be needed to make background checks for new applicants for positions as guards or other sensitive spots. They may be needed to combat industrial espionage or to reduce theft. Industrial espionage is extremely widespread, and it will probably never be completely eliminated. However it can be reduced through compartmentalization of information, prompt destruction of scrap paper, and other procedures which the agencies will recommend.

When theft is suspected, it is usually a grave mistake for management to attempt to make its own investigation. Accusing a man of theft is an extremely dangerous proposition. If he is innocent, he will be insulted, his morale will be shattered, and he may quit. If he is guilty, he will be forewarned and will be more careful to conceal his behavior. In any case, he may well be in a position to sue the investigator and the company for slander.

It is better for management to notify the local police of the problem and to call in a private investigative agency if it persists. The police cannot do a great deal inside the plant, but they are in a position to circulate descriptions of the stolen material and be on the outlook for it in pawnshops, junkyards, and the like. The private investigator may assume the role of an employee and work under cover to discover the thieves.

In making initial contact with the investigative agency, a great deal of care must be taken. In undercover work, any type of written record should be avoided. Memoranda and letters have a way of becoming public information. Everyone can then recognize the "company spy," and he becomes an object of ridicule. At the best, the company's money is being wasted; at the worst, the investigator is subjected to serious injury. Personal contact is the best way of initiating the investigative program. Reports and telephone calls should be to the home rather than the plant. A handwritten letter is entirely acceptable under these circumstances. The investigation should be known only to you and your superior.

The success of the investigator is not necessarily limited to the catching of the thieves. Often the thieves will move on to other employment because they know that an agent is working on the case and will eventually catch up with them. Additionally, the agent can make recommendations to cut down on opportunities for theft. For example, he can suggest closing off the employees' parking lot from the receiving and shipping docks, forbidding shipments in personal cars, requiring passes for all packages, sealing truck shipments, and so on.

One measure which has been found effective in reducing theft is the issuing of personal property passes in triplicate. The supervisor signs the pass at the request of the employee, sends the second carbon copy to the security office, and keeps the third carbon copy for his files. When the employee reaches the gate he surrenders his pass to the guard. Later, the guard matches the surrendered pass against the security office's file copy and notifies the security officer if there is any discrepancy. The supervisor's file copy eliminates any argument about when and by whom the pass was changed.

Still another method for reducing theft is the serialization of units. At the point where components are assembled to make up a finished unit, a serial number should be assigned. These serialized units should be kept in a secure area, and when released should be checked out against the log book. This serialization may not prevent the units from being stolen, but it makes them a great deal easier to trace if they should be recovered and pinpoints the area and time when they were stolen. If possible, the serial numbers should be metal die stamped or marked with an electric pencil, as these markings are much more difficult to alter.

When solid evidence is gathered against the thieves, the company should prosecute them. It is not sufficient to simply discharge the offenders. To do so is serving notice to all other employees that the worst that can happen to them if they are caught stealing is that they will lose their jobs. The great bulk of the millions of dollars worth of goods stolen each year in industrial plants is the work of employees. This loss to industry will not be substantially reduced if management refuses to take a hard line with the offenders.

Chapter 8

The Future Challenge

The future challenge to the plant engineer will lie in the direction of greater specialization. Instead of a general understanding of a great variety of subjects, he will be expected to know more thoroughly a shorter list of responsibilities. The department he works in will be larger relative to the overall plant. He will spend considerable time in dealing with outside consultants and specialists.

INCREASED IMPORTANCE OF PLANT ENGINEERING

Industrial expansion and the rapid rate of change fostered by technology makes the plant engineering function one of the fastest growing areas of American industry. The staff of the plant engineering department must be always on the lookout for, and receptive to, improved equipment and methods which will cut costs and lead to increased productivity.

The pressing need to achieve greater productivity in the face of constantly rising costs has radically altered the nature of the plant engineering function. Most plant maintenance problems of twenty years ago could be handled by a master mechanic. He needed little formal education to maintain the relatively, simple equipment for which he was responsible. The current complexity of automated production lines or process control systems will require the services of a qualified engineer. He will often require special skills in metallurgy, chemistry, electronics, or civil engineering. These special skills may be represented by various individuals in the plant engineering office, depending upon the size and nature of the plant. In addition to the cost pressures of the times, the plant engineer has the additional problem of equipment wear and obsolescence to keep him constantly on the alert for new ways to improve operations.

The plant engineering function in many companies is a professional service which is gaining increased recognition. One of the most effective ways of gaining recognition is for the plant engineering staff to meet regularly and frequently

---

This chapter draws freely from the Bibliography items by Donald H. Denholm, David E. Nuttall, Dave Entrekin, and F. A. Logan.

with the managers of the production departments. The staff listens to the service requirements of the managers, proposes approaches to problems, and then establishes mutually agreed upon objectives to satisfy the manager's needs. Management by objectives has proved to be an excellent way in which to evaluate supervisors by using commitments and results as a measuring tool. There is no reason why this technique cannot be applied to a service group such as plant engineering.

Management needs to turn its attention to the many opportunities that are available for reducing maintenance costs. High maintenance costs are usually the result of poor management. Of all the major budget items that are found in American industry, none shows weaker return than maintenance. Even in well-managed companies, maintenance is often not as efficient as it could be.

However, maintenance losses are not inevitable. The knowledge and tools for their control are already at hand. We know a great deal about scheduling, planning, and material control. All that needs to be added is the determination to bring maintenance costs under control. The widespread availability of data processing equipment will facilitate establishing this control in many of the larger plants. The whole concept of keeping maintenance costs in check can best be implemented by a combination of common sense, well-established management principles, and cooperation with the production departments.

The best way to increase effectiveness is in labor utilization. Supervision needs to concentrate a great deal in this area. Top management should encourage first-line and middle management supervisors to receive training in modern management techniques. Improving the quality of supervision is highlighted by the fact that a first-line maintenance supervisor directing a crew of 15 men will spend perhaps $250,000 annually on direct labor, materials, tools, and supplies. Of this amount, labor costs are about half. Numerous publications and seminars are available to help supervisors achieve better results through better planning and delegation.

Manpower development is a serious problem facing industry today, and the fastest growing need is in maintenance. Training is the tool of manpower development, and it must be used to its fullest extent if the maintenance manpower situation is to be kept from becoming more critical. There is a great deal of pressure on industry to accept employees from the lowest socio-economic level—people who have never held a steady job. Only through a long-term, far-reaching program can these people be effectively trained.

A number of programmed training courses have been developed by the Plant Engineering Training Division, E. I. du Pont de Nemours & Company; Industrial Training Service; and the Society of Manufacturing Engineers. These materials can be used as individual home study courses in which the student evaluates his own work. As each frame is completed, he compares his response with the accepted response shown.

Programmed materials are also adaptable to supervised group study. The maintenance supervisor is frequently the key man in the training program. Using these materials, the trainees can share the benefits of group participation and discussion of actual applications within their company. Supervisors should supplement manual skill development on the equipment that maintenance workers will encounter in the plant.

Increased profitability in maintenance can be achieved through the reduction of breakdowns, particularly on high-capital-investment equipment. This requires the development and implementation of a reliable preventive maintenance program, increased utilization of skilled craftsmen, and control of supply and spare parts inventories.

Modern, efficient methods are being developed to bring about more efficiency in work control and scheduling. Data processing equipment is providing easier and better means of maintenance control. This lessens the clerical burden and allows the supervisor more time to direct the activities of his subordinates. He should be encouraged to take advantage of the skills of the higher-classified craftsmen and attempt to delegate the less-skilled jobs to lower-classified men and trainees. This type of program will bring long-range results as older men retire and are replaced by trained people.

Data processing equipment is fast becoming an efficient tool for the plant engineer. Maintenance costs are tabulated for use when analyzing equipment replacement. Preventive maintenance scheduling can be accomplished with a minimum of clerical work. Future possibilities in the use of this equipment include its use in establishing maintenance work standards.

The majority of industrial equipment and building repairs are not done until serious problems develop. Of course, by that time damage is quite often extensive. When these problems do occur, it is usually clear that they could have been prevented by remedial work done a few years earlier. A preventive maintenance program may appear to cost more initially, but in the long run it will more than pay for itself.

The control of supply and spare parts inventories has been improved by updated systems and techniques. Data processing equipment has brought greater efficiency in handling and purchasing procedures. This allows the manufacturer to achieve better results with considerably less paper work. The development and production of numerically controlled machine tools is growing faster than technicians can be trained to maintain them. Industry cannot expect to hire enough experienced men to satisfy their needs. Training programs will have to be implemented to secure sufficient manpower for this requirement.

COMPUTER ASSISTED MAINTENANCE

Computer controls have been in use in certain process industries for some time. However, only recently has the computer been used as a controller of machines producing individual parts and as a monitoring device and analyzer of machine operations. Analysis suggests three major obstacles that have stood in the way of progress in applying computer control to production machines. Cost was one problem, but integrated circuits, miniaturized computers, and new approaches to programming have cut into the cost advantages once enjoyed by magnetic controls.

The second problem was the lack of special talent. The computer controls require a new breed of people. Not only must they be computer experts, but they must understand the complicated logic of machine controlled networks and supervisory ideas and precepts which enable many machining operations to be combined into a single system.

The third problem has been the absence of established concepts of computerized control of machining systems which would offer reasonable assurance that the equipment would be ready for production when placed in a plant. Consequently, there was reluctance on the part of production management to get involved as long as the final form was in doubt and end reliability was only conjecture. Here, the solution required a packaging concept which offered strong advance indication of reliability and adaptability. These concepts have now evolved.

While the computer initially may be limited to monitoring and display purposes, it has the potential for taking corrective action so that production can continue uninterrupted. When tests for product quality are involved, the computer can monitor the tests and make adaptive control adjustments in the related machining operations. When trouble occurs, the computer can check all sensing inputs to pinpoint the problem area for the operator. In many cases it can summon help from its memory of preestablished service routines to give advice about the problem. Since all machine actions can be constantly timed and compared to standards, the causes of loss of efficiency can be spotted immediately. All operating data on the machine becomes available to managers in summarized form so that it can be studied away from the equipment and the pressures of production.

Some of the conditions in which computer control is attractive are as follows:
1) Operations in which downtime is especially costly
2) Systems involving testing and/or feedback of test results to make adaptive machine adjustments
3) Systems having considerable interaction between operations, particularly where such interactions make it difficult and time-consuming to trace down the origins of problems
4) Systems which experience very costly downtime when standard maintenance routines are overlooked.

The three types of computer installations of concern here are: (1) computer control, (2) computer monitoring, and (3) the combination of computer control and monitoring. These types can be differentiated as follows:
1) *Computer control* alone implies that the computer is serving the same general function that the magnetic controls have been serving on the machines up until now. Although various improvements can be realized in this substitution, it may be practical to consider a straight substitution of one form of controller for another.
2) *Computer monitoring*, on the other hand, means that the machine is being controlled in a conventional manner, but the computer is acquiring data about the various actions of the machine and perhaps is also providing diagnostic information about troubles. Bear in mind that the machine remains entirely under the control of the conventional magnetic relays.
3) *Computer control and monitoring* is just that—a system which both controls and monitors. Ordinarily, the conventional magnetic controls are not included (except perhaps in a pilot installation where it makes sense to have alternate control modes as a learning aid).

Looking at these three possibilities on a cost vs. benefit basis, the monitor-only system is, on the surface at least, the most expensive. It implies that the computer cost will be in addition to the conventional magnetic controls. The reason why decisions have been made to monitor only is the value of good ana-lytical data. Systems managers and engineers are finding that they can keep their systems operating at a high level, thereby offsetting the cost premium by production increases.

A question which might be raised is why magnetic controls should be re-tained if a computer is to be employed as a monitor. Why not use computer control in place of the magnetic control and let monitoring be a secondary func-tion of the computer? This question is one which will be increasingly answered by combined computer control and monitoring. The reason some are choosing monitor-only systems at this stage is that they find it more convenient to let the computer function alongside the magnetic controls while they become more confident of the computer and their programming ability.

To illustrate why computer monitoring is less effective in conjunction with magnetic controls than when the computer is also controlling the machine, consider the case of programming the computer monitor to aid in trouble-shooting. A program can be written to detect off-standard machine performance and offer diagnostic particulars, but when it's only a monitor, the computer cannot stop the machine. This can only be accomplished by use of magnetic controls on the operator.

In case of difficulty, the machine continues to run until a report is issued by the computer and acted upon by the operator. This means that the maintenance man will not see the machine in its original mechanical position when the diffi-culty occurred. But if the computer also happened to be in control, it would stop the machine at the moment the difficulty occurred — in addition to printing a diagnostic report — thus retaining the problem conditions for examination by the maintenance people.

Before considering the topic of computer and controller configurations, two more points are relevant. First, experience has shown that users can adapt them-selves more easily to the combination of computer control and monitoring than to the hybrid system of magnetic control with computer monitor. Second, re-gardless of whether or not both control and monitoring are performed with the computer, another choice becomes necessary — whether to rely entirely on one large, costly computer, associated with all of the machine's functions, or break up the system between two or more computers. Fig. 8–1 shows these two alter-nate approaches.

Two or More Computers

It is felt that the advantages weigh heavily on dividing up a job in the satellite/information center configuration. Under this concept, a small computer is assigned to all control and/or monitoring functions for a section of the line. It accepts all inputs from the machine and, if controlling as well as monitoring, makes all logic decisions before output control signals are relayed to all motors, solenoids, and switches on its assigned section. It functions as a satellite to a master computer, the information center.

Regardless of whether the satellite is a controller as well as a monitor for its section, it does not accumulate data permanently or issue reports. Those func-tions are performed at the information center computer. Additional sections of the line have their own satellites and they, too, report to the information center,

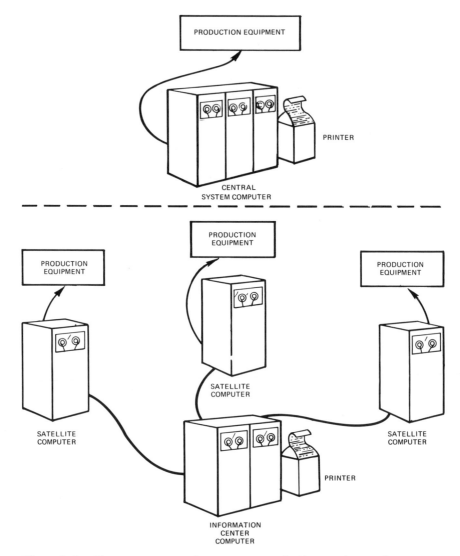

Figure 8–1.   Alternate concepts of computer control. Above, a large-scale computer controls the entire production system; below, several smaller computers each control part of a production, and a separate computer serves as a data center.

where the filing and various print-out functions can be economically centralized. There are a number of advantages to this arrangement.

System Integrity and Reliability. Each individual section of the system has absolute data retention. Thus, if it should have a failure, the data it has stored will not be lost. And, of course, if a satellite goes down for any reason, it has no effect on the rest of the system. The other sections and the information center will keep operating. Moreover, if a satellite does go down, the information center, which has been following every step of its operations, not only has a record of its data on file but can call in troubleshooting programs to speed its reactivation. When the problem has been corrected, the information center also reprograms the satellite because it maintains each satellite's individual programs on file at all times.

System Expandability. In a satellite system, the core configuration does not exceed the core capabilities of the system. The amount used is generally 25 to 50 percent, allowing for expansion at low cost. The computer, due to its lower utilization, will operate at lower duty cycle requirements. Generally, only 50 to 75 percent of the core provided is utilized in the process.

System Flexibility. One satellite can be used to pilot new techniques and additions such as future on-line gaging, on-line control, and adaptive control that will be included in the systems of the future. All of this can be accomplished with total isolation from the rest of the system, since it is linked to the main system only through its data link to the information center.

System Changes. Each satellite is programmed for the particular lines it is monitoring or controlling. Often, only some lines are changed when the part is changed. Therefore, on a revamp only the satellite or satellites involved would have program changes. Reworking a program for the entire system would be unnecessary. Any change is much easier in the satellite/information center configuration.

System Complexity. The satellite system is much easier to troubleshoot, revamp, maintain, or expand because it is modular in construction. In troubleshooting, the problem is automatically narrowed down to one computer. Since it is well interrelated, almost any change in one part of the program will have an effect on another part of the program. Therefore, with smaller programs the extent of these effects and the time required is decreased. In expanding, program complexity is less, as previously mentioned, and if desired another satellite can be easily added.

Reporting Formats

When the tremendous data-collecting ability of computers is considered, their reporting formats must be a major concern. Even though we are still utilizing only a small portion of the computer's potential data-collecting ability, the reports could swamp an operator or process engineer if they were not carefully planned to be few in number and right to the point.

Of course, this does not mean that it is not possible to provide detailed and very definite reports to suit special analytical needs. This is certainly feasible, because the information accumulated in the data base is very inclusive. It does, however, mean that printouts are normally restricted to summary reports that are related to machine management. Exceptional condition reports would be generated when off-standard conditions, such as overtime cycle, or malfunctions occur. A cathode-ray-tube display might be an alternate method of displaying these exceptional condition reports to avoid the generation of voluminous paper records.

New Computer Developments

After examining the benefits available, some may ask why the computerized machine controls are just now appearing on the scene. There are two main reasons: (1) the advent of integrated circuits to replace conventional electronic components has cut computer costs while making computers far better suited to shop operating and maintenance programs, and (2) the programming of automatic machining systems has been simplified by the development of special software.

Three years ago, if it were desired to have a computer-controlled machining system, it would have been necessary to start the program from scratch. Highly trained computer programmers would have had to spend thousands of man-hours developing new computer programs to simulate conventional control arrangements. They would have had to write these programs in the language of the computer, laboriously spelling out the scores of individual computer operating steps necessary to call for each individual machine action. Changes that were later required would also have been a job for programming experts.

With the new special software, it is no longer necessary to follow this routine. Now process control engineers can learn in four weeks how to write programs for machining operations. This capability can be acquired rapidly because the software system allows them to develop computer flow-chart analogies for ordinary wiring diagrams. From these diagrams the control engineers can easily write a symbolic program of subroutines to computerize the flow chart. The important point here is that the common machine control conventions have been broken down into computer-assembling subroutines, and the executive programming does exist that permits the subroutines to be programmed by lightly trained people.

Advantages of Computerizing Machining

Downtime reduction, and the resultant increase in machine productivity, is one area in which dollar payoffs can be checked by justification of the increased costs of computer control. A recent study of machine downtime, its causes, and the improvement potential of computer control and monitoring provided the analysis for Table VIII–1.

Table VIII–1. Example of Savings Resulting from Computerization.

Cause of Downtime	Downtime, Conventional (percentage)	Downtime, Computer (percentage)
Electrical	5.5	3.0
Mechanical	5.2	4.0
Scheduled tool change	7.0	2.0
Unscheduled tool change	9.3	9.3
Tool adjustment, inspection	5.9	5.9
Other	4.1	4.1
Total downtime	37.0	28.3
Running time	63.0	71.1

The study shows that mechanical downtime can be reduced by 23 percent as a result of reduced electrical failures, which can cause mechanical damage, and the detailed analysis and tuning provided by accurate cycle timing.

The savings in electrical downtime, which represents 45 percent of the downtime attributed to this cause, is ascribed to the following:

1) Ground checking
2) Circuit checking and trouble analysis
3) Reliable limit switch application
4) Computer self-test routines
5) Simplified wiring.

The major savings realized is the potential 30 percent reduction in overall tool change time—all in the area of scheduled tool changes. This is simply due to improved tool and man-power management, and the summary reporting provided by the computerized system. Field experience tends to validate the figures developed in the study. Additionally, there are other benefits for which it is difficult to assign dollar values. These include improved tool life, reduced weekend maintenance, reduced cost for repair parts, reduced floor space requirements, accurate management reports, and high reclamation value.

COMPUTER ASSISTED DESIGN

No one will seriously dispute that the application of computers to commercial data processing has been very successful, particularly in the last ten years. The advantages of extending similar techniques to the drafting room, to planning, and to manufacturing engineering are now being developed. People in the industrial control field, who have devoted years of effort toward the solution of industry's manufacturing problems, are now working with a radically new and effective tool. They can use this tool to drastically cut new-product design-to-prototype lead time.

Presently, attempts are being made to re-examine the basic manufacturing system itself and to study at least partial removal of the paper-work curtain imposed on current N/C systems by engineering drawings and specifications. An attempt is being made to devise a total symbolic control system to automate the handling of engineering numbers as a continuous flow process. The N/C programmers have devised a way of removing the major N/C bottleneck, the geometric language barrier which would otherwise have greatly hampered such a control system.

Operations management in engineering-oriented companies indicate that the cost of direct machining labor represents only a small percent of the total costs. However, the belief is widely held that cutting the machining time in half cuts the cost in half, not including the cost of the material. The point that a substantial increase in overhead may have been necessary to accomplish this reduced machining time is rarely considered. In actuality, a 50 percent reduction in machining time may affect total costs by less than 1 percent, assuming overhead is not affected by the change. Clearly, industry must automate engineering to remain competitive and to reduce prices in a world of constantly escalating costs.

One design system which has been developed is called ADE, an acronym for automated drafting equipment. This system is characterized by the following four features: (1) a semiautomated design extraction system, (2) automated design detailing equipment, (3) automated drawing equipment, and (4) an automated N/C and inspection machine programming system.

To illustrate the capabilities of the system's software, the N/C machine-tool paths recorded on tapes for one typical machining problem are computer software derived from a relatively small number of coordinates and geometric definitions digitized directly from the designer's layout drawing. The elapsed time for this tool path preparation was three days; only eight man-hours were expended.

Conventional detail drawings for this class of work, at least, need not be used at all for transfer of manufacturing information to the modern N/C workshop equipped with computer-aided inspection machines. When they are needed, they are written on microfilm aperture card film in 15 to 20 seconds as a by-product of the machining tape computation. Standard microfilm aperture card facilities may be used to store, retrieve, and issue prints and parts lists.

Manual labor content is minimal and for many parts is less than one hour. Even more important, only one person needs to be involved. This individual completes his tasks all in one setting by programming and operating symbolically identified keys on the ADE reader (see Fig. 8–2, upper left) to program metal cutting, fixturing, tool listing, and detail drawings. Tape-fed machines and software combine to do all the rest.

ADE System Operation

Normally this operation originates with the designer's layout drawing, albeit one prepared with 10 percent more care than exercised in the past. The object is to allow the draftsman/planner to prepare semiautomatically a tape for each part involved in the assembly, suitable for feeding to a computer any part which requires calculations. The layout drawing, which is to be measured, is placed on the surface, aligned with the X axes, and then fixed. A probe can be moved to any position on the surface and can be locked in either the X or Y axis or both. As the probe is moved, an electronic system measures the distance moved in X and Y from any preselected datum point, at any position, and the absolute coordinates of any line or point can be printed out on the associated teletype by pressing a button on the control panel.

The accuracy of measurement of penciled lines or points is about ±.005 in., but more accurate "demand" dimensions can be fed in either by means of the teletype keyboard or by setting the probe to the desired readings on the automatic digital readout (accuracy .001 in.). Alternately, the cursor or probe can be moved from point A to point B and edge-numbered dials on the control panel can be used to override the .001 and .0001 decimal places. Six-digit counters and a precision measurement system maintain absolute position relative to datum. Subdatum counters are usually provided for incremental working. The drawing scale will accommodate ranges from 10:1 to 1:10. Information is produced in the form of a hard copy and a punched paper tape. Editing by software is facilitated.

A continuous flow process from designer's layout to computer machining tapes is set in motion by operator extraction of a PP (point-to-point) and/or a CP (continuous path) tool-path. If detail drawings are required, the operator extracts a third short tape, which when processed by the computer rapidly

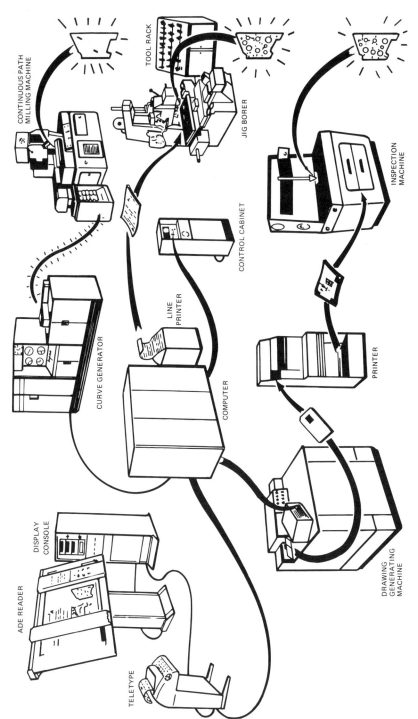

Figure 8–2. Position of automated drafting equipment (ADE) in the total computer-controlled N/C system.

"writes" via a microplotter a dimensioned part outline drawing on microfilm aperture cards as a by-product of the above machining data handling process.

A selected drawing format on a simple slide is optically mixed with tape input information "written" by a flat-faced CRT in 15–20 seconds. The aperture card film is processed within the microplotter in one minute. When prints are required, 18 × 24-in. prints are prepared via a commercially available aperture card printer. Electrostatic copy machines can enlarge, as desired, and reproduce the drawing on vellum for printing on standard reproduction equipment. This latter process permits manual additions, such as overall dimensions, etc. A single microplotter is designed to serve the drawing/quick-look needs of a group of programmers.

Carrying the numerical definition a stage further, it is possible to deal with three-dimensional parts. If these are studied, it will be found that the machining usually breaks down into manageable blocks. This is because the designer tends to work within the limitations of the existing machine tools. Typically, each face is defined relative to a subdatum, preferably at the corner of each face, and the view on the face together with a table of coordinates is given. A tape is normally provided for the machining of each face.

Economic Gains with ADE

The reduction in overall project time utilizing the ADE approach represents a very substantial improvement as compared to similar projects processed via conventional design/drafting room and manual N/C programming routes. Similar gains can be expected by organizations who manufacture a variety of partially standardized products and who are plagued by customizing-to-order problems, that is, by many variations of a family of basic designs. The great advantage of the ADE system is that it provides output suitable for efficient programming of N/C machine tools and should accelerate the absorption rate and write-off of such machines in industry.

WASTE AND POLLUTION CONTROL

The costs of pollution control must be built into the cost of every industrial product. It is as normal a cost as those associated with raw materials, manufacturing, packaging, distribution, warehousing, advertising, selling, and other cost increments that make up the total product cost. Every citizen must understand that if he is to enjoy the fruits of our technology, he must be willing to pay for the disposal of the unwanted by-products.

Industry can provide important and meaningful assistance in the field of pollution control. Air quality standards should be designated on a land usage concept to meet the needs of each particular region or area. The standards must be adequate to prevent damage to health, vegetation, and property. A great deal can be done by periodically reviewing all the effluents from the plant with the industrial suppliers to learn what less toxic products have been developed or what recycling equipment is available.

All industrial plants should have a clearly stated management policy which requires plant managers to have active pollution abatement programs in effect.

The policy should include cooperation with governmental agencies, responsible participation in the work of associations concerned with air pollution, and the carrying out of all practical actions to eliminate or reduce the concentration of pollutants. The position of industry has been mainly that they will confrom with whatever laws are laid down; while this is better than opposition, it is far better if industry takes the lead so that more and stronger unneeded regulations are not enacted.

Effective education and advertisement are needed to make every person aware of his contribution to the pollution problem. We can have clean air if everyone will devote serious and conscientious efforts to do his part in maintaining a rational control over his own emission problems.

Management personnel are confronted with ever-increasing expenditures for plant environmental equipment. These new costs will affect future product unit costs and will be passed along to the entire society. Unfortunately, not all geographical areas of manufacturing will experience these expenditures at the same time. Product cost will be affected by this overhead and may create unequal competitive atmospheres. The need to improve in-plant environmental conditions is required for a number of reasons. Excessive uncontrolled contamination is an issue with employees, organized unions, and state industrial commissions as well as health insurance carriers. These pressures to improve in-plant conditions will multiply in the future.

The need for ventilation has been apparent in the heavy industries where foundry furnaces, welding shops, and cleaning processes contribute heavily to plant contamination. Exhaust systems including dust collectors are required to control this contamination at acceptable levels. In order for these systems to operate effectively, it is necessary to introduce tempered make-up air through air-handling equipment. It is not uncommon to introduce volumes of one million cfm of process air in foundries, auto production areas, breweries, and chemical production areas. The expenditure for this equipment can exceed $500,000. Operating costs for this equipment can exceed $50,000 annually.

Increased product quality often requires rigid control of space conditions not only to guard against contamination, but also for close control of temperature and humidity. An example of rigid temperature control is maintenance of the temperature within a few degrees over an entire year. Air changes or turnovers of 25 per hour can be installed to ensure uniform temperature on a product being machined. In recent years, humidity control has been found necessary to ensure product quality. The chemical, electronic, and electrical industries are now utilizing moisture control. Miniaturization has brought about greater use of thin dielectrics and made humidity more critical. The pharmeceutical industry has found humidity control in the range of 5 to 10 percent necessary in the packaging of effervescent tablets.

One of the newer challenges to face plant and industrial engineers is the field of noise abatement. Medical studies have indicated that prolonged exposure to the noise from industrial machinery results in hearing damage. Heavy industry will no doubt be faced with sizable expenditures for noise reduction when the result of these studies becomes more widely understood as a factor in plant safety.

Still another problem which is becoming increasingly troublesome is the treatment of industrial waste. While this was covered in some detail in the previous chapter, it may be well to note that a great deal of emphasis will be placed on the problem in the coming years. The approach will be toward the treatment or recycling of wastes rather simple disposal of the material. The day in which an industrial plant could dispose of its wastes in the nearest stream is past, and strict enforcement of standards will become the rule.

Liquid Wastes

While large industrial plants can afford to install treatment facilities for their liquid wastes, small plants can not economically do this. The average machine shop, for example, must make a choice of several available approaches:
1) Hauling away and dumping in landfill sites
2) The use of biodegradable products which cannot be dumped in public waterways but which would be acceptable to municipal sewage systems.
3) Contracting with a service organization capable of handling the waste which would collect it with the waste from several small plants and dispose of it in accordance with one of the basic processes (separation, segregation, alteration, combination, or elimination).

Hauling away and dumping is at best only a temporary way of handling the problem and will be practical for only a few more years. Modern plant management will have to find more positive answers to the problem. Eventually, all the landfill sites will be filled, and the time to find acceptable alternates will have all but vanished.

Biodegradable aqueous solutions used as machine coolants are one of the immediate solutions to be considered. If uncontaminated with machine tramp oil, this material will be acceptable to most sanitary systems. Unfortunately, surveys have shown that an average machine shop with approximately 100 tools using a biodegradable coolant can put as much load on a sanitary system as a town of 7,000 residents. Since these solutions must be treated with a great deal of oxygen before they can be allowed in the public waterways, this approach will also be short-lived in usefulness.

Contracting with specialists in disposal is probably the best answer for the small manufacturer. As laws become more stringent and as public pressure becomes stronger, retaining this type of service will insure all concerned of complete, adequate, and safe disposal. The method which will be employed to meet the standards set down by the city, county, state, and federal governments will be determined by the plant engineer, based upon his judgement of the economics of the situation.

Management should be preparing one-year, five-year, and ten-year plans for environmental control. In order to plan wisely for these future needs, and to eliminate duplication or haphazard emergency expenditures, management should hire or contract with outside consultants who are in tune with future needs. Additional nonproductive overhead for these assignments is not readily acceptable to management. However, the total expenditure for future outlays may run into the millions of dollars for large production areas. The cost of the planning personnel not only could, but would save large amounts of money by eliminating crash programs.

Management can expect to provide money outlays for temperature control (both heating and cooling), humidity control, internal air filtration, noise abatement, and the control of effluents into the streams and the atmosphere. New technological changes in processes in the metal industries are helping to reduce air pollution. Although these new processes are expensive, economically they are less costly than the mechanical collection of contaminants in older methods. Product quality has improved in many cases, and increased production has resulted.

Solid Wastes

The solid waste disposal problem will certainly receive more attention in the future than it is receiving now. The problem of the industrial plant is roughly comparable to that of the small community concerned with household refuse. The major differences are that a higher percentage of industrial waste is metal, and it contains smaller amounts of paper, glass, and organic material. In the industrial plant, a good deal of segregation of metal scrap can be performed, and this should enjoy a steady market over the coming years.

For the majority of industrial plants, the solid waste disposal problem is taken care of by turning the problem over to an outside contractor. If the municipality is willing to take this step, it would be the ideal solution, but this is increasingly difficult. The solution of trucking the solid refuse to a dump, either private or municipal, is going to become more of a problem as available sites become filled up and as residents become progressively more resistant to dumping being performed in their neighborhood.

One of the more recent developments in disposal technology has been equipment for pulverization and shredding of solid waste. Although equipment of this type has been in use in Europe for many years, it is just recently being introduced into the United States. Wherever it has been put into use, it replaces the sanitary landfill operation which has many undesirable features, such as odors and fires.

The pulverization process begins with dumpage of the solid waste into a hopper at the front of the machine. This is the start of a conveyor feeder system which then lifts the material and discharges it into the grinder. Once inside the machine, the hammers in the prebreaking section cut up the waste and ready it for the next step. The throat of the mill narrows just below the hammers. A clearance of one-and-one-half inches exists between them and the walls of the machine. The hammers pass within that distance of the throat 80 times per second, choking off any possible burning. Objects too large to continue through the process are ejected through a special adjustable chute. These rejected materials can be combined with milled refuse and buried or can go to a separate scrap collection point.

The results of large-scale operations in Madison, Wisconsin, and Montreal, Canada, have been very promising. Some of the advantages are:

1) The milled refuse is not attractive to flies and rodents and need not be covered.
2) The site has much greater density and settles uniformly.
3) Milled material allows operators to work closer to definite grades and contours.
4) No winter problems exist with frozen cover material, since none is used.

5) Trucks can operate on milled material; they do not get mired in mud as they do in landfill operations.
6) Money is saved by not having to buy or move earth cover, since milled waste does not require it.

While the purchase of such milling and pulverizing equipment would probably be economically unfeasible for all but the largest plants, it is possible that some kind of arrangement might be arrived at with a municipality or a group of other plants to purchase such equipment for shared use. A small service company might be willing to start such an enterprise if financial details could be worked out.

Bibliography

Accident Prevention Manual for Industrial Operations. 5th ed. Chicago: National Safety Council.

Adams, Richard N., and Jack T. Preiss. *Human Organization Research.* Homewood, Ill.; The Dorsey Press, 1960.

Anderson, T. D. "The Operation of an Integrated Treatment System for Cyanide and Chrome in Plating Waste." Paper given at the 37th annual meeting of the Ohio Water Pollution Control Conference, Toledo, Ohio, 1963.

Argyris, Chris. *Understanding Organizational Behavior.* Homewood, Ill.: The Dorsey Press, 1960.

Armand, H., ed. *Safety Maintenance Directory and Manual of Modern Safety Techniques.* New York: Alfred M. Best Company, 1968.

Baumeister, Theodore, and Lionel S. Marks, eds. *Standard Handbook for Mechanical Engineers.* 7th ed. New York: McGraw-Hill Book Company, 1967.

Beeman, Donald. *Industrial Power Systems Handbook.* 2d ed. New York: McGraw-Hill Book Company, 1955.

Berman, P. A., P. O. Thoits and A. J. Uijlenhoet. "Gas Turbine Package Provides Both Power Plant Startup and Peaking Service," *Westinghouse Engineer,* Vol. 28, No. 5 (Sept., 1968), 130–34.

Besselievre, E. B. *The Treatment of Industrial Wastes.* New York: McGraw-Hill Book Company, 1969.

Bethel, Lawrence L., et al. *Industrial Organization and Management.* New York: McGraw-Hill Book Company, 1956.

Bird, Frank E., and George L. Germain. *Damage Control.* New York: American Management Association, Inc., 1966.

Blake, Robert R., and James Mouton. "Managerial Grid," *Advanced Management,* Sept., 1962, 12–15.

Blake, Roland P., ed. *Industrial Safety.* 3rd ed. Englewood Cliffs, N.J.: Prentice-Hall, Inc., 1963.

Broadwall, Martin M. "Planning – Key to Successful Maintenance Training," *Plant Engineering,* Apr. 18, 1969.

Brown, W. *Exploration in Management: A Description of the Glacier Metal Company's Concepts and Methods of Organization and Management.* New York: John Wiley & Sons, Inc., 1960.

Ceresa, M., and L. E. Lancy. "Waste Water Treatment," in *Metal Finishing Guidebook.* 37th ed. Edited by N. Hall. Westwood, N.J.: Metals and Plastics Publications, 1969.

Chamberlin, Robert C. "Centralized Computer System Controls Maintenance at Remote Plants," *Maintenance Engineering,* Aug., 1969.

Chuse, Robert. *Unfired Pressure Vessels.* 4th ed. New York: McGraw-Hill Book Company, 1960.

Cleland, David I. "Why Project Management," *Business Horizons,* winter, 1964, 83.

"Course in Maintenance Management #4504." New York: American Management Association, Inc.

Deehan, R. H. "Plant Security," in *Handbook of Modern Manufacturing Management.* Edited by H. B. Maynard. New York: McGraw-Hill Book Company, 1970.

Denholm, Donald H. "Network Planning: A New Shop Tool," *Iron Age,* Feb. 15, 1968, 105–107.

209

———. "Systematic Dollar Decision," *Proceedings of the SAVE Conference*, 1968, 251–57.

Duffy, Daniel J. "Authority Considered from an Operational Point of View," *Journal of the Academy of Management*, Dec., 1959, 167–76.

Eckenfelder, W. W., Jr., and D. J. O'Connor. "Chemical Treatment of Paint and Pigment Wastes," *Tenth Proceedings of the Industrial Waste Conference*, Purdue University, LaFayette, Indiana, May, 1955.

Entrekin, David A. "Computer Control—Why, How," *American Machinist*, Mar. 9, 1970, 87–94.

———. "Machine Control Computers," *Automation*, Oct., 1969.

Febles, Edvardo. "How to Implement Plant Maintenance Planning," *Plant Engineering*, Sept. 4, 1969.

Fire Protection Handbook. 12th ed. Boston: National Fire Protection Association.

Fletcher, R. H. "Exhaust Heat Gas Turbine Bonus," *Power Engineering*, Vol. 73, No. 7 (July, 1969), 39–41.

French, J. R. P., Jr., and R. L. Kahn. "A Programmatic Approach to Studying the Industrial Environment and Mental Health," *Journal of Social Issues*, Vol. 18 (1962), 1–47.

Gaddis, Paul O. "The Project Manager," *Harvard Business Review*, May–June, 1959, 91.

Gardner, J. E. *Safety Training for the Supervisor*. New York: Addison-Wesley Publishing Co., Inc., 1969.

Gocke, B. W. *Practical Plant Protection and Policing*. Springfield, Ill.: Charles C. Thomas, Publisher, 1957.

Grant, Eugene L., and W. Grant Ireson. *Principles of Engineering Economy*. 4th ed. New York: The Ronald Press Company, 1960.

Gurham, C. F. *A Plant Engineer's Guide to the Literature on Air and Water Pollution*. Cincinnati: American Institute of Plant Engineers, 1970.

Handley, William, ed. *Industrial Safety Handbook*. New York: McGraw-Hill Book Company, 1970.

Harrison, R., D. T. Tomblen and T. A. Jackson. "Profile of the Mechanical Engineer," *Personnel Psychology*, Vol. 8 (1955), 469–90.

Hartung, Frank E. *Crime, Law, and Society*. Detroit: Wayne State University Press, 1965.

Healey, Richard J. *Design for Security*. New York: John Wiley & Sons, Inc., 1968.

Hicks, Herbert G. *Management of Organizations*. New York: McGraw-Hill Book Company, 1967.

"How Maintenance Managers Use Automatic Data Processing," *Plant Engineering*, Oct. 2, 1969.

Jasinski, Frank J. "Adapting Organization to New Technology," *Harvard Business Review*, Jan.–Feb., 1959.

Jones, D. B. "Can You Afford Your Cooling Water Treatment Programs?" *Materials Protection*, Vol. 4, No. 3 (Mar., 1965), 62–65, 67.

Katz, Daniel, and Robert L. Kahn. *The Social Psychology of Organizations*. New York: John Wiley & Sons, Inc., 1966.

Kelly, T. P. "Should You Computerize Maintenance Record Keeping?" *Modern Manufacturing*, April, 1969.

Knight, Paul E., and Alan M. Richardson. *Scope and Limitation of Industrial Security*. Springfield, Ill.: Charles C. Thomas Publishing Company, 1963.

Koop, John E. "Effective Distribution of P.M. Time," *Plant Engineering*, Aug. 7, 1969.

Kreamer, W. H., and John L. Sanders. *Installing an Effective Preventive Maintenance Program*. Management Bulletin, No. 97. New York: American Management Association, Inc., 1967.

"Labor Relations Know-How," *Mill & Factory*, Jan., 1964.

Lee, John F. *Theory and Design of Steam and Gas Turbines*. New York: McGraw-Hill Book Company, 1954.

Leibenstein, Harvey. *Economic Theory and Organization Analysis*. New York: Harper and Brothers, 1960.

Leyson, Burr W. *The Miracle of Light and Power*. New York: E. P. Dutton and Company, Inc., 1955.

Logan, F. A. "CAD as a Tooling Aid." Paper presented at the Computer Assisted Design Conference, Southampton University, Apr. 15–18, 1969.

"Maintenance Cost Control," *Plant Engineering*, Mar. 6. 1969.

"Maintenance Organization: What's the Best for You?" *Mill & Factory*, Dec., 1967.

March, James G., and H. A. Simon. *Organization*. New York: John Wiley & Sons, Inc., 1959.

——— and ———. *Handbook of Organizations*. New York: Rand McNally & Co., 1965.

Maynard, H. B., ed. *Industrial Engineering Handbook*. 2d ed. New York: McGraw-Hill Book Company, 1963.

Momboisse, Raymond M. *Industrial Security for Strikes, Riots, and Disasters*. Springfield, Ill.: Charles C. Thomas, Publisher, 1968.

Morrow, L. C., ed. *Maintenance Engineering Handbook.* New York: McGraw-Hill Book Company, 1966.

Newbrough, E. T. *Effective Maintenance Management.* New York: McGraw-Hill Book Company, 1967.

Nuttall, David E. "An Operational Computer-Aided Design System," *Supplement to NCS Proceedings, From Tape to Time Sharing,* The 6th Annual Meeting and Technical Conference of the Numerical Control Society, Apr., 1969.

Partridge, Everett. *Your Most Important Raw Material.* Philadelphia: American Society for Testing and Materials, 1968.

"Plant Maintenance Management System." White Plains, N.Y.: International Business Machines Corporation, Technical Publications Department.

Potter, A. A., and J. P. Calderwood. *The Elements of Steam and Gas Power Engineering.* New York: McGraw-Hill Book Company, 1969.

Riccardi, Michael F. "Maintenance and the Supervisor," *Supervisory Management,* July, 1968.

Rogers, Keith M. *Detection and Prevention of Business Losses.* New York: Arco Publishing Co., Inc., 1962.

Rubenstein, Albert H., and C. J. Haberstroh. *Some Theories of Organization.* Homewood, Ill.: The Dorsey Press, 1960.

Rudolfs, W. *Industrial Wastes – Their Disposal and Treatment.* New York: Reinhold Publishing Corporation, 1953.

Safety Engineering Specifications and Procedures Manual. 3rd ed. Cedar Rapids, Iowa: Collins Radio Company.

Sawyer, John W., ed. *Gas Turbine Engineering Handbook.* Stamford, Conn.: Gas Turbine Publications, Inc., 1969.

Sax, Newton J. *Dangerous Properties of Industrial Materials.* 3rd ed. Princeton, N.J.: D. Van Nostrand Company, 1970.

Schooler, R. L. "Application of Predetermined Time Standards for Planning Maintenance Work," *Plant Engineering and Maintenance,* Vol. XX (1969).

Shull, Fremont, Jr. "The Nature and Contribution of Administrative Models and Organizational Research," *Journal of the Academy of Management,* Aug., 1962, 124–38.

Siemon, K. O. *Directory of Safety and Construction Codes, USA States and Cities.* Westfield, N.J.: Code Publishing Company, 1965.

Simonds, Rollin H., and John V. Grimaldi. *Safety Management: Accident Cost and Control.* Rev. ed. Homewood, Ill.: Richard D. Irwin, Inc., 1963.

Skeith, Ronald. "Simulation Checks Problem of Machine Interference," *Industrial Engineering Journal,* May, 1969.

Smith, Gordan W. "Maintenance Planning/Scheduling: Measuring the Results," *Plant Engineering,* Feb. 6, 1969.

Sorenson, Harry A. *Gas Turbines.* New York: The Ronald Press Company, 1968.

Staniar, William, ed. *Plant Engineering Handbook.* 2d ed. New York: McGraw-Hill Book Company, 1959.

Stieglitz, Harold. "Optimizing Span of Control," *Management Record,* Sept., 1962, 25–29.

Stires, David M., and Maurice M. Murphy. *PERT/CPM.* Boston: Farnsworth Publishing, Inc., 1962.

"Tested Yardsticks for Measuring Maintenance," *Mill & Factory,* May, 1964.

Turban, Efraim. "The Complete Computerized Maintenance System," *Industrial Engineering Journal,* Mar., 1969.

Vaughn, Richard C. *Introduction to Industrial Engineering.* Ames, Iowa: Iowa State University Press, 1967.

Wade, Worth. *Industrial Espionage and Misuse of Trade Secrets.* Ardmore, Pa.: Advance House Publishers, 1964.

Walsh, Daniel S. "Work Sampling Study Saves 16% Maintenance Labor," *Plant Operating Management,* Aug., 1969.

Wilkinson, John J. "How to Manage Maintenance," *Harvard Business Review,* Mar.–Apr., 1968.

———. "Maintenance Management," *Plant Engineering,* Jan. 9, Apr. 17, May 15, and June 12, 1969.

Index